INDELIBLE IMAGES
New Perspectives on Classic Films

BERT CARDULLO

UNIVERSITY
PRESS OF
AMERICA

LANHAM • NEW YORK • LONDON

Copyright © 1987 by

University Press of America,® Inc.

4720 Boston Way
Lanham, MD 20706

3 Henrietta Street
London WC2E 8LU England

British Cataloging in Publication Information Available

Library of Congress Cataloging-in-Publication Data

Cardullo, Bert.
  Indelible images.

  Bibliography: p.
  1. Moving-picture plays—History and criticism.
I. Title.
  PN1994.C333   1987   791.43'75   86-34014
  ISBN 0-8191-6149-7 (alk. paper)
  ISBN 0-8191-6150-0 (pbk. : alk. paper)

Film stills courtesy of National Film Archives, London,
and the Museum of Modern Art, New York.

All University Press of America books are produced on acid-free
paper which exceeds the minimum standards set by the National
Historical Publication and Records Commission.

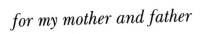

for my mother and father

TABLE OF CONTENTS

INTRODUCTION

This book is a collection of essays written between 1980 and 1985 (with the exception of one, written in 1975). The arrangement is by subject, even though there was no such plan from the beginning behind these independently written items. After the fact, I have discovered the subjects of major interest to me.

The first is literary genre and film. Much has been written on the adaptation of drama and fiction into film; I choose to treat two works that are improvements on their sources, that exemplify the reverse of the maxim, "The better the work of literature, the more it resists transmutation into film." *Room at the Top* and *Way Down East* are in addition exempla of a different sort: each is an implicit philosophical reflection on the nature of the film form as it differs from the novel and the drama respectively. Much has also been written about the so-called "screwball" comedies of the 1930s and 1940s—Stanley Cavell has recently devoted a whole book to taking them too seriously.[1] I discuss film comedy of a different kind: one "serious" comedy, *The Last Laugh*, and one farce, *Some Like It Hot*—both works of vision, not simply surface, of dynamism, not mere mechanics.

Little has been said about film as a medium for tragedy, or what must approximate genuine tragedy in the modern era. As I argue in my essay on *Way Down*

East, this is perhaps because action in film is more of a journey in the present than a confrontation based on the past (the usual form of tragedy in drama); the one is filled with possibility or promise, the other with suspense or foreboding. By its very form, film reflects for spectators in the twentieth century the belief that the world is a place in which man can leave the past behind and create his own future. I don't mean by this that there aren't tragic possibilities in film, just that they are formally different from the tragic inevitabilities we encounter in drama (except when film deliberately takes over the tragic form of drama, as in the adaptation of a play); they are *possibilities* and therefore do not attract the attention of critics following the scent of tragedy as we know it in drama. Tragic characters in film are more often makers of their own destinies in the present than they are victims of the past. In this section I analyze *Day of Wrath* and *Hiroshima, mon amour*—each a unique blend of dramatic inevitability and cinematic possibility—as well as *Shoeshine* and *The Rain People*—the former a tragedy of society, of a society's tragic brutalization of itself in the person of its future, represented by two boys; the latter a character's tragic journey of self-discovery. Moreover, I treat *The Seven Samurai*, a film of circumstance as opposed to a drama of fate, and thus a kind of anti-tragedy.

Of all literary movements, German Expressionism can claim the closest ties to film. This is partly because film gave an easier outlet to the "cinematic" form of Expressionist drama than did the stage; film also permitted more artful lighting of the painted sets favored by the Expressionists. Jack C. Ellis has written that, "in their quest for means to objectify inner consciousness, [these artists] created a world on film that represents not so much a physical reality . . . but the projection of a state of mind: the universe distorted and stylized to express what one might feel about it."[2] This is not abstract film—the human form is still present—nor is it realist cinema: it is a special mixture of the real and the fantastic, of the truly felt and the fantastically imagined. I treat one indisputably Expressionist film, *The Cabinet of Dr. Caligari*, but give it something of an anti-Expressionist reading; one supposedly marginal work of Expressionism, Murnau's *Nosferatu*, that I regard as both a fully realized product of the movement and a novel variation on it; and lastly, an Italian film, *L'avventura*, that uses Expressionist form to portray, less anti-Expressionist sentiments, than distinctly *un*expressionist ones.

Cinematic departures from traditional notions of character and empathy interest me precisely because this sort of experimentation has been going on wholesale in literature for some time, but seems to occur only sporadically in films. The reason, clearly, is that, unlike literature, film embodies rather than evokes the human figure; and unlike theatre (where such experimentation has a long and continuing tradition), film most often photographs actual physical reality instead of attempting to re-create it or reorder it. We see real people (be they actors or not) in real settings, and as a result we search for the common bond between ourselves and them; we seek to know them and their surroundings, in order to have them, in their allure and complexity (but ultimate knowability), tell us something about our own lives. Thus a work like *Une femme douce*, or almost any other Bresson film, in its refusal to make its characters accessible and in its spiritual, nearly mystical qualities, disorients if not exasperates many viewers: they are unable or unwilling to see that Bresson is indeed trying to tell them something about their lives as well as about how those lives have hitherto been depicted on screen. His methods are not conventional, but neither are his perceptions. Orson Welles's methods in *Citizen Kane* are not conventional, either, but those methods—of narrative and of characterization—and their meanings have been obscured over the years by overemphasis on this film's dazzling technique. Something similar can be said about *Shoot the Piano Player*: its mixture of tones and genres has too often been applauded for itself, apart from its relationship to character and action and apart from its effect on an audience. *The Nights of Cabiria* is the most conventional of the works considered in this section, but it is deceptively conventional: in the guise of realism Fellini has given us a film that tends to rescue character from plot, to present character for itself, at the same time as it makes that character accessible yet finally inscrutable. In other words, Fellini has made a film that is more truly realistic than most so-called realist works of literature and film—than even the films of his immediate forbears, the Italian Neorealists, which were sometimes highly plotted (e.g., *Shoeshine*) and which sometimes oversimplified character to make their political and social points (e.g., *Open City*).

I am attracted to the idea of space as a kind of character or commenter in cinema for two reasons: (1) film can make space live, can endow it with meaning, in ways that painting and the theatre (let alone literature) cannot, simply because the camera can select what it wants the eye to see; and (2) few filmmakers exploit this ability of the medium to the fullest: they treat cinema more as the incarnation of literature, of stories, and as the fluid extension of plays over space and time, than as the medium of *moving pictures*. Claude Goretta could easily have transferred Pascal Lainé's novel *The Lacemaker* faithfully to film; instead, he has chosen not only to tell Béatrice's story well, but also to transform her through images, through the careful framing of her in relation to objects, settings, and people. Robert Altman does not transform the characters of *Nashville* through images, he exposes them: what people are in close relation to their space, how they are its empty reflections—at once its products and producers, its pawns and manipulators—is offered up for our scrutiny more than are these individuals' own thoughts, actions, and interactions in time.

Clearly, some of my subject headings overlap. For example, I group *Room at the Top* under "Literature into Film," but I give the film a tragic reading. And I consider *Une femme douce* as an experiment in characterization and empathy, but I also discuss this film as an adaptation of Dostoyevski's novella "A Gentle Spirit." My hope, of course, is that such essays will do double duty, will contribute an understanding to two subject headings instead of only one.

As my subtitle indicates, most of the essays are reconsiderations of already acknowledged masterpieces by directors whose careers have been well documented. In some cases, I feel that these "masterpieces" have been misunderstood, or have been praised for the wrong reasons; in other cases, I simply offer another perspective on a great film. In the instance of *Room at the Top*, I argue implicitly that the film deserves upgrading to masterpiece status, which it has heretofore been denied by critics who otherwise acknowledge its historical importance in introducing into British films a sexual candor as well as a disenchanted view of provincial working-class life. Three of the essays strike notes of regret: the ones on Coppola's *Rain People* and Truffaut's *Shoot the Piano Player* do so out loud, the one on Altman's *Nashville* tacitly or in retrospect. In my view, the careers of all three directors have fallen off since they made these films. I attempt to give reasons for Coppola's decline, since no other critic besides me perceives the early *Rain People* as his best work. My regret at Truffaut's decline, which I try to account for at the end of my essay on *Shoot the Piano Player*, is surpassed only by my regret at his untimely death in the fall of 1984. I wrote "The Space in the Distance" almost at the time that *Nashville* appeared and haven't added a postscript on Altman's subsequent, significantly lesser films because such an addition would turn into an essay in itself, and because not many critics would argue that Altman became a better director after *Nashville*. This film is a major achievement in any event and thus merits consideration on its own, apart from what preceded or followed it in its director's career. The same can be said of *The Lacemaker*, which marks the high point of Claude Goretta's work. Goretta, born in 1929, did not make his first feature until 1970; none of his handful of other films measures up to *The Lacemaker*, but then again, none embarrasses its director in the way that *Quintet* does Altman and *One From the Heart* does Coppola.

I offer this collection as evidence of my continuing relationship with cinematic art, by which I mean not only stylistic signature, but also style wedded (inseparably) to substantial content. I realize that this statement sounds clichéd, if not in fact naively humanistic to many, but it bears repeating again and again in an era in which the study of film has become more the study of the art of making films than of film art, and beyond this, (1) more the study of sociology than of art, more an examination of how film supports the status quo than of how it reflects upon society; and (2) more the consideration of individual films (or parts thereof) as exemplifications of an overarching theory of film than as works of art unto themselves.

Bert Cardullo
New Haven, Connecticut
September 1986

NOTES

1. Stanley Cavell, *Pursuits of Happiness: The Hollywood Comedy of Remarriage* (Cambridge, Mass.: Harvard Univ. Press, 1981).
2. Jack C. Ellis, *A History of Film* (Englewood Cliffs, N.J.: Prentice-Hall, 1979), p. 96.

PREFACE

A number of these essays have been previously published in the *New Orleans Review*, *Literature/Film Quarterly*, *Film Criticism*, and *Post Script*. These pieces have all been revised and in some cases expanded for this volume. My thanks to the editors of these journals for permission to reprint.

I would like to thank here Stanley Kauffmann for his example and friendship (and for his judgments with which I quarrel!); Richard Gilman for his encouragement and support; and John Mosier and Sarah Spain for their kindness and generosity. I want also to remember Joseph P. Strelka and Bert O. States, early teachers of mine whose ideas continue to influence me. My family knows that this work would not have been possible without their love and understanding. And my friends at Yale know how much their friendship has meant to me.

B.C.

I

LITERATURE INTO FILM

PRIDE OF THE WORKING CLASS:

Room at the Top Reconsidered

At least three critics have written that Jack Clayton's *Room at the Top* (1958) leans toward melodrama, particularly from the moment the industrialist, Mr. Brown, offers Joe Lampton his daughter, Susan, in marriage.[1] According to this view, the "evil," greedy Joe agrees to the marriage, which causes his "good," abandoned lover, Alice, to get so drunk that she kills herself in a car accident. I want to go against this reading of the film, and I want to do so primarily through an investigation of Joe's behavior at several crucial moments. I will consider only the film of *Room at the Top*, not John Braine's novel of the same title on which it is based, because the film version is, in my view, better than the original at the same time as it is essentially true to its source. Neil Patterson's screenplay, of which Braine approved, strengthens the story line of the novel through the rearrangement of some incidents, the cutting of others, and the development of still others and of certain characters, Susan in particular. In other words, the film heightens the *drama*, the clash and interaction of character, of the story; it pares the plot down to the essentials while it keeps, and enhances, the detail and atmosphere of the novel's locations simply by photographing them. (Clayton, the cameraman Freddie Francis, and the art director Ralph Brinton all had a hand in choosing the evocative locations.)

The film also does something else that will be vital to my discussion, and that all films do: it places life on the screen, life that becomes automatically fascinating for having been framed, and by thus attracting our interest in the protagonist, Joe Lampton, it confers a kind of importance on him, on a working-class man whom we wouldn't normally give second thought to in real life. The novel of *Room at the Top* attempts to do the same, but, I am arguing, it is not as successful as the film because in the book Joe remains an abstraction, a composite of words. The pleasure we take in paying rapt attention to, and caring a lot about, such a man *on film* (or, to a slightly lesser, in the theatre, if Joe's story were to be adapted to the stage) is as damning as it is astonishing. Film in this way holds a special, intriguing power over us: the power to engage by the act of isolating and framing, by embodying images.

. . .

Before receiving Mr. Brown's offer over lunch at the exclusive "Conservative Club" of Warnley, Joe had declared his love for Alice Aisgill during a weekend at the coast. She is a Frenchwoman of obscure origins, perhaps from a working-class background similar to his (she tells him early in their relationship that he reminds her of a boy she once knew), who is married to an upper-class Englishman; Alice is thus, like Joe, an outsider in Warnley. Upon returning home from the coast for work, Joe was confronted by her husband, George, with the latter's knowledge of the illicit affair. George tells him that he will not grant Alice a divorce and that Joe must never see her again. If he does not comply, George declares that he will drag him into court, which will break Joe financially and cause both his and Alice's names to be smeared in the local newspaper. In addition, Alice's husband says that he will withhold support from his wife, so that it will become impossible for her and Joe to remain together—they will be completely destitute. When he meets with Mr. Brown, therefore, Joe is in a somewhat desperate situation: he knows that he does not love Susan—chasing her had been more fun than "having" her—and loves Alice, but may not be able to remain with her. Mr. Brown at first offers Joe a proposition to set him up in business and make him a rich man in exchange for leaving Susan alone. Mr. Brown is testing Joe, but he also means what he says. Joe is presented, in other words, with a way out of his desperate situation: if he gives up Susan for good, which he wants to do anyway, her father will buy him his own accounting firm, the income from which will enable Joe to fight George Aisgill in court and take Alice away from him (if she does not love her husband, neither does George love her—he holds on to her out of spite).

Out of pride, out of a desire not to be manipulated in such a way by a member of the moneyed class, *not* out of love for Susan, Joe refuses her father's first offer, despite Mr. Brown's threat to ruin him if he does not accept. Impressed with Joe's show of character and with what appears to be his love for Susan, Mr. Brown then offers him both his daughter in marriage and a top job in the Brown family business, provided he never see Alice Aisgill again. Susan is pregnant by Joe, Mr. Brown reveals. Himself once a member of the working class, the father has been testing this working-class young man's suitability for marriage. Had Joe taken the accounting firm in return for leaving Susan, Mr. Brown would have let him go. Ironically, at the same time as Joe shows his British "pluck" by refusing Mr. Brown's first offer, he traps himself. He is now confronted with the choice on the one hand of a good job in the Brown firm and Susan as a wife whom he cannot betray for Alice and whom he will not be able to cheat on with other women very easily, and on the other hand with remaining in his job as an accountant for the city and risking everything by continuing to see Alice. Joe's pride—his belief in himself as the equal of his so-called "betters"—his consequent desire to love and be loved by one of them, and additionally his desire to share, through marriage, their power and fortune, had in the first place caused him to seek Susan's favor upon his arrival in Warnley from his dreary hometown of Dufton. Now Joe's pride has placed him in a terrible dilemma: either he weds Susan and lives comfortably if miserably, or he refuses to marry her and attempts against all odds to win Alice as his wife. And one can be certain that if Joe refuses Mr. Brown's second offer, the latter will ensure that George Aisgill succeeds in his attempts to ruin Joe and Alice, whom Susan's father calls an old whore. As Mr. Brown says, he can fix just about anything. (Joe no longer has the choice of giving up Susan in return for his own accounting business, since her father now believes that Joe loves his daughter—if he suddenly disillusions Mr. Brown by rejecting

Susan for an "old whore" and still asks to be set up with his own firm, he will be refused and will have provoked Mr. Brown to support George Aisgill against him and Alice.) Joe chooses Susan and a job in the Brown business, but he needs a double Scotch in order to do so; later he courageously decides to tell Alice of his decision in person rather than writing her a letter, as Susan suggests. That he says to Alice over and over again, "*I'm going to marry Susan!*" seems to me to indicate more that he is talking himself into this decision than that he is declaring his mind made up.

So, far from veering toward melodrama at the end, *Room at the Top* moves into tragedy. Joe is no villain who gets what he wants at some poor woman's expense. His spiritual life, awakened by his love for Alice, began its descent once he gave up his love for her and is over the moment she dies in the automobile crash. The film suggests this in the office scene at Town Hall and its aftermath. Amidst congratulations from the secretaries and his fellow workers on his impending marriage to Susan and his appointment to the Brown firm, Joe overhears a conversation in which Alice's death is reported. He smashes his champagne-filled glass to the floor and hastily exits, winding up late that night at a working-class pub, where he gets thoroughly drunk in the company of a local girl. Her jealous boyfriend and some of his cohorts later viciously beat Joe up, then throw him into a dirty canal whose surface reflects the neon sign of one of Mr. Brown's factories. Joe's descent is complete, for the moment physically as well as spiritually. His spirit will remain in the gutter, despite the place he will soon take at the top through marriage to Susan. Correctly, he blames himself for Alice's death;

just as correctly, he has chosen unhappy marriage with Susan over bankruptcy and disgrace for himself and Alice at George Aisgill's hands.

At the time of *Room at the Top*'s release, Penelope Houston posed the following question without answering it: "Is [Joe] the victim of his own character, or of a social system which has formed him and given him bitterness?"[2] Joe is the victim of his own character *and* of the English social system; his tragedy is at once of his and his society's making. The pride that makes it impossible for him to accept Mr. Brown's offer of an accounting firm in return for leaving Susan alone, was born, not in a vacuum and not to every working-class man in England, but of the resentment Joe in particular felt as a member of the oppressed laboring class in his native Dufton as well as in the Royal Air Force (where officers bossed him about).

When *Room at the Top* was released in America, Robert Hatch wrote that "the film repeatedly suggests that there is something important about Joe Lampton, but what it is never comes clear."[3] Philip Hartung echoed Hatch with the line, "I'm not sure that Joe Lampton is worth all this attention."[4] Joe would argue, as he does in the film, that he is "working class and proud of it"; that is, that he is important by virtue of *his*, and by extension the film's, belief in his importance, in his special humanity. His tragedy is that he remains working class at heart at the same time as he assumes the manners and dress of, first the middle class, then the upper class—he remains working class in his *pride*. Further, his tragedy is that, not satisfied with his own sense of self-importance as the son of working-class parents who gave their lives during the war, and as the ward of a loving aunt and uncle, he strives to become important to people like the Browns and, by extension, to critics like Hatch and Hartung. The great irony is that at the moment he becomes "important" through marriage into the Brown family, he has ceased to be of importance to us. At the moment he reaches the top, he has in fact reached the bottom. Joe hesitates a long time before uttering a tepid "I do" during his wedding ceremony. It is as if he is completely aware of the finality of the "sentence" he is imposing on himself and wants to extend his freedom just a few more moments before losing it. His hesitation here is the externalization of the hesitation he inwardly felt at his decision to wed Susan and tried to dispel by affirming again and again, "*I'm going to marry Susan!*" The tears Joe sheds in the car as he and his bride are driven away from the church are for himself as well as for Alice. Seemingly encapsulated in the limousine, alone in spirit if not in body, Joe sees nothing but deserted road ahead as we watch the open road quickly disappear behind him through the rear window.

The inevitability of Joe's fall is contained within his character, which, as I have indicated, has been formed by his experience during the war as well as by his life of poverty and social humiliation in Dufton. The war gave Joe a taste of freedom, a kind of holiday. According to the director Jack Clayton, "Holidays abroad for the English . . . prior to 1939 were basically for rich people. But in the war there was this enormous flowing population, going all over the world, having totally new experiences."[5] The war also fueled Joe's feelings of resentment toward the upper class, represented by his haughty, sneering superior officers in the Royal Air Force. He admits that he did not try to break out during his three years in a German prisoner-of-war camp, unlike Susan's suitor Jack Wales, an officer who was successful in his escape attempt. Joe's pride caused him to wait out the war in prison; he preferred detainment in one place by the Nazis to subjugation all over Europe by British officers. On account of his pride, in other words, he chose to "entrap" himself. Similarly, after experiencing the freedom of a larger, more variegated town like Warnley, he traps himself in marriage to Susan, albeit unwittingly, as the result of his pride: he refuses Mr. Brown's first offer during lunch at the Warnley "Conservative Club." Just as Joe did not want to be ordered around willfully and contemptuously by Royal Air Force officers, he does not wish to be told what to do, for a price, by the commanding Mr. Brown.

The inevitability of Joe's fall is reflected in *Room at the Top*'s visual style. Even though he is ostensibly enjoying his relative economic and social freedom in "cosmopolitan" Warnley, the camera is "trapping" Joe the whole time through tight framing in restrictive settings. He lives in very cramped quarters, just as he did in Dufton—when he visits his aunt and uncle there, the scene is confined to one dark, dreary room whose low-hanging ceiling presses down on the characters. When he gets on the bus for work with his fellow employee and housemate Charles Soames and has to stand, not only does the camera cut him off just below the waist, but also many other passengers crowd around, hemming him in. The camera presses in on him when he telephones Susan after his return from Dufton, only to be told by her mother that she is vacationing in the south of France. We get a close-up of his face here, less to emphasize his emotional state than to stress his confinement, in personality if not in career, within the working-class world of his origins—this close-up is harshly juxtaposed against the full-body shot of Mrs. Brown answering her telephone in a spacious living room. Joe jumps for joy after this call, ironically declaring to Charles that the Browns are falling into his trap, that by removing their daughter from his sight they are only increasing her fondness for him. Joe barely has space to express his happiness, since the low walls and angled ceiling of his attic room seem to be collapsing in on him.

The camera's tight framing of Joe continues during his love scenes with Alice. Naturally, when they are so framed in bed, their intimacy is underlined. But when the lovers are photographed sometimes from the neck up, at other times from the waist up, as they walk about their trysting place (the tiny apartment of Alice's friend, Elspeth) during an argument, clearly something other than intimacy is being indicated. The camera is cutting them off, limiting their already limited space, suggesting the world closing in on them. At issue here, significantly, is Joe's pride, which has flared up in response to Alice's revelation that she had once posed nude for a photographer. Just as he was too proud to be subjugated by Royal Air Force officers during the war and will later be too proud to capitulate to Mr. Brown by accepting his offer of an accounting firm in return for breaking off with Susan, Joe is too proud to submit, in a manner of speaking, to all the men who are "having" Alice (through nude photographs) at the same time as he does, and "having" her younger, more voluptuous self at that. So upset is he at Alice's revelation that he ends the affair, only to reunite with her after his conquest of Susan. It is after they get back together that they sojourn on the coast, where, even after it stops raining and they can leave their small cottage, they seem confined: as they walk on the beach in the middle distance, the piles of a pier frame them on either side in the foreground.

. . .

I do not think *Room at the Top* argues that Joe Lampton should have stuck to his own people, as his uncle advises him to do; that he should have been happy to live among the working class of Dufton at the same time as his accountant's salary enabled him to live above them, so to speak. (At one point in the film, in order to get Joe away from Susan, Mr. Brown arranges a very good job for him back in Dufton, which Joe refuses when he learns who is responsible for it.) *Room at the Top* is not reactionary, it is not a cautionary tale; and neither is it revolutionary. The film does not emphasize the class struggle, as Peter Cowie maintains.[6] It does not give, in Thomas W. Bohn and Richard L. Stromgren's words, human form to social protest through the character of Joe Lampton.[7] Joe knows that he is any man's equal, if not his better. He comes to Warnley with the city accountant's job in hand, so "equal opportunity" is not an issue in the film. As Stanley Kauffmann has written, in his pursuit of Susan, Joe "yearns for power, not equality,"[8] yearns to *join* the upper class, not dismantle it. Joe is out for himself, not for the class of his origin; he is out to avenge past wrongs done to *him*, to get what is coming to *him*. His alienation from the working class becomes clear when, back in Dufton for

12

the job interview Mr. Brown has secretly set up, he returns to his boyhood home, which is now a bomb site. When he tries to be friendly to the mother of a little girl with whom he had been talking and tells the woman that he used to live next to her house, she dismisses him as a total stranger and slams the door in his face.

For better or worse the social classes are in place in *Room at the Top* and on the evidence will remain in place, *have* remained so. The issue is not the proletarian revolution on the one hand or the preservation of the class system on the other, but Joe Lampton's attempt to rise through the classes. The film is timeless, not timely; its subject is a complex human being, not an oversimplified sociopolitical cause. Paradoxically, Joe's working-class pride drove him to educate himself out of the working class, then compelled him to try to get a piece of the upper class. Tragically, the pride that enabled him to endure years of poverty and social humiliation is the same pride that undoes him spiritually. In a sense, the class of his origin has its revenge on him in the end for leaving it, while he proves that class is no barrier to someone with strength, ability, and determination. Of course, Joe pays a great price in order to do so—he "wastes" Alice Aisgill. She may be the "tragic waste" of this story, but one could argue that in killing herself she has also "killed" Joe and thus has had her revenge on him, too. In short, far from cheapening its action by resolving it through melodrama, *Room at the Top* enriches that action throughout by consistently suggesting its tragic underpinnings. There are no black-and-white characters in the film, no heroes or villains. Each character wins, and each one loses.

NOTES TO
"Pride of the Working Class: *Room at the Top*
Reconsidered"

1. Penelope Houston, "Room at the Top?", *Sight and Sound*, 28, No. 2 (Spring 1959), p. 58; Adam Garbicz and Jacek Klinowski, *Cinema, The Magic Vehicle: A Guide to Its Achievement* (Metuchen, N.J.: Scarecrow Press, 1979), p. 402; and George M. A. Gaston, *Jack Clayton: A Guide to References and Resources* (Boston: G. K. Hall, 1981), p. 10.
2. Penelope Houston, "Room at the Top?", p. 57.
3. Robert Hatch, "Films," *The Nation*, 25 April 1959, p. 395.
4. Philip Hartung, "The Screen: All the Sad Young Men Are Angry," *The Commonweal*, 3 April 1959, p. 22.
5. Gordon Gow, "The Way Things Are: Jack Clayton in an Interview," *Films and Filming*, 20, No. 7 (April 1974), p. 13.
6. Peter Cowie, *Seventy Years of Cinema* (South Brunswick, N. J.: A. S. Barnes, 1969), p. 224.
7. Thomas W. Bohn and Richard L. Stromgren, *Light and Shadows: A History of Motion Pictures*, 2nd ed. (Sherman Oaks, Calif.: Alfred Publ. Co., 1978), p. 306.
8. Stanley Kauffmann, "Movies: Angry Man on the Make," *The New Republic*, 13 April 1959, p. 21.

WAY DOWN EAST:

Play and Film

In his book *Dynamics of Drama*, Bernard Beckerman distinguishes between "plot," which "signifies the sequence of events, or incidents, in a play," and "story," which "designate[s] all incidents and activities that occur before, after, and during the play, onstage *and* off-stage."[1] In *Way Down East* (1920) D. W. Griffith tells the story that occurs before the play of the same name, by Lottie Blair Parker, Joseph R. Grismer, and William A. Brady, in addition to recounting the plot. I would like to consider Griffith's possible reasons for telling Anna Moore's entire story chronologically and to examine his adaptation of dramatic techniques to film.

It should not be overlooked that *Way Down East* was made during the silent era. That is, even if the director had wanted simply to film the play as it stood, he would have been unable to do so without the heavy use of titles. Naturally, Anna's past is revealed through dialogue in the play, which begins when she arrives at Squire Bartlett's farm in Maine looking for work, after her baby has died and she has been evicted from the rooming house.[2] Lennox Sanderson, who had seduced her in Boston, is staying at his country estate nearby; his visit to the Bartlett place provokes the drama. Griffith must tell Anna's story from the beginning through pictures (and the discreet use of titles). Beyond this, he uses nature to evoke characters' inner states where the drama would use, for instance, the soliloquy; and he uses nature as a silent but expressive character. Two examples are the scene of Anna walking down a country road after her eviction and the one of her meeting with David, the squire's son, near a falls. In the former—a long shot—the environment underlines Anna's desolation by seeming to overwhelm her, a tiny figure by contrast who becomes even smaller as she walks away from the camera. In the latter, the gleaming, tranquil river reflects the couple's contentment, while the falls that pours into it is a representation of the passion surging inside them.

The sources of tension in the play *Way Down East* are the gradual revelation of Anna's secret and the definition of her relationship with Sanderson. These tensions disappear in the film because we follow her from her first meeting with him, after she has arrived in Boston from the country to visit a rich aunt. Perhaps believing that an equivalent of dramatic suspense would be necessary to hold the audience's interest in his chronological tale of Anna's ordeal, Griffith creates tension in the first half of the film, before his heroine leaves Boston, through visual means as well as creating literal visual tension. The first type is produced when, several times, a scene from life on Squire Bartlett's farm is inserted into the action. We do not know that this is where Anna will eventually seek refuge and find salvation through David; we look forward to an explanation of the farm's presence in the film. Literal visual tension is created in two ways. Life in the city, in Boston, is filled with verticals—tall doorways, spiral staircases, high ceilings—whereas life in Maine, in the inserted country scenes, is composed mainly of horizontals—the long porch of the Bartlett family house, the flat land, the background action that crosses the screen from right to left (e.g., a man riding past the farm on a horse). In addition to this horizontal-vertical juxtaposition, there is the larger, even more striking one of outdoors against indoors. Almost all the shots of the country in the first half of *Way Down East* take place outside, in the fresh air and sunlight. By contrast, all the shots of the city occur indoors, in darkened, smoke-filled rooms. The atmosphere in Boston is frenetic: there seemingly are round-the-clock parties. The inhabitants of Bartlett village are so relaxed that they are constantly falling asleep during the day; this may explain the otherwise curious shot of David in bed on a sunny afternoon, awaking only when Anna, as yet unknown to him, is entering into the bogus marriage with Sanderson miles away.

Filming the whole of Anna's story, as opposed to solely the plot of the play, gave Griffith one large advantage: he could make it appear less melodramatic, or better, he could enhance the *realism* of the melodrama. In the play, Anna seems doomed. If it were a tragedy, she would be; since it is a melodrama, she is not. She is trapped in what Bernard Beckerman calls an "intensive structure":

If critical actions are effects of the past, man is a prisoner of his past. He is caught in a highly contracted situation, his end foretold before the plot begins, for the plot is enmeshed in the toils of the story. . . . Subject to overwhelming circumstances his initiative is limited to *how* he will act not *what* he will do. As the action progresses, his range of choice is increasingly reduced, and he *discovers* that it is so reduced. (pp. 187–188)

David pulls Anna miraculously from this structure at the last minute.

In the film of *Way Down East*, Anna is placed in something resembling Beckerman's "extensive structure":

> In contrast to the practice of commencing the plot after the story is well-advanced is the practice of commencing story and plot almost simultaneously. . . . The full story unfolds within the duration of the plot, with the result that the characters are not victims but makers of destiny. Whatever blows fall are consequences of events we clearly see. Responsibility is evident. . . . There are always possibilities open for the characters, insofar as action is concerned. . . . The time and space covered in the course of such a play militates against highly compressed circumstances. . . . As a result, the human being is not enmeshed in circumstance but passes through them. Action becomes journey rather than confrontation. Hence, it can always take a new turn. (pp. 187–189)

Clearly Anna is enmeshed in circumstances in the film, but, just as clearly, she passes through them, and we see her do so. Although she is victimized by Sanderson on account of her rustic innocence, she struggles to make her own destiny: she endures the disgrace of giving birth out of wedlock and the grief of her baby's death, then creates a new life for herself through hard work at Squire Bartlett's farm. Circumstance intervenes again in the persons of her erstwhile seducer and of her former landlady, who betrays her past to the squire, and again Anna fights against it: she rightly accuses Sanderson of deception in front of his neighbors, then walks out of the farmhouse defiantly into a huge snowstorm. Because we witnessed her strength and bravery immediately after she was deserted by Sanderson and were not simply told about them, we find those qualities in her at the end more believable. Because we witnessed her journey from the Maine countryside (where she lived with her impoverished mother) to Boston, then from there back to Maine and Squire Bartlett's farm, where she found a home, we are more ready to view her foray into the snow as possible escape rather than probable death. In the play, we only hear of Anna's incredible rescue. In the film, her rescue becomes credible because *we see it happen*, seemingly without gimmick: David searches for her in the blizzard, sees that she has fainted on the ice of the river as it is breaking apart, and follows her from floe to floe until he snatches her from the falls at the last possible moment. After this, her forgiveness by Squire Bartlett (since she is indeed not immoral) and marriage to David can be only anticlimax; in the play, they are meant to be epiphany.

I do not mean to imply that Griffith increases the literary value of the Parker-Grismer-Brady script by expanding it in time and space. It is still a melodrama. What he accomplishes, however, in adapting the play to film is to point up a significant difference between the two forms. Not the most obvious one—that drama is verbal and cinema visual—but the difference in structure and philosophical assumption between the two. The paradigm of dramatic form in the West up to Ibsen, with the exception of Shakespeare and his coevals, has been intensive or Aristotelian. Shakespeare's plays are often called "cinematic" precisely because their structure is extensive. Film form is by its nature extensive: the camera easily extends itself over time and space. In adapting *Way Down East* to film, Griffith essentially dropped an intensive structure into an extensive one, with favorable results. Plays are still being "opened up" on film, but it is clearer to us now that they belong on stage, not on the screen.

What Griffith and his audience were discovering was that film not only satisfies the craving for physical reality but also for freedom—from the restrictions of time and place, from the limitations of language, and *from the past*. To use Beckerman's terms, action in film is more of a journey in the present than a confrontation based on the past; the one is filled with possibility or promise, the other with suspense or foreboding. If melodrama, in which villainy is punished and virtue rewarded, was a last-second escape from the past, film is nearly an obliteration of it. Melodrama provided its audiences in the nineteenth century with momentary relief from a world in which man felt himself a prisoner of his past, of his origins, and in which justice was most often not done. By its very form, film reflects for spectators in the twentieth century the belief that the world is a place in which man can leave the past behind and create his own future: justice does not enter into the question, because man no longer need be the victim of his mistakes. *Way Down East* represents a landmark in the transition between the worlds of intensive and extensive structure, of Aristotelian drama and film, of the nineteenth and the twentieth centuries. It is as if, in filming *Way Down East* after the seminally cinematic *Birth of a Nation* (1915) and *Intolerance* (1916) and late in the historical process that saw film make over theatrical melodrama, Griffith were going back to mark simultaneously his own beginnings in the nineteenth-century theatre (as an actor and a playwright) and his movement from theatre into film in 1908 when he took a job with the Biograph company in New York.

NOTES TO
"*Way Down East*: Play and Film"

1. Bernard Beckerman, *Dynamics of Drama: Theory and Method of Analysis* (1970; rpt. New York: Drama Book Specialists, 1979), p. 171. Hereafter cited by page number in the text.
2. Actually, Anna does not arrive at the Bartlett farm until fairly late in the first act. Arthur Lennig sees this as a flaw in the play, which, he believes, spends too much time introducing the Bartlett family as well as the local people and thus unwisely splits the focus between this group and Anna. (Lennig, "The Birth of *Way Down East*," *Quarterly Review of Film Studies*, 6, No. 1 [1981], p. 107.) Griffith's film doesn't have this problem, since, as I go on to say in the second paragraph of my essay, he tells Anna's story from the beginning, showing what in the play is only referred to; in this manner, she is established as the center of the action from the start.

II

COMIC VISIONS

DER LETZTE MANN GETS THE LAST LAUGH:

F. W. Murnau's Comic Vision

The key to the fullest interpretation of F. W. Murnau's *The Last Laugh* (1924) is an understanding of the German concept of "Beruf," which means not simply profession but calling or station as well. Indeed, the entire film can be seen as a parody of the idea of "Beruf," culminating in the Emil Jannings character's escape, through sudden wealth, from the rigidity of all social and professional standing. The point of the final sequence (often called the "comic epilogue") is to establish conclusively the film's parodic intentions: ironically, even though Jannings, the former doorman and washroom attendant, is now very rich, he does not behave with the dignity and reserve, not to say smugness, of a rich man. He gives his money away most freely to the new washroom attendant, to all the bellboys, and to the former night watchman, who is now his bosom companion. He gives a bum not only a few coins, but also a ride in his carriage! That is to say, Jannings enjoys his wealth and makes it enjoyable to others; he does not wear it on his sleeve for all to admire. Significantly, he gives nothing to the man who took his place as the doorman, because the latter is all efficiency, no heart, and because the new doorman treats him not as the good and friendly person he has always been, but, begrudgingly, only as a rich man.

To emphasize that the Emil Jannings character behaves outside his new "calling" during the final sequence, Murnau shoots the reactions of upper-class hotel patrons to the sight of him and the night watchman eating, drinking, and smoking with gusto in the dining room: the wealthy guests find the two men ridiculous. To point up the craziness and unbelievableness of Jannings' good luck—he inherits the fortune of Mr. Monney, an American, by being the man in whose arms this eccentric millionaire died down in the washroom—Murnau slyly shoots the incredulous and laughing reactions of the hotel's occupants to the news in the paper. Murnau is aware of the contrived nature of the inheritance, so instead of shooting Mr. Monney's collapse into Jannings' arms and Jannings' later receiving news of the bequest, the director *reports* these events. He thus makes them seem more believable for their being given special status or framing in a newspaper and for their being mocked, even as we would mock them.

Jannings' sudden wealth *is* funny, and I think that the only way to see it is as a comic device, not as an intrusion on the otherwise "real" world of the film. The German title of the film supports this view of the Jannings character as the victim/beneficiary of a comic plot, not as the tragic victim who gets the "last laugh" on his former tormentors when fate suddenly decides to smile his way for a change. Jannings doesn't get the last laugh on anyone at the end. He returns to the place of his former employ, the Atlantic Hotel, not to "give it back" to the

manager who demoted him from doorman to washroom attendant at the first sign that his age was catching
up to him, not to lord his new wealth over the patrons of
many years who quickly forgot him, but to enjoy from
the point of view of a guest, or simply of a "retired
doorman," the hotel that was for so many years the
place of his "Arbeit," the all-important German work.
Murnau entitled the film *Der letzte Mann* (*The Last Man*),
not *The Last Laugh*: the title signifies that the Jannings
character was the last man in the company of the rich
American when he died and therefore would inherit all
of his wealth according to the terms of this millionaire's
will.

I call *Der letzte Mann* a parody of the idea of "Beruf,"
but by no means do I mean to suggest that this parody is
at the Jannings character's expense. On the contrary,
Jannings' humanity, both his pride and his humility,
work throughout the film to suggest that he is above this
parody and that Murnau has other plans for him. What
gives *Der letzte Mann* its permanence and power is this
curious tension that exists between the work's parodic
intentions and Jannings' portrayal of the doorman-
washroom attendant. The tension is often mirrored by
Murnau's camera. At the beginning of the film, we note
the camera's identification with the point of view of the
person (Jannings?) going down in the elevator and then
walking out the door. This movement portends what
will happen to Jannings, who, so secure in his job, is
precipitously "kicked" down into the washroom, if not
out the door of the hotel. The benevolent camera
photographs him only from the neck up, however, as he
is putting on the jacket of his new "Beruf" down in the
washroom: it thus conceals from our view the reason for

his shame. The camera makes much of the revolving doors at the entrance to the hotel and of the swinging door leading downstairs to the washroom: the implication, for Jannings as for us all, is that one must go out the same way one came in, or go down the same way one came up. But the camera gives equal space to the night watchman's searchlight: normally used for searching out thieves and bums, it finally finds Jannings' face and with it the soft truth of his kindness and generosity, in contrast with his doorman's coat and its cumbersome façade of pomp and authority.

The Emil Jannings character's whole life rests on his belief that he is performing well at the job he was meant to do and that he is a responsible and loving family man. This is Germany at the height of the Weimar Republic. So hand in hand do job and family go that Jannings cannot think of giving his daughter away in marriage if he is not in his doorman's uniform. So important is his uniform to his identity that he wears it religiously to and from work, despite its bulk. The uniform *becomes* Jannings to the extent that, once he takes it off, he is diminished, he *feels* diminished. When he goes to work on the morning that he is to be demoted and sees his replacement at work in front of the hotel, he reacts as much to seeing the uniform on another man as to the man himself. In fact, he never has any words with the new doorman; but he does seem genuinely crushed, disbelieving, at the idea that a duplicate of his uniform exists. When his aunt brings Jannings some lunch after he has been demoted to washroom attendant (but has kept the news from his family), she gets all the way to the front of the hotel without realizing that it isn't her nephew hailing cabs and greeting guests: to her, the uniform she sees *is* her nephew. Murnau brilliantly has her close her eyes and girlishly hold out the lunch bag, *then* realize, when she gets no response, that it is not her nephew at the door. (This is a strange "aunt": she is not much older than Jannings and often seems to behave like a wife toward him; she lives with him and his daughter. My guess is that Murnau intended her to be Jannings' wife, but relented for fear that his German audience would not be able to accept any parody that would have a *wife* do what this aunt was about to.)

His demotion to washroom attendant is the beginning of the end for Jannings and the point where we realize completely what Murnau is attempting to do. The director wants us to see the man beneath the "Beruf," the feeling beneath the form, something that the Expressionists before him wanted to accomplish on a much grander scale. They wished to crush bourgeois "forms," bourgeois rigidity, completely and to cultivate the expression of the unconscious, the "Seele" or soul, the "true" self. The Expressionists were essentially serious, so serious, I would add, that at times they were unintentionally comical and may in this way have contributed to their own decline. Although Murnau uses some expressionistic techniques in *Der letzte Mann* to project the state of Jannings' mind, the exaggerated seriousness with which this character views his situation, the director is pursuing a fundamentally comic vision. His concern is not with the expression of the individual unconscious, but instead with the individual both as a reflection of the society in which he lives and as an untarnished or immutable entity unto himself.

Thus, when Jannings' family virtually kicks him out of the house for losing his job, he seems, incredibly, to accept this sentence. What is important to the family above all else is that he turn in his doorman's uniform, which he has continued to wear to and from his new job as washroom attendant in order to keep the bad news from them as long as possible. When Jannings' neighbors in the tenement complex (Murnau sets his residence here because it is important that we get the idea of petty bourgeois conformity in numbers: women constantly cleaning, men rushing off to work every morning, children forever at play) learn that he has lost his job, they taunt him cruelly for wearing a uniform he no longer has a right to wear, for assuming a false identity, for attempting to remain a part of their community.

Earlier in the film, a group of children had excluded a child from their midst, but this child seemed banished less for anything it had done than because its sex was indeterminate: neither fully male nor fully female. Like Jannings, in other words, it seemed excluded because it was *without identity*. Jannings befriended this child on his way to work, giving it a piece of candy. The night watchman, who is oddly child- or doll-like in behavior and appearance (falling asleep at dinner with the rich Jannings in the hotel, for instance, and reacting to his newfound status as "friend to the rich" with typically childlike aplomb) and who, for me, even slightly resembles the excluded child, returns Jannings' gesture, befriending him when he sneaks back into the hotel to hang the doorman's coat back in the manager's closet. From this point on, the night watchman is Jannings' family, his "son," if you will. We never see Jannings' aunt, daughter, or son-in-law again. This is parody of the highest order: a man loses his job and with it his identity, and, it could be said, from that moment on his family does not recognize him. "Beruf" is family, iden-

tity, *life*. Murnau has almost imperceptibly demolished
the very idea at the heart of both the Weimar Republic's
success and its subsequent duping at Adolf Hitler's
hands.

I say "imperceptibly" because what we are drawn to,
all the time that Murnau is shattering the idea of
"Beruf," is the thoroughly human character of Jannings. As a result, a lot of what happens in the film,
though improbable in hindsight, is completely believable *while it is happening.* (This is why the tension I
described earlier was "curious," why it is perhaps better
called a "suspension.") *Der letzte Mann* thus does not
make the mistake of many films with comic, parodic, or
satirical *intentions*: the directors of these films assume
that as long as they photograph actual (but not characterized) people engaged in acts that in reality would be
improbable (e.g., a family's total rejection of the father
for losing his job), disbelief will be suspended and they
will get their point across. They are wrong. Their work
is rejected because it appears ultimately ridiculous; it
contradicts unrelievedly what we know about human
beings in the real world. These films differ from ones
such as *The Gold Rush* (1925) or *The General* (1927),
which are purely comic in style as well as structure and
many of whose "improbable acts" are clearly intended to
be seen as the products of their performers' exceptional
athletic-acrobatic skills.

One can get away with a film that has comic, parodic,
or satirical *intentions*, but only for very short periods of
time, in a skit or something comparable. Brecht wrote
such a skit and may have had it filmed, but I can't be
sure of its filming and I have not been able to find it in
his writings.[1] Nevertheless, I will give what I remember
of it, only because its theme is Murnau's, if Brecht does

execute this theme a bit more savagely: the parodying or burlesquing of "Beruf," or of simple propriety and respectability. A white-collar worker of the Weimar Republic comes home after work. He enters his apartment and begins to set it in order: he hangs up clothes, puts other things in their place, cleans up generally. Next he goes to the mirror atop his dresser and grooms himself, combing his hair, straightening his tie, and brushing off his jacket. He puts the brush and the comb back where they belong. He then takes off his watch and carefully lays it on the dresser. After doing this he goes to the window, opens it, and promptly jumps out. . . . Without the identity of "Beruf," Jannings is turned out by his family. Possessing this identity completely, and completely in loathing of it (however much, or *because*, he is under its spell), the Brecht character or "construct" turns *himself* out: he commits suicide.

So the Emil Jannings character, or perhaps it is better to say the acting of the great Jannings himself, rescues *Der letzte Mann* from the "ridiculousness" I have described in films with similar parodic intentions. Murnau, in turn, miraculously rescues Jannings from the world of parody and places him in the more salutary world of comedy. Or rather, the director has the worlds of parody and comedy converge with Jannings as their focal point, because at the same time as Jannings breaks out of the bounds of "Beruf"—by transcending "Beruf" through wealth, then transcending wealth (or the conventional synonyms for it: greed, exploitation, or even crime) through generosity and kindness—he is actually remaining the kind and generous person he was at the start of the film, when he was still the looked-up-to doorman. Matters have changed, but matters have remained the same. Even as Murnau has rescued him and the night watchman himself has saved him from possible further humiliation over the return of the doorman's coat, so too does Jannings now rescue the night watchman from the loneliness of the night. Jannings does not simply give this man his money, he gives him *his friendship.*

Der letzte Mann is not a tragedy gone wrong, as some critics think.[2] Jannings loses his job because of advancing age, not because of some flaw inherent in his character. He does not come to any great awareness about the roller coaster-ride that we call life; he is not a thinker or a rationalizer. Something bad happens to him, and something good happens to him, and he remains constant throughout. This is the sense in which he is "comic": he endures, ready to go through the same experience again if he has to; he is renewed. Tragedy is death- or end-like; comedy, life- or commencement-like. Those who still feel that Murnau tacks a happy ending on to *Der letzte Mann,* that he mixes tragedy and sentimentality or contrivance to the detriment of high seriousness, might look at Jannings' remaining the same man in wealth that he was on the doorman's salary as the suggestion that, even had he not struck it rich, he would have remained essentially the same good-hearted person in his lowly, miserable position as a washroom attendant, shunned by his family. Murnau *avoids* sentimentality by not having the washroom attendant Jannings comforted by, and comforting, the night watchman in their mutual isolation. Just think how we would have totally rejected such a scene as a stacking of the deck. Then think how natural and breathtaking it is to see the rich Jannings freely dispensing his wealth to others and fully enjoying himself in their company.

All of this in total silence. Not a word is heard during

the film, which, of course, was made before the advent of sound. There is only one title (see note 2). Its silence is perhaps what is truly breathtaking about the film. If for Robert Bresson the soundtrack invented silence, needed it, that is, then for Murnau silence had no knowledge of sound, did not need it: the uniform, the face, the body, the gesture tell all. Words could only come between us and the doorman. *Der letzte Mann* is discursive in a way that much silent film is not. Some of its expressionistic techniques contribute to the discursiveness, as does Murnau's fluid camera. But above all, it is the expressiveness of Emil Jannings' acting that is responsible for this effect, this telling or leading. We accept Jannings' silence without question from the start, because we know intuitively that we are in the presence of the comic mode.

The attention Jannings pays to himself in his preening, his isolation in the position of head doorman, his uniform that makes him stand out almost grotesquely: these elements signal subliminally that we are in the world of comedy, where concentration is on the individual in reflection of others (commonality) more than in action upon them (exceptionality), and where fate is less a thing that everyone has or wants control over than something that simply is, is accepted, and is moved on from. For all Murnau's isolation of him, Jannings has more in common with those around him and is more dependent on them than not: he pays attention to himself so that others will pay attention to him; he lives for the life of the hotel and that of his neighborhood. Film is ideally suited as a form to Murnau's "serious comedy," or comedy with a vision, because it can place the individual in the wide company and action of others, thereby stressing almost effortlessly what he has in common with them, as well as isolate him in the frame, thereby designating him as the victim/beneficiary of its motions. If much of the film comedy of Chaplin is criticized for being uncinematic, this criticism should emphasize less that Chaplin was not innovative in technique than that he did not exploit the medium's ability to show us what the Tramp has in common with other people as well as what he has peculiar unto himself. If much of the film comedy of Keaton is praised for being innovative in technique, this comedy should also be criticized for its excessive, almost narcissistic, concentration on the idiosyncrasies of the Keaton persona.

Silent acting is ideally suited to "serious comedy" and film comedy in general, as several critics have noted before me, because its silence is unreal in the same way that comedy's movement is artificial or improbable. Emil Jannings' silent acting may be unreal, but it is nevertheless wonderfully compelling, even mesmerizing, because it is accomplished without words. *Der letzte Mann*'s movement may be artificial or improbable, but precisely this quality enables the film to make so biting a comment on the society out of which it arose.

NOTES TO
"*Der Letzte Mann* Gets the Last Laugh:
F. W. Murnau's Comic Vision"

1. The Brecht scholar James K. Lyon, now of the University of California at San Diego, related the action of the film or the script in a seminar in which I was enrolled at the University of Florida in the fall of 1971.

2.   Critics' and historians' views of the "comic epilogue" in
Der letzte Mann fall into three groups: there are those who
praise the film exclusively as a tragedy, without attention
to the "comic epilogue"; those who praise the majority of
the film as tragic and puzzle over why Murnau added an
epilogue; and those who praise the addition of the "comic
epilogue," which they claim by its very improbability
reinforces the sense that the body of the film is about real
life and that only stories have happy endings. Murnau
himself contributed to this last view, since the only title in
the film whimsically reads: "Here at the scene of his last
disgrace the old man will slowly pine away, and the story
would really have ended there had not the author taken
pity on the forsaken old man and added an epilogue in
which he makes things happen as, unfortunately, they do
not happen in real life." I stand by my interpretation of
the epilogue as organic to the film's meaning, rather than
as a mere distancing device that reminds us, through the
artificiality of its happy ending, of the reality of the
Jannings character's disgrace and suffering.

    Some critics and historians in the first group men-
tioned above are: Lotte H. Eisner, *The Haunted Screen:
Expressionism in the German Cinema and the Influence of Max
Reinhardt*, trans. Roger Greaves (Berkeley: Univ. of Calif.
Press, 1969), pp. 207–221 [first publ. in French in 1952];
Lewis Jacobs, *The Rise of the American Film* (New York:
Teachers' College Press, 1967), pp. 309–310 [first publ.
1939]; and Maurice Bardèche and Robert Brasillach, *The
History of Motion Pictures*, trans. Iris Barry (New York:
W. W. Norton, 1938), pp. 255–256.

    Critics and historians in the second group mentioned
above: Gerald Mast, *A Short History of the Movies*, 3rd ed.,
rev. and enl. (Indianapolis: Bobbs-Merrill, 1981), pp.
143–144; John Fell, *A History of Films* (New York: Holt,
Rinehart and Winston, 1979), p. 144; and David A.

Cook, *A History of Narrative Film* (New York: W. W. Norton, 1981), p. 122. In *Murnau*, which she wrote over ten years after the publication of *The Haunted Screen*, Lotte Eisner accused the director of catering to the lowest common denominator in his audience by offering them the "comic epilogue": "The comic happy ending . . . has been thrust arbitrarily on to the film, rather as a comic afterpiece used to be appended to the performance of a tragedy. . . . [In] the platitude of the banal happy ending, the modern commercial fairy tale, . . . Murnau becomes as gross as his German audiences. This is . . . authentic tasteless glossiness" [(Berkeley: Univ. of Calif. Press, 1973), pp. 154, 158; first publ. in French in 1964, and presumably translated into English by the author, since no translator is listed on the title or copyright pages].

Critics and historians in the third group mentioned above: Siegfried Kracauer, *From Caligari to Hitler: A Psychological History of the German Film* (Princeton, N. J.: Princeton Univ. Press, 1947), p. 101; Jack C. Ellis, *A History of Film* (Englewood Cliffs, N. J.: Prentice-Hall, 1979), pp. 100–101; and John D. Barlow, *German Expressionist Film* (Boston: Twayne, 1982), pp. 146, 153.

THE DREAM STRUCTURE OF
SOME LIKE IT HOT

Some Like It Hot (1959) is film farce of the highest rank. Stanley Kauffmann may not have been the first to call it a farce, but he was the first to *understand* it as one:

> Farce . . . begins with a ridiculous but engaging premise (Wilder's "nugget": two male musicians latching onto an all-girl band), then builds on this improbable premise with rigid logic. . . . Farce gives us the thrill of danger (when Joe forgets to take off his bandstand earrings, racing to a date as a millionaire) and the thrill of split-second neatness (when he whisks them off just in time). Basically, that is the greatest joke of all: absolute order has been imposed on the chaos of life. Farce, as an artistic form, is identical with that order. We know that life, on either side of these two hours, is chaotic: there is pleasure here in seeing how neatly things fit together for people we like.[1]

The order Kauffmann speaks of has to do with the characters' achievement of their goals in the face of many obstacles: Jerry and Joe escape death at the hands of the mob; Joe gets the girl; and Sugar and Osgood each find love. But there is another, larger order created at the end of the film, and it has to do with the main characters' fulfillment of their repressed wishes.

Eric Bentley wrote in his famous essay "The Psychology of Farce" that "like dreams, farces show the disguised fulfillment of repressed wishes."[2] He was speaking primarily of bedroom farce, where "one is permitted the outrage [of adultery] but is spared the consequences."[3] And in *Some Like It Hot* one does indeed find Jerry telling Joe of his childhood dream of "being locked in a pastry shop with goodies all around"; in the film that dream becomes realized in adult terms when he finds himself surrounded by the beautiful girls of Sweet Sue's band on the train bound for Florida. But *Some Like It Hot* is no bedroom farce, and, since they are both disguised as women, neither Jerry nor Joe is able to take advantage of his situation on the train. Jerry almost drops his disguise in an attempt to seduce Sugar in his berth, but the pair are interrupted by other band members looking for a party. Joe beats Jerry to Sugar at the Miami Beach hotel and seduces her, or rather, in the guise of a millionaire uninterested in women, he is seduced by her; but he is hardly fulfilling any repressed wish of his or the audience's here: he is simply behaving like the typical womanizer that he is. The repressed wishes of Joe, Jerry, Sugar, and Osgood have to do less with the bedroom than with the *living* room, less with sexual relations than with the social relationships between members of the opposite sex and of the same sex. If bedroom farce shows the disguised fulfillment (disguised because the fulfillment takes place onstage, not in real life) of its audience's repressed sexual wishes, *Some Like It Hot* shows the disguised fulfillment (literally as well as figuratively) of its audience's repressed social wishes. Transvestism is used in the service of this fulfillment, not to make a point about latent tendencies in Jerry and Joe.

Jerry's repressed wish, and by extension that of some men in any audience of the film, is for a better relationship with a man. Joe clearly dominates him in Chicago, gambling their money away, involving Jerry in schemes against women, causing the both of them to witness the Saint Valentine's Day massacre. In Florida, Jerry, disguised as Daphne the bass fiddle player, suddenly becomes aggressive and fun-loving, attracting the millionaire Osgood Fielding. Fielding woos him/her doggedly and they eventually get engaged; when Jerry and Joe must flee the hotel where the band is playing because gangsters have arrived who want to kill them for being the only witnesses to the Saint Valentine's Day massacre, Jerry says of Osgood, "I will never again find a man so good to me." Osgood has treated Jerry/Daphne with respect, showered him/her with gifts, and made promises that he intends to keep. He regards Jerry/Daphne as a partner, not as a pawn in a game. Jerry has finally achieved parity with another man—ironically, through allowing the feminine side, or let us simply say another side, of his character to come to the surface. When Osgood tells him "nobody's perfect" after Jerry/Daphne reveals that he/she is really a man, what is being said is that the masculine side of Jerry's personality, or the side that he showed when dressed as a man, is the weakest, the most negligible. This is not to suggest that Jerry is a woman trapped in a man's body or a repressed homosexual. It is to say that, in disguise as a woman, he has been freed to express parts of himself that he learned to suppress in his dealings as a man with other, more assertive men. One could argue that *Some Like It Hot* is Jerry's dream of a better relationship with a man, his own disguised fulfillment in a dream of a repressed wish. I have always imagined Jerry awakening from his dream, just as the audience does from its own, when the film ends abruptly on Osgood's "nobody's perfect"-line, as the motorboat carries the two couples (Osgood and Jerry/Daphne, Joe and Sugar) away from the gangsters stranded on the dock.

Sugar Kane is Jerry/Daphne's double in the film. They are both blondes, they get along like sisters, and they have the same repressed wish-dream. Sugar has always fallen for saxophone players in the past, and they have all treated her badly; she says that she now wants to forget about love and find some retired as well as retiring Miami Beach millionaire to make life easy for her. But it is her double, Daphne, who finds the millionaire. Sugar gets Joe, the man who has been treating Jerry badly and who is another saxophonist. Joe poses as a shy millionaire so that he can make Sugar another of his conquests; whenever Osgood gives Jerry/Daphne a gift, Joe quickly seizes it and offers it to Sugar. What Sugar really still wants, like many women in the film audience, is a good relationship with a sensitive man of her social station and interests—in Sugar's case, a reformed saxophonist. She gets him, and when Joe makes his magical transformation on the bandstand before fleeing the gangsters, she wastes little time thinking about the logic of events up to this point. Before her "dream" ends, she is going to make the most of it: she races down to the dock on a bicycle, jumps into the motorboat, and falls into Joe's arms. The last we see of them, they are kissing passionately in the back seat as

Osgood and Jerry/Daphne discuss marriage in the front.

Joe, like Jerry, is dressed as a woman (Josephine) in order to escape detection by the gangsters, who are looking for them in every male band in the country. In addition, the boys are broke, so even work in drag in an all-girl band is acceptable. On top of this, it is in Joe's interest for them to stay in drag because he is using the Jerry/Daphne-Osgood relationship to further his own with Sugar Kane: for example, he has Daphne lure her gentleman friend onto land so that he can entertain Sugar on Osgood's yacht. But Joe's repressed wish, as opposed to his ostensible wish for sexual conquest of Sugar, is to get rid of his callous, exploitative attitude toward women and become a gentle, compassionate man—surely this is also the repressed wish of a good number of male audience members of *Some Like It Hot* today, just as it was of at least some men in the audience when the film was released in 1959. Joe becomes a different man in the film, in his "dream," by living in disguise as a female and experiencing firsthand how women are treated by men as well as secondhand, through his own observation and through talks with band members. For instance, when Jerry/Daphne complains about being pinched in the elevator, Joe responds in complete seriousness, "Now you know how the other half lives." As Josephine, Joe has the opportunity on the train to hear Sugar's lament about her many abortive affairs with saxophone players. It is true that he will subsequently use against her his own charm as a saxophone player and the knowledge that Sugar is looking for a millionaire to marry; but the seeds of his later sympathy for her are planted on the train. Instead of just departing with Jerry and forgetting about Sugar once the gangsters arrive at the hotel (for a convention of "The Friends of Italian Opera"!), he solicitously telephones her in his millionaire's voice that he must leave for South America immediately to supervise his family's oil concerns. Pursued by henchmen after they have seen through his and Jerry's disguise (and after Jerry and Joe have witnessed yet another execution, of Spats Columbo and his men, who themselves carried out the Saint Valentine's Day massacre), Joe hears Sugar singing "I'm Through with Love," a moving response to his telephone call, and risks his life by walking onto the stage, kissing her on the lips, and saying, "None of that, Sugar. No guy is worth it." Significantly, Joe is still in disguise as Josephine when he says this in his own masculine voice. He is addressing Sugar woman-to-woman, as a man. In disguise as a woman, Joe has been freed to tap parts of himself that he had suppressed in order to get ahead in the cruelly competitive world of men. Though he has torn off his wig by now, he is still dressed and made-up as Josephine when he and Sugar embrace at the back of the motorboat. It is as if the film, and his dream, must end here, before he can turn completely into a man again—not one of whom, as he has said, is worth it.

Osgood Fielding is Joe's double in *Some Like It Hot*. They dress alike (Joe has stolen a suitcase containing the fashionable summer clothing of the band's manager, Beanstalk, which the former wears when posing as a millionaire), use the same yacht, and give the same gifts. Like Joe before he met Sugar, Osgood was a philanderer until he met Daphne. When Osgood begins to pursue Daphne at the hotel, he is ostensibly up to his old tricks. But she (naturally) resists his immediate physical advances, and this sparks his interest; she then resists his polite *social* advances, and this makes him even more determined to win her over. By the time Daphne accepts a date with him to go dancing, he is so enamored of her that at the end of the evening he proposes marriage. Osgood's repressed wish is precisely for resistance from a woman—resistance to the temptation of falling for him on account of his money and social connections. Like Joe, he wants to stop taking advantage of women, wants to treat them with respect and sensitivity. He gets his opportunity with Daphne, who behaves the way women should have behaved toward him all along: not with more propriety or less femininity, but with a demand for equality, for give-and-take. Daphne is Osgood's dream of the ideal woman—someone with whom he gets along so well that sex becomes beside the point. In their discussion in the motorboat speeding away from the gangsters on the pier, Daphne actually threatens an unconsummated marriage without dampening Osgood's desire to make her his wife. So much does he like her that when she goes on to say, "Damn it, I'm a man," he regards her change of gender as incidental to their marriage, as a foible that he will simply overlook.

He is dreaming, of course. Just as Sugar, Jerry, and Joe have been dreaming—of a world in which their unconscious desires are granted, in which perpetual action replaces burdensome thought, and in which the only people who suffer consequences for their acts are the non-dreamers (the perpetrators as well as the victims of the Saint Valentine's Day massacre). We in the audience have been dreaming, too, not only in the sense that, identifying with Jerry, Joe, Sugar, or Osgood, we have had our own repressed wishes come true, but also in the sense that we have absolutely believed every improbable, if not impossible event that has taken place on screen, while it was taking place. Like the characters, we had no time to think. We awaken from our dream at the same time as the four main characters do from theirs—when they all meet together in close quarters for the first time, in the motorboat, their submerged longings gratified.

. . .

Disguise or impersonation plays a part in many of Wilder's films—certainly in all of his comedies. And in the comedies *The Major and the Minor* (1942) and *Kiss Me, Stupid* (1964), for example, as in *Some Like It Hot*, it is only in disguise that characters discover suppressed aspects of themselves or perceive their society from a point of view denied to someone who always looks at it through the same eyes. In *Kiss Me, Stupid*, Polly the prostitute plays her role as Orville J. Spooner's wife— for which he has hired her as part of a plot to keep the lecherous pop singer Dino away from his real wife—so well because she has a genuine desire to get married and settle down. By the end of the film, she has left the town of "Climax," Nevada, determined to quit prostitution for a life of domestic tranquility. In *The Major and the Minor*, Susan Applegate, posing as the twelve-year-old Sue-Sue and in love with Major Philip Kirby, is able to see Kirby's fiancée, Pamela, for the scheming, selfish woman she is only with the help of Pamela's sister, Lucy—a real twelve year-old.

But *Kiss Me, Stupid* and *The Major and the Minor* are hardly on a level with *Some Like It Hot*, nor are other Wilder comedies with a disguise motif, notably *One, Two Three* (1961) and *Irma la Douce* (1963). This is partly because, unlike *Some Like It Hot*, these films give us time to think, to consider the improbability of their characters' disguises and/or conversions. The farce *Some Like It Hot* gives us no such time: it succeeds by virtue of its continuous motion. Appearances in real life are deceiving, so the cliché goes, despite the time we have to penetrate them; in the dream world of farce, disguises are, paradoxically, revelatory, precisely because we have so little time to question them. They are not meant to appear real or believable—they are intended as transparent, psychic symbols. And they therefore move at the pace at which the mind is capable of moving when it is unencumbered by its own powers of cogitation, by the burden of consciousness.

NOTES TO
"The Dream Structure of
Some Like It Hot"

1. Stanley Kauffmann, "*Some Like It Hot*," in his *Living Images: Film Comment and Criticism* (New York: Harper and Row, 1975), pp. 328, 331–332.
2. Eric Bentley, "The Psychology of Farce," Intro. to *"Let's Get A Divorce" and Other Plays*, ed. E. Bentley (New York: Hill and Wang, 1958), p. x.
3. Eric Bentley, "The Psychology of Farce," p. xiii.

III
TRAGIC VARIATIONS

THE SYMBOLISM OF
HIROSHIMA, MON AMOUR

I want to consider *Hiroshima, mon amour* (1959) on the level at which it seems to me most interesting, and most successful: the symbolic.[1] Resnais was approached after the appearance of *Night and Fog* (1955) to make a documentary about the atomic bomb. *Night and Fog* was a documentary about Auschwitz; *Hiroshima, mon amour* would turn out to be a fiction film, with the script by the novelist Marguerite Duras. *Hiroshima* does, of course, include footage of the city and its people after the dropping of the bomb, and half of the film is shot in modern-day Hiroshima. But the aesthetic impulse behind it was not to document or fictionally to re-create the horror of the atomic bomb; that impulse was foremost, I believe, to create through the character of the Frenchwoman a metaphor for the tragedy of the bomb.

Resnais decided to make a fiction film instead of a documentary or a fictionalized documentary (the Frenchwoman in the film is an actress who has come to Hiroshima to make a fictionalized documentary about the bomb, in which she plays a nurse), because he wanted, I think, to make his film more accessible to the Western audience for whom the dropping of the bomb meant the end of war with Japan. Indeed, he began to make a documentary but did not complete it, stopping work after only a few months. To make a documentary about the horrors perpetrated by the Nazis at Auschwitz is one thing. But to have made a documentary about the horrors perpetrated by the Allies, specifically the Americans, at Hiroshima would have been quite another, Resnais seemed to sense, because unlike the Jews in the concentration camps, the Japanese were aggressors in World War II. The atomic bomb was designed to stop them once and for all. A Resnais film documenting the devastation and suffering caused by the bomb would have been incomplete and unacceptable to a Western audience. Even a film fictionalizing both the devastation and suffering caused by the bomb and the pressing reasons for its dropping would seem inevitably to be creating more sympathy for the victims than for the victors. A film that created the two sides to the dropping of the bomb—the tragedy of its dropping, that is—through metaphor would reach, and affect, its audience. Camus was right to say that "it is better to suffer certain injustices than to commit them even to win wars."[2] The Americans were equally right to inflict great suffering on the Japanese rather than continue to suffer themselves.

The Frenchwoman comes to Hiroshima thinking that she knows all there is to know (through newsreel footage, books, interviews, etc.) about the bomb and the effect it had on the city. The Japanese architect with whom she has a torrid affair asks her how she can know what she has not experienced, either directly or indirectly (he is a native of Hiroshima but was not there when the bomb was dropped; the rest of his family was there, and all were killed). There is naturally something to what he says—we get footage of the leveled Hiroshima to *underline* his meaning, not to give us the experience of the havoc wrought by the bomb—but the real point is that the Frenchwoman, in her private life during the war, underwent an experience similar to the experience of those who *dropped* the bomb, not those who received it. And she has undergone an experience since the war openly comparable to the experience of the conscience-stricken airmen who dropped the bomb, if not to the one undergone by the leaders and citizens of the triumphant nation that decided to use it.

The Frenchwoman (neither she nor the Japanese is ever named), living in occupied Nevers, fell in love with a German soldier and had a long affair with him. Shortly before the liberation of the town, the soldier, waiting to meet his lover at an appointed place in the countryside, was killed by Resistance fighters. The Frenchwoman, identified as the lover of a German, had her head shaved by the citizens of Nevers and was paraded through the town to verbal and physical abuse and to the disgrace of her family. In order to avoid further censure by the townspeople, her family virtually kept her prisoner in the cellar of their home. Finally she was allowed to move to Paris and did not see Nevers or her family again. Although she eventually married, it is clear from her statements that the Japanese is the first man she has been able to love since the German. (She says to the Japanese at one point, "Oh! How good it is to be with someone, sometime"; and she tells him about her affair with the German, although she has never told her husband.)

The Frenchwoman's love affair with the German was tragic, if one defines tragedy as the conflict of two goods. She fell naturally in love with him, yet she should not have carried on a love affair with an enemy of France. To love is good; to support one's country is good also. Likewise, the Frenchwoman's fellow citizens naturally punished her for fraternizing with the enemy. Yet they should not have punished her, since she did not collaborate with the Germans against the French— indeed, her boyfriend may have treated the people of Nevers better for his relationship with one of their daughters—and since she was so young and inexperienced. The tragedy of the Frenchwoman's love is analogous to the tragedy of the atomic bomb. The Americans had to drop the bomb, because the Japanese refused to surrender and a land invasion of Japan would have meant the loss of hundreds of thousands of American lives. Yet they should not have dropped it, because of the unprecedented destruction and long-term suffering it would bring about; because their use of the bomb would stigmatize them in the eyes of the world; and because they would be introducing a weapon that would be copied by other nations and would undergo further development, to become the hydrogen bomb. To defend one's country is good; to "love thy neighbor" ("thou shalt not kill") is good also, or at least to do so to the extent that one does not subject him to atomic weaponry is good.

The title of the film expresses the tragedy of the bomb as well as of the Frenchwoman's love. The juxta-position of "mon amour" against "Hiroshima" is star-tling. The love the Americans should have had for the Japanese is juxtaposed against the horror (immediately called forth by the word "Hiroshima") they should have inflicted, and did inflict, upon them. The love the

Frenchwoman had for the German is juxtaposed against the death he should have suffered, and did suffer, at the hands of Resistance fighters. "Hiroshima" in the film becomes a metonym, not only for the Japanese architect but also for the German soldier, since the Frenchwoman talks to the Japanese as if he were the German a number of times. When she does so, he does not act surprised. Through this device, as well as through the device of having the Frenchwoman and the Japanese speak in incantatory tones, Resnais encourages us to view his film on the symbolic rather than the realistic level. To this end also he does not name the characters, does not permit them to engage in small talk, and has the Frenchwoman say a line like this to the Japanese, in which she describes the meaning of the film's title from her point of view: "You destroy me, you are good for me".

Although it may at first seem strange that Resnais has chosen the tragedy of the Frenchwoman's *love* to be a metaphor for the tragedy of the *bomb*, his choice is actually entirely appropriate. Loving the enemy is the only thing that *approaches*, in its seeming incomprehensibility, grotesqueness, or even monstrosity, utterly annihilating (as opposed to simply defeating) the enemy by means of the atomic bomb. Although it may seem equally strange that Resnais has included someone French in a metaphor for the tragedy of the bomb, this too is entirely appropriate. America is never referred to by name in *Hiroshima, mon amour*. For purposes of distancing it is left to a foreigner, from a country that was almost non-combatant in the war, to incarnate America's presence—one implied by the very word "Hiroshima." The French are the apparent opposites of the Americans who dropped the bomb, just as the Frenchwoman's love is the apparent opposite of the bomb's destruction. But the French capitulation to the enemy is the only thing that *approaches*, in *its* seeming incomprehensibility, grotesqueness, or even monstrosity, the American annihilation of the enemy by means of the bomb. Like the woman's love for the German, the French capitulation was tragic—one knows that they could not have won if they had fought; yet one senses that they should have fought anyway, lost, and maintained their honor.

Even as the French have suffered since the war from the tragedy of their capitulation, so too has the Frenchwoman been suffering from the tragedy of her love affair with the German soldier. Not only has she not been able to love another man until she meets the Japanese; she has also not been able to love herself— love for another presupposes love for oneself—out of guilt for having had an affair with one of the enemy. John Ward believes that the Frenchwoman has been "psychologically deformed" by her experience at Nevers[3] and that her psychosis flaws *Hiroshima, mon amour*:

> The experiences of the girl were not of a kind that would give rise to normal personal memories, or even to the kind of memories which, just because of their extremeness, could serve as a paradigm of a class of 'standard' personal memories. Hers were in fact traumatic. It is not just her relationship with her Japanese lover that is affected: her whole life has been crippled. . . . The simple fact is that, in various ways, she is not free to choose what she wants to do; and to that extent the film, as an analysis of how even lovers are kept apart by their pasts, is weakened. It is weakened

because instead of developing the conflict between them, it assumes this conflict by making her the kind of woman any man would fail to get on with.[4]

To the extent that *Hiroshima, mon amour* is a realistic film, Ward is correct. The Japanese is "normal" and the Frenchwoman is "psychotic." *That* is what keeps them apart. But if we look at the film symbolically, as being less about the lovers themselves than about the two sides in World War II they represent, then I think that the flaw Ward speaks of disappears.

This particular Japanese is the perfect one to place in service as a symbol for his people, since he did not suffer any physical harm himself from the bomb and since his looks are more Western than those of the average Japanese. Thus we are distanced sufficiently through him from the actual suffering caused by the bomb, just as we are distanced through the French-woman from those who actually dropped it. This frees us to contemplate and lament the tragedy of the atomic bomb's creation and use. The Japanese and his French-woman are stand-ins for the genuine articles, symbols by detraction. Unlike traditional symbols, which are intended to enrich our perceptions of what in real life we take for granted, they are meant to make us contemplate in art what we otherwise could or would not. All film characters are literally "figures of light"; the Japanese and the Frenchwoman are figuratively so in the sense that they are shadows of the substance on which Resnais means to shine his light.

The Japanese is more precisely a symbol for his defeated people who, in rebuilding their country, were at the same time externalizing their wartime experience, working off their suffering, if you will. He has adjusted to his experience of Hiroshima and has been involved, as an architect, in rebuilding the city. His fellow Hiroshimans live so well with their past that they erect museums and give guided tours to commemorate it. The Frenchwoman, by contrast, has not adjusted to her experience at Nevers, has never returned to the city, and has been involved as an actress in living her life, on stage or on the set, through others and thereby negating her past. In her joy at-guilt over loving the German soldier, she is a symbol for the victorious Americans, who, overjoyed at saving their own country and the countries of the Allies, were at the same time internalizing their guilt for destroying Hiroshima with the atomic bomb. (This guilt was externalized in the suffering after the war of the crew members of the Enola Gay, the plane that carried the bomb.) The Americans—in Indochina in particular, where they followed the French—were later to attempt to negate *their* past by playing the role of peacemaker or savior in foreign conflicts, all the while continuing to build up arms and set themselves up for the same dilemma they faced in World War II, this time with the added danger that they themselves might be destroyed by the bomb.

The Frenchwoman faces her World War II dilemma again in Hiroshima—to remain or not to remain with her Japanese lover, a one-time enemy, like the German. Far from being merely a relationship between a psychotic woman and a normal man doomed to failure from the start, the relationship between the Frenchwoman and the Japanese is symbolic of the difficult rapprochement between a repressed America and a reconstructed Japan (remember that *Hiroshima, mon amour* was made only thirteen years after the war). The Japanese wants to find out all he can about Nevers, so that he can know the Frenchwoman better. The Frenchwoman, thinking she knows all there is to know about Hiroshima before she gets there, learns that she herself must come to terms with what happened at Nevers. Like the American "peacekeepers" abroad, the actress in the film about peace must return home to find herself.

Even as she could not tear herself away from the dead German's body in Nevers, she cannot leave the Japanese. But she must, and will. Even as the German courted death by continuing to see the Frenchwoman with the Americans approaching and the Resistance fighters becoming braver, the Japanese risks psychological damage by continuing to woo the Frenchwoman in the face of her dilemma. He must, and will, give her up, in order himself to survive. The Japanese must return to rebuilding Hiroshima—significantly, he has stopped work completely while conducting his affair with the Frenchwoman. On the realistic level, their love would not have existed without the bomb—recall that the Frenchwoman comes to Hiroshima in the first place to make a film about the bomb, "about peace," she says. On the symbolic level, their love cannot continue to exist *because* of the bomb: the Frenchwoman, in returning to Nevers, symbolizes America "coming home" to confront its romance with atomic warfare.

The Frenchwoman's love for the German isolated her in Nevers, has isolated her since the war, and will continue to isolate her: she must return to Nevers alone, a heroine who has, through contact with the searching Japanese in the present, experienced tragic recognition about her past. (He may be seen, in this sense, as a purely dramatic device; we have already seen him as the German's "double" and as a symbol in his own right for Japan.) Just so, America's atomic bombing of Japan alienated her from some of her own people, separated her in power from the rest of the world, and has continued to separate her. Although other countries have had the bomb, only America has ever used it. Now America has a stockpile of nuclear weapons that is matched only by the Soviet Union, with whom she is isolated in perpetual conflict. Like the Frenchwoman, America has had to return home alone, a heroine who has, through "involvements" abroad as well as post-war occupation of Japan, again and again comprehended the tragedy of the bomb, of the conflicting demands (destructive, reconstructive[5]) of absolute power.

NOTES TO
"The Symbolism of *Hiroshima, Mon Amour*"

1. *Hiroshima, mon amour* is most often discussed as an experiment in modernist style. Roy Armes is representative of those who take this approach to the film and praise it for its achievement:
    It was not until nine years after *Orphée* and *Rashomon* that the European cinema took further decisive steps forward in its self-imposed task of freeing itself from the bonds of an aesthetic based on the nineteenth-century novel and the 'well-made play': Alain Resnais's *Hiroshima Mon Amour* is a good example of the total novelty that now became possible.

(*The Ambiguous Image: Narrative Style in Modern European Cinema* [Bloomington: Indiana Univ. Press, 1976], pp. 27–28.)

[*Hiroshima Mon Amour* partakes of] certain stylistic methods which may be taken as characteristic of modern film-making—a refusal of psychological explanation, a stylization of acting and an interest in novel combinations of image and music. (*The Ambiguous Image*, pp. 83–84.)

Charles Thomas Samuels, on the other hand, is representative of those who attack the film for its experimenting in style at the expense of substance:

Daring as an innovator, and . . . unsatisfactory as an artist, is Alain Resnais, whose major achievement is an editing style that represents the flux of memory—with its confusion of tenses and yearning for the subjunctive. Unfortunately, Resnais neither invents nor writes the scenarios on which this technique is lavished, and he has deplorable taste in collaborators. Marguerite Duras's script for *Hiroshima Mon Amour* is portentous and melodramatic. (*Mastering the Film and Other Essays* [Knoxville: Univ. of Tennessee Press, 1977], p. 9.)

2. Albert Camus, *Resistance, Rebellion, and Death*, trans. Justin O'Brien (New York: Knopf, 1961), p. 114.
3. John Ward, *Alain Resnais or The Theme of Time* (Garden City, New York: Doubleday, 1968), p. 37.
4. John Ward, *Alain Resnais or The Theme of Time*, pp. 34–35.
5. Godelieve Mercken-Spass, "Destruction and Reconstruction in *Hiroshima, mon amour*," *Literature/Film Quarterly*, 8, No. 4 (1980), p. 244. While I am indebted to Professor Mercken-Spass for the pairing of these two words in the title of her essay, my ideas about *Hiroshima, mon amour* differ substantially from hers.

TAKE COMFORT, TAKE CAUTION:

Tragedy and Homily in *Day of Wrath*

James Agee was right. One of the attributes of *Day of Wrath* (*Vredens Dag*, 1943) to respect most is "its steep, Lutheran kind of probity—that is, its absolute recognition of the responsibility of the individual, regardless of extenuating or compulsive circumstances."[1] Critics speak often of Dreyer's austere style and his treatment of religious themes,[2] but few recognize any tragic intentions on his part.[3] The director himself, however, writes that in the four films *Passion of Joan of Arc* (1928), *Vampire* (1931), *Day of Wrath*, and *The Word* (1955)— those that are generally believed to be his best—he "ended up with a dramatic form which . . . has characteristics in common with that of tragedy. This applies particularly to *Passion of Joan of Arc* and *Day of Wrath*."[4] Dreyer was convinced there was a need for a "tragic poet of the cinema," and he felt that this poet's "first problem [would] be to find, within the cinema's framework, the form and style appropriate to tragedy."[5]

David Bordwell's plot summary of *Day of Wrath* is characteristic of most writing on the film in that it ignores the subject of Absalon's responsibility:

> *Day of Wrath* is the story of how, in seventeenth-century
> Denmark, Anne falls in love with the son of Absalon, the
> old pastor whom she has married. A subplot involves
> Herlofs Marthe, an old woman accused of witchcraft
> and persecuted by the church elder Laurentius. After
> Herlofs Marthe is executed, Anne and Martin share a
> furtive idyll. When Anne tells Absalon of the affair, the
> old man dies. The pastor's elderly mother Merete ac-
> cuses Anne of witchcraft. When Martin abandons her,
> Anne finally confesses to having been in Satan's power
> and is burned as a witch.[6]

Because the pastor Absalon is reticent and because we
never see him lust for his wife Anne, it is easy to fail to
consider *Day of Wrath* as his tragedy. Dreyer begins the
film with the ferreting out and burning of Herlof's
Marthe as a witch so that attention will focus immediately on Absalon and his actions. Absalon seems almost
to have forgotten that he pardoned Anne's mother, also
accused of being a witch, years before when he was
widowed so that he might marry Anne, half his age. But
his young wife is no different in function from his first
wife: she is his companion and the mistress of his house,
not the object of his sexual desire. Anne married Absalon out of obligation; if she does not love him, she has at
least accustomed herself to him.

All is apparently well in Absalon's world, then, at the
start of the film. The Herlof's Marthe incident changes
matters. It reminds Absalon of the sin he committed to
obtain Anne as his wife, and it places him in the position
of sinning again: Marthe asks him to pardon her in the
same way that he pardoned Anne's mother. Absalon is
faced with a tragic choice: spare Marthe and sin again in
the eyes of God, or let her go to her death and incur

guilt for having spared one witch (for selfish reasons) and not another. He lets her go to her death, and she in turn pronounces the curse that he will soon die and prophesies for Anne a fate similar to her own.

Even though Absalon dies and Anne herself will be burned as a witch, *Day of Wrath* is not a testimony to the powers of witchcraft. Witchcraft, rather, is something Dreyer contrasts with the piety of Absalon.[7] Witchcraft—setting oneself up as a rival to God—is the gravest sin to Absalon, just as forgiving witchcraft, which he did for Anne's mother, is the gravest sin that he, as a representative of God, can commit. I hesitate to use the term "tragic inevitability" with regard to this film, for it is not simply a tragedy of character. There is too much "arranging" going on in it. Absalon to a large extent brings on his own doom, but there is a sense in which Dreyer is making an example of him for all the world to see and be encouraged by. I stress that Dreyer, not witchcraft or "fate," is making an example of him. Or Dreyer the artist is his own witch-god, which explains the choice of a pastor as tragic figure and of witches as his antagonists: Dreyer wishes to register the artist's power in the universe alongside the forces of evil and the wrath of God.[8] The event that clarifies Dreyer's purpose is the entrance of Martin, Absalon's son by his first marriage, into the film.

Martin, who has recently graduated from the seminary, is the favorite of his grandmother, Merete, just as her son Absalon was once her favorite. (She lives with Absalon and Anne.) Like his father before him, Martin falls in love with Anne and appears to "choose" her over Merete. It all seems a little too pat: father and son love the same woman; the woman prefers the son; disapproving mother-grandmother looks on. In this way Merete is a kind of chorus to events; she disapproves of Anne from the start, and thus, for all her sternness and stridency, we find ourselves sharing her opinion. But the deck is stacked in *Day of Wrath* for a good reason, even as it is in *Hippolytus* and *Phaedra*, to whose love-triangle plot the film is indebted. Dreyer wants his Absalon to go through the worst possible ordeal before dying; he wants the worst that can happen to him to happen. Absalon the pastor is Dreyer's sacrificial lamb. Like his Biblical counterpart, Absalon rebels against his father, God, when he pardons a witch and marries her daughter, and he must be killed for his sin. Moreover, he will be permitted by Dreyer to utter barely a word of protest throughout his ordeal. This is part of the strategy of outrage: Absalon committed an outrageous act in marrying the young Anne; he sincerely repents his sin of pardoning Anne's mother, but only when he is confronted, outrageously, with the possibility of committing the same sin again; and he dies at the outrageous admission by Anne that she has betrayed him with his own son. Even as he suffers silently the guilt of his original sin of pardoning Anne's mother, so too he suffers silently the revelation of his betrayal: he simply dies.

It was Johnson, I believe, who first complained of the improbability of Lear's proposal to divide his kingdom among his three daughters according to how much each loved him. The same complaint could be made about the staid pastor Absalon's proposing to pardon a witch and marry her young daughter: nothing in Absalon's behavior during the film, and no information Dreyer gives us about him, can account for his going to such extremes to marry so young a woman, especially when one considers the time and place in which he lives. But demands for this kind of believability in a work of art miss the forest for the trees. Like *King Lear, Day of Wrath* could be called, in J. Stampfer's term, a "tragedy of penance,"[9] in which the enormity of the offending act provokes the enormity of the punishment. Stampfer makes the important point that *King Lear* is not a tragedy of hubris, like *Oedipus Rex*, but of penance:

> [The] opening movement [of *King Lear*] leads not to dissolution, exposure, and self-recognition, as in *Oedipus* and *Othello*, but to purgation. And Lear's purgation, by the end of the play's middle movement, is so complete as to be archetypal. By the time he enters prison, he has paid every price and been stripped of everything a man can lose, even his sanity, in payment for folly and pride. As such he activates an even profounder fear than the fear of failure, and that is the fear that whatever penance a man may pay may not be enough once the machinery of destruction has been set loose, because the partner of his covenant may be neither grace nor the balance of law, but malignity, intransigence, or chaos.[10]

Absalon repents, but it is too late, and there is no evidence that matters would be different had he repented long before the film begins. Marthe would still have dabbled in witchcraft and she would still have sought sanctuary in Absalon's home, since she herself had hidden Anne's mother and felt that the same favor was due her in return.

Dreyer has Absalon repent only when faced with the possibility of committing the same sin again, and not earlier, not because this is why he is being destroyed in the first place—for sinning monumentally *and living peacefully with that sin*—but because Absalon's late repentance "rescues him from perfection in the process of being doomed."[11] That is, Dreyer singled out the pastor for destruction and invented his sin but had to have him repent belatedly to remind us of its seriousness. The sin is dim in Absalon's own memory at the beginning of the film and in our minds, for having occurred so long ago and offscreen. (Dreyer keeps it offscreen and in the past, I believe, because of its very improbability). Absalon, in other words, had to appear flawed beyond his original sin of pardoning a witch and marrying Anne. And his flaw is his tardiness in repenting, his willingness to tolerate it in himself but not in his congregation, and least of all in Marthe. Thus Dreyer makes him appear something less than irreproachable—no small accomplishment in the case of Absalon, who strikes one at first as being irreproachable. This is important, because the less irreproachable Absalon becomes the easier it is for us to witness, if not finally condone or participate in, his destruction. The destruction of a flawless or completely and quickly repentant man is too easily rationalized as pure accident or pure evil; of a bad man, as poetic justice. Neither is paid much attention. But the destruction of the man in the middle—the good man who has done wrong, yet has neither been perverted by his wrongdoing nor has atoned for it—*this* is more terrible, precisely because it is deserved, yet not deserved, and therefore inexplicable. We pay attention to it.[12]

Ironically, then, even though Absalon chooses God in choosing not to pardon Marthe for her witchcraft and so could be said to be attempting to atone for the sin of pardoning Anne's mother, he still receives the maxi-

mum punishment. He chooses God and dies, unforgiven (but still loved) by his mother for having married Anne in the first place, unforgiven by Anne for
having robbed her youth, alienated from his son who
loves Anne as much as he does. And he is without a
fellow minister at his side, as he was at Laurentius' side
when the latter died in fulfillment of another of
Marthe's curses.

Laurentius' sudden death must not in itself be looked
on as a testimony to the powers of witchcraft. Rather, it
should be seen as one more punishment inflicted upon
Absalon, one more price he has to pay for the "folly and
pride" of coveting a young woman and pardoning her
witch-mother in order to get her. He pays the final price
in remaining unforgiven by God Himself, Whom one
might have expected to show some mercy toward Absalon. That He does not is not an argument against God;
it is an argument, using one of God's own as an example, for the fallibility of the human and the inscrutability of the divine. It is an argument that the worst in
man—the worst or the flaw in a good man—is combated
by the worst in God or simply the universe, and as such
it is a form of purgation: this is *the worst that can happen*,
and from that we can take comfort. What will happen to
us cannot be as bad. Dreyer, finally, has been the engi-
neer of all this, as much to fortify himself against the
many forms of disaster, to use Bert O. States's words
(see note 8), as to assert his own imagination's place as a
force in the universe.

.   .   .

J. Stampfer remarks that "there is no mitigation in
Lear's death, hence no mitigation in the ending of the

play. . . . *King Lear* is Shakespeare's first tragedy in which the tragic hero dies unreconciled and indifferent to society."[13] Lear dies, and there is no one from his family to carry on in his place: with him have died Goneril, Regan, and Cordelia. Absalon dies unredeemed and bewildered, but there is someone from his family to carry on in his place: his son, who turns on Anne and, with his grandmother, accuses her of witchcraft in willing the death of his father. *Day of Wrath* ends with our knowledge that Anne will burn as a witch and with the suggestion that Martin will take over his father's duties as pastor. Martin will occupy the role Absalon filled after the death of his first wife, before he met Anne and pardoned her mother: that of pastor, living with his (grand)mother. Anne's mother has been dead for some time (presumably of natural causes), Absalon is dead, and Anne will die: the sin will be completely expiated. Matters will be returned to a state of grace. But we do not *see* them returned to a state of grace. We do not see Anne burn, as we did Marthe, and we do not see Martin become pastor. Dreyer's overriding concern is still with Absalon's destruction, not his society's redemption. Whatever reconciliation we get at the end of the film, then, is less in the sense that wrong is righted than in the sense that wrong is counterpointed. Absalon yielded to temptation with Anne; Martin does not, ultimately. Dreyer juxtaposes the chaos of Absalon's life against the newfound order of Martin's so as to point up the irrevocability of that chaos and the tentativeness of that order.

Dreyer uses this technique of counterpoint again when he intercuts the scene of Absalon returning from the dead Laurentius' house with the one of Martin and Anne in the parsonage, where she wishes Absalon dead.

The relationship between these two scenes might seem too obvious: Absalon comments at one point on the strength of the wind, "It was as if death brushed against my sleeve."[14] But Dreyer is not telling us here that Anne is willing Absalon's death, that even as she wishes his death, he feels it coming. He is portraying Absalon's own sense of his impending doom, of his punishment for his sin. He sees trouble coming, or at least feels very uneasy, outdoors as well as indoors—he can find no peace anywhere. Earlier Dreyer had intercut a scene of him at home, full of remorse for having pardoned Anne's mother to marry her daughter, with a scene of Anne and Martin wandering blissfully in the fields at night. She feels no guilt indoors or outdoors for betraying her husband and for wishing him dead. Absalon can feel guilt for his sins; Anne cannot. She is, in this way, less the instrument of his doom than its counterpoint. She incarnates evil; he, good gone wrong. Absalon's mother, at the other extreme from Anne, incarnates good, or at least righteousness; Martin, contrasted with his father in the middle, good that is tempted but finally abstains.

Even the way that Anne accepts her witchcraft and her sentence to burn at the stake, after Martin renounces her, is in direct counterpoint to the way that Absalon receives the revelation of his betrayal and her accusation that he robbed her youth; and this contrast makes the circumstances of Absalon's death clearer. He dies immediately of a heart attack out of guilt and out of shock at the extremity of his punishment. Anne accepts-chooses death-by-burning coolly. She wants to die, not so much because she thinks she has played any part in her husband's death or that this would matter anyway, not so much out of guilt, as to spite Martin, who has betrayed her for his grandmother. She will die out of spite, out of selfishness; Absalon has died for his sins, for his belief in a higher law than the law of self.

Day of Wrath counterpoints witchcraft with piety, indulgence with abstinence, evil with good. The film "gorges" itself on Absalon's destruction, but all the while it reassures us that what happens to him cannot happen to us, it warns us that some form of destruction or misfortune lies in wait for everyone. That is its underpinning: Dreyer not only takes out his frustrations absolutely on Absalon, he is also sure to include himself and, by extension, the audience as a potential, if less serious, victim of a malevolent universe. This he does through the character of Martin and the film's visual style. Dreyer is careful not to have Martin succumb in the end to Anne's temptations. He must have a scare but must survive, his virtue, or at least good intentions, intact, as the character we identify with most. Anne herself is too evil, too devious to identify with; Absalon's mother so good as to be a caricature of goodness, rightness, and caution; and Absalon, of course, too victimized. Through Martin, Dreyer posits the existence of two separate worlds, the one safe, rational, certain, the other dangerous, irrational, uncertain; and he shows how simple it is to cross from one world to the next with a single action. Martin rejects Anne at the last minute and remains on the safe side.

I said at the start that many critics have remarked on the austerity and stateliness of Dreyer's visual style. Paul Schrader, for example, writes that

> the late nineteenth- and early twentieth-century Kammerspiele (literally, chamber plays) were the immediate

stylistic precedents for Dreyer's films. . . . In each of Dreyer's films one can detect elements of Kammerspiele: intimate family drama, fixed interior settings, unembellished sets, long takes emphasizing staging, the use of gesture and facial expression to convey psychological states, plain language, and a thoroughgoing sobriety.[15]

But no one has remarked on how Dreyer contrasts in *Day of Wrath* the seeming sureness and reason of this style with the disorientation and unreason of another style that he puts side by side with it.

Often Dreyer will shoot a character from one angle and then cut to a shot of the same character from the reverse angle; or he will cut from one character to another, then return to the first at an angle that confuses the viewer as to the place of the characters in the room and their relation to each other. The effect of this is less to suggest that objective reality does not exist, that people and things can be looked at and interpreted in any number of ways, than to give the viewer a sense of the changeability of matters from moment to moment, a sense of a world in which a fixed position or a complete knowledge of oneself is impossible. In other words, as with his characterization of Martin, so too with his visual style is Dreyer attempting to posit the existence of two separate worlds, the one orderly, the other chaotic.[16] Even as the camera can change worlds from shot to shot, so too can a man change his "world" from one action to the next—except that the camera can go back, can reclaim the orderly after a plunge into the chaotic. That is not so easy for a man. Martin comes as close as possible to doing it at the end of *Day of Wrath* when he goes from loving Anne and swearing that she is not a witch to despising her and swearing that she is.

Dreyer has written:

> All good films are characterized by a certain rhythmic tension, which is induced partly by the characters' movements as revealed in images . . . For [this] kind of tension, much importance is attached to the lively use of a moving camera, which even in close shots adroitly follows the characters; so that the background constantly shifts as it does when we follow somebody with our eyes. . . . It is of some significance for the adaptation of stage plays that in each act of most plays there is as much action off stage as on, which can yield material for . . . new rhythms.[17]

One senses that by "good films" Dreyer means those (like his own masterpieces) that attempt to create tragedy, where the kind of tension he speaks of is essential and underlines another kind, which is perhaps the essence of tragedy: the viewer feels that the outcome of the action is inevitable at the same time as he feels a certain measure of control over his own fate, that he is not himself inevitably doomed. He feels right up to the end, furthermore, that even though the outcome of the action is inevitable, something could be done to alter the course of events. (Cf. dramatic terms like "turning point" and "moment of final suspense.") Or that alternative values or an alternative world exists somewhere. The alternative world is peopled by Martin in *Day of Wrath*, as I have stated. The chaotic world of Absalon is suggested not only by the cutting but also by the moving camera that, in following clearly one object or person, turns everything else into a dizzying blur.

Day of Wrath is an adaptation of a play. Dreyer includes in it the offstage action that he refers to in the above quotation—scenes that in the film's source, the historical drama *Anne Pedersdotter* by the Norwegian playwright Hans Wiers-Jenssen,[18] are only reported by characters. I am thinking specifically of Anne and Martin's meeting in the fields at night and Absalon's return home from the dead Laurentius' house. These outdoor scenes create a rhythmic tension in the film. But the tension here does not derive from the intercutting of outdoor and indoor scenes. It comes from the tilting upward of the camera one moment to the trees above the lovers Anne and Martin, implying that God is judging their sinful actions below; and the leveling of the camera the next moment at the unhappy, fearful, penitent Absalon in the same outdoors to the exclusion of the heavens above, implying that God is not present and will not grant mercy to him. In one instance it seems that the world is inhabited by a just and rational God, in the other that no such God exists. The outdoor scenes give Dreyer further opportunity, then, to dramatize the two separate worlds he demarcated so tellingly indoors.

.   .   .

I have remarked several times on the reticence of Absalon, his lack of reflection on, and of exasperation with, what is happening to him compared with Lear. This is the factor that has, up to now, caused critics to look outside his character—namely, to witchcraft and the mysterious—for the key to the film's intentions.[19] I want only to explain more precisely Absalon's silence, almost his *absence*, since it is so unusual a trait in a character so important and so obviously intelligent.

Dreyer makes Absalon silent and passive because *we are not so*, or we think we are not. Absalon's behavior in the face of his misfortune is, to us, one of the worst things that can happen: he does not object (like Lear), he does not run (as Oedipus did from Corinth), he does not suspect or seek counsel (like Othello). We can picture ourselves in all these actions. This is a comfort: we think that we would fight back and perhaps escape; we forget momentarily what happened to Lear, Oedipus, and Othello. Part of the art of *Day of Wrath* is that it beguiles us into thinking we are different, and therefore better off, in a way that Shakespeare and Sophocles do not, and then it reminds us, through the character of Martin and through its visual style, that we are vulnerable. It gives us the greatest comfort, and it gives us good caution. If *Day of Wrath* was, as Robert Warshow and Paul Schrader believe, one of the first films to attempt to create a "religious system,"[20] it succeeds less in the sense that it evokes God for us than in the sense that it does for us what religion, at its best, and art, only rarely, do for us: it makes us feel that we are chosen at the same time as it makes us feel we are expendable or incapable.

NOTES TO
"Take Comfort, Take Caution: Tragedy and Homily in
Day of Wrath"

1. James Agee, *Agee on Film: Reviews and Comments* (Boston: Beacon Press, 1958), p. 304.

2. See, for example, Jack C. Ellis, *A History of Film* (Engle-wood Cliffs, N. J.: Prentice-Hall, 1979), pp. 88–89; Leo Braudy and Morris Dickstein, eds., *Great Film Directors: A Critical Anthology* (New York: Oxford Univ. Press, 1978), p. 209; Paul Schrader, *Transcendental Style in Film: Ozu, Bresson, Dreyer* (Berkeley: Univ. of Calif. Press, 1972), pp. 114–115; and Tom Milne, *The Cinema of Carl Dreyer* (New York: A. S. Barnes, 1971), pp. 12–15.

3. Those that do speak of tragic intentions on Dreyer's part, do so only in passing, like Tom Milne (*The Cinema of Carl Dreyer*, p. 13), or in vague terms, like Jean-Louis Cornolli (Cornolli quoted in Mark Nash, *Dreyer* [London: British Film Institute, 1977], pp. 58–59).

4. Carl Theodor Dreyer, Foreword, *Carl Theodor Dreyer: Four Screen Plays*, trans. Oliver Stallybrass, intro. Ole Storm (Bloomington: Indiana Univ. Press, 1970), p. 7.

5. Dreyer, Foreword, *Four Screen Plays*, p. 7.

6. David Bordwell, *The Films of Carl-Theodor Dreyer* (Berkeley: Univ. of Calif. Press, 1981), p. 117.

7. David Bordwell seems to support my view here when he writes:

> The film, set during the worst years of the European witch-hunts, relies on a general historical awareness of the Church's persecution of witches. . . . But what is significant is that at crucial points Dreyer's film refuses to define a position with respect to the historical phenomenon of witchcraft. Gone is most of the paraphernalia of traditional witch-lore: the witch's ability to confound neighbors, the witches' sabbath, etc. Although the apparatus of Church repression is well summarized in Laurentius's interrogation, the film remains silent about the various causes which historians have proposed for the witch-craze (religious strife, the rise of the medical profession, the

retention of pagan religious customs). (*The Films of Carl-Theodor Dreyer*, pp. 125–126.)

8. The view of tragedy I take in this essay is the one first propounded by Bert O. States in *Irony and Drama: A Poetics* (Ithaca, N. Y.: Cornell Univ. Press, 1971). States writes:

> The idea that the victory inherent in tragedy arrives primarily in the earned nobility of the defeated-victorious hero is actually much overrated as the key to catharsis; the victory is rather in the poet's having framed the definitive fate for his hero-victim. In turning the tables on his hero so *exactly*, getting the all into his one, he shows wherein the imagination is a match for nature in getting her to participate so thoroughly in the fault. This seems the most complete statement that can be made about destructiveness, and when the poet can arrange to make it, as Shakespeare and Sophocles have, he has posed the unanswerable argument against reality in his effort to fortify men against the many forms of disaster. In effect, he has said, "You may destroy me, but I have gone even further. I have conceived the impossible destruction." In other words, the force of tragic catharsis consists in the poet's having conceived a power beyond Power itself; as such, it would seem to be not only a purgation but something of a gorging as well. (p. 50)

Let us not forget that Dreyer made *Day of Wrath* in 1943 during the German occupation of Denmark: one huge form of disaster for the Danes, without a doubt. Ole Storm notes that while

> *Vredens Dag* can hardly be regarded as a Resistance film, . . . it contained unmistakable elements of the irrationality that was characteristic of Nazism: witch-hunting, mass hypnosis, assertion of power,

and the primitive, always latent forces which, in certain conditions, can be exploited by any authority that knows how to license the gratification of blood-lust as an act of justice; whereby a judicial process conducted without witnesses or counsel for the defence culminates in a death sentence passed on the sole basis of a forced confession. (Intro., *Four Screen Plays*, p. 19.)

9. J. Stampfer, "The Catharsis of *King Lear*," *Shakespeare Survey*, 13 (1960), rpt. in Leonard Dean, ed., *Shakespeare: Modern Essays in Criticism* (New York: Oxford Univ. Press, 1967), p. 375.

10. Stampfer, "The Catharsis of *King Lear*," in Dean, p. 375.

11. States, *Irony and Drama*, p. 54. See note 12.

12. Bert O. States on dramatic flaw is worth quoting at length again; my ideas here and some of my language come from the following:

> What we notice about the great tragic heroes is that their truly dramatic flaws are not such as to worsen their characters in the moral sense, but to make them ambiguously fallible. We would not, therefore, emphasize the fact that in Sophocles' version Oedipus' temper hastens his doom, but that it rescues him from perfection in the process of being doomed. . . . Here, perhaps, is the true sense of Aristotle's own idea: to mark the excellent and flawless man for destruction, or conversely the utterly bad man, is to make a statement that is less complete, less *infinite*, than to mark for destruction the median man who simultaneously deserves it (but not quite), yet does not deserve it (but not quite). (*Irony and Drama*, pp. 53–54.)

13. Stampfer, "The Catharsis of *King Lear*," in Dean, pp. 366, 371.

14. Oliver Stallybrass, Trans., *Four Screen Plays*, p. 211.

15. Schrader, *Transcendental Style in Film*, pp. 114–115.

16. David Bordwell notes Dreyer's "systematic changes of camera orientation" (*The Films of Carl-Theodor Dreyer*, p. 124) and the discontinuity that results from such changes, and even documents Dreyer's need to reorient the audience to the action through the use of long shots (p. 121). Yet he concludes the opposite of what I do: that Dreyer is seeking only to produce varied shot patterns for their own sake (p. 121), and that in fact Dreyer is unifying space by separating it into its component parts, which the audience will then naturally join together (p. 124).

17. Dreyer quoted in Ole Storm, Intro., *Four Screen Plays*, pp. 13–14.

18. I want to stress that *Anne Pedersdotter* was an historical drama. Dreyer transformed it into tragedy. Storm writes that "the historical element is emphasized in Wiers-Jenssen's play, which is concerned with the delusions, superstitions and ignorance that existed in the past." (Intro., *Four Screen Plays*, p. 17.)

19. See, for example, Robert Warshow, "*Day of Wrath*: The Enclosed Image," in his *The Immediate Experience: Movies, Comics, Theatre and Other Aspects of Popular Culture* (Garden City, N. Y.: Doubleday, 1962), pp. 265–266; Braudy and Dickstein, *Great Film Directors*, p. 209.

20. Warshow, *The Immediate Experience*, p. 266; Schrader, *Transcendental Style in Film*, p. 127.

THE CIRCUMSTANCE OF THE EAST, THE FATE OF THE WEST:

Notes, Mostly on *The Seven Samurai*

I must categorize the films of the world into three distinct types. European films are based upon human psychology, American films upon action and the struggles of human beings, and Japanese films upon circumstance. *Japanese films are interested in what surrounds the human being.*

—Masahiro Shinoda[1]

Kurosawa's *The Seven Samurai* (1954) is such a Japanese film as Shinoda describes, one that portrays the power of circumstance over its characters' lives. The major "circumstance" in the film is this: with the invention of the gun and the development of the horse as an instrument of warfare, the samurai have been rendered obsolete as the warrior figures in Japanese society of the Sengoku Period (1534-1615). Whereas it is the samurai swordsmen who once would have raided the peasant village for rice and women, it is now the gun-toting bandits on horseback who do so. This places the peasants in an enviable position: they can hire the samurai to defend them for the price of three meals a day and a place to sleep. But it also places them in a precarious position: the samurai will also teach them to defend themselves, which the peasants have never done before. Circumstance has forced a new role on them. They are farmers by nature, fighters by chance (and by necessity). Circumstance forces the dignified samurai to go about in shabby clothing and even to chop wood for a meal; it compels them to work for the very class of people that they once had the most contempt for. Circumstance puts a gun in the hands of anyone who can pay for it (unlike a sword, which only a master can wield, a gun can be mastered—especially at close range—by almost anyone) and thus turns the petty thief into the roving, deadly, greedy bandit, part of a larger robber band or "army." Circumstance then dictates that three guns—all that the bandits possess—are not enough against the expertise of the samurai combined with the total number of peasants. The day will come when all the bandits carry guns, however, and that day will spell the extinction of the samurai and the rise of the military, and later of the civilian police, to protect the people.

The force of circumstance is clearly at work throughout *The Seven Samurai*. But the film is hardly a treatise on man's helplessness before circumstance, his dwarfing by it. The art of the film, for me, is in man's playing out his destiny before circumstance at the same time as it seems to engulf him. The farmers fight and die for their freedom. The samurai defend the farmers nobly and fiercely, no differently than they would defend themselves. The bandits fight to the last man against unbeatable odds, apparently forgetting that their initial objective in storming the village was to seize the farmers' crops: their own honor and fighting ability have become the issue. We see ironies in the situation, but the farmer, the samurai, and the bandits do not, or they do so only in passing. They *act*, and in action are ennobled. *The Seven Samurai* is perhaps truly an "action" or "epic" film in this sense: that action occurs not for its own sake or for the sake of mere spectacle, as is often the case in American films, but in the service of ennoblement. The different protagonists act, no matter what they think or don't think about their situation. If they are aware of "circumstance," they pay no attention to it. The concentration is thus always on the human struggle more than on the existential dilemma. What matters is the present and the human more than the historical and the circumstantial. In this manner, the human transcends the circumstantial: those dead at the hands of circumstance are not mourned (farmers, samurai)[2] or rejoiced over (bandits) at the end of the film; the living go on living— the farmers plant rice, the surviving samurai move on, unheralded—the dead are dead (the final shot of the burial mounds).

The point must be made again, for the sake of contrast: *The Seven Samurai* is about circumstance, or about man and his relationship at his best to circumstance; it is not about fate. In tragedy man acts, often stupidly if inevitably, and then reflects on his actions, wisely. In the artwork of circumstance, man acts wisely in the face of the stupidity and unpredictability of circumstance. In a way, tragedy focuses unnaturally on man and his deeds. It presumes the authenticity and absolute rule of fate, then sets man happily against fate or against himself (in whom fate may reside). The work of circumstance focuses more naturally on the vagaries of circumstance and on man's often instinctive response to them. The folly is in the universe; the wiseness, if not the temperance or caution, is in man. Man assumes a more modest position in this kind of art and, in my estimation, appears as a result in a better light. Circumstance is the real force, the real enemy lurking at all times in the background of our lives. Fate is the straw man in tragedy: one senses often that it has been invented merely for the display of man's vanity, his self-obsession. Fate seems dominant in tragedy, but man apart from fate is the actual star (one hears him calling out, "Look at me!"). Fate is something that man has created to *explain away* his own obsessions and inadequacies. Circumstance is real or tangible; man is most often defeated by it. At his best, he meets adverse circumstance on equal ground, and if he does not triumph, he does not lose, either. He distinguishes himself in the fight. That is all, and that is enough. Of the three groups of characters in *The Seven Samurai*— the farmers, the samurai, and the bandits—this can be said with almost tactile sureness.

The work of circumstance is interested in what surrounds the human being and in how he reacts under stress to his surroundings. Tragedy is interested in what it believes is immutable in each human being and in the world, and in how this immutability leads to man's destruction. Tragedy is interested, in other words, in man above all else, in all his flaw. Circumstance places man squarely in the world; fate pushes him back into himself. The one art looks out, the other in. The difference between them is the difference between East and West, self and other. Accordingly, tragedy focuses on one character; the work of circumstance, on several or many characters. Indeed, *The Seven Samurai* is not about the seven samurai themselves, it is about the characteristics of samurai—courage, honor, dignity—that circumstance conspires to bring out in others. The farmers are the ones who first decide to fight the bandits; only then do they think to hire samurai to help them.

One example from the film will suffice to distinguish between Western tragedy and the Eastern work of circumstance. Near the end, circumstance presents the young woman Shino with a difficult choice. By now she is in love with the samurai initiate Katsushiro; she must go with him, a man of a higher class, or stay behind in her native village. She chooses to remain at home. Even though she loves Katsushiro, she makes a wise choice. She will forget him in time—indeed, she seems to forget him immediately—and marry a man of her own class. She will suffer momentarily but prosper in the long run. Shino suppresses self for other, for her relationship with her family and her village, with the world she has known since birth.

What would have happened in a tragedy, given a similar situation? This situation would have been the basis for *the entire film*. Shino would have been irresistibly drawn to Katsushiro and would have planned to run off with him. Her parents would have disapproved of the relationship (if they had known about it—it will be kept secret from them until the end). Shino's love for Katsushiro would have been true, but doomed by its own intensity as well as by the intensity of his love for her and by the lovers' consequent willingness to go to any lengths to marry. Shino and Katsushiro would both end up committing suicide, and only in sorrow would their families, separated by class, be joined. We are in the world of *Romeo and Juliet*, where foolish, if sincere and inevitable, action on the part of the protagonists leads to the wisdom of reconciliation between their long-feuding families. Romeo and Juliet choose self-fulfillment over duty to family, and they pay for their decision with their lives. To a Westerner, theirs is a noble sacrifice; to someone like Kurosawa, it is a senseless one. Senseless, because it is the very intensity, if not obsessiveness, of Romeo's love for Juliet that causes him to kill himself upon finding her "dead." Even as he was irresistibly drawn to Juliet despite the serious feud between their families, so too is he compelled to commit suicide without investigating the circumstances of her "death." Romeo does not sacrifice himself for Juliet; he sacrifices himself to his own ideal of romantic love. His suicide is, paradoxically, a form of self-endorsement: if he can't have Juliet, then no one can have him. He places himself before the other members of his family and community, and it is this absorption with himself, this retreat into self, that makes him commit suicide when he finds Juliet's body. Romeo is finally all alone, with no reference outside himself once Juliet is "dead," therefore he fancies suicide as the only way to remain "alone" without suffering. He cannot think of anyone but himself, and that is what kills him: he exhausts his powers of reason and measure.

Clearly, I am not trying to say that characters in Japanese films do not commit suicide or otherwise come to ruin. Think only of Shinoda's own *Double Suicide* (1969) and his more recent *Ballad of Orin* (1978). But there is a great deal of difference between lovers' delib-erately *choosing* suicide as a means of escape from society's strictures—killing themselves because they cannot fathom society's harsh workings or, possibly, so as not to rend the fabric of society—and Romeo's killing himself in an hysterical moment of grief because he thinks his Juliet dead, or her stabbing herself because she knows that her lover has expired. Romeo and Juliet's suicide is an *accident.* It would never have happened if not for the intervention of Friar Laurence. It is a "tragic" accident in the sense that it was inevitable that Juliet, in her consuming love, would go to such extremes to be with Romeo, and in the sense that her family will not relent in its feud with the Montagues; but it is an accident nonetheless. The reason for Juliet's taking the potion in the first place is to appear dead *to her family,* so that she will be buried, freed from her tomb by Friar Laurence, and met by Romeo for the escape to Mantua. She rejects her family and city, that is, for her lover.[3]

Shakespeare, then, devotes a whole play to the actions of Romeo and Juliet. Kurosawa makes the relationship of Shino and Katsushiro a small part of a work devoted to illustrating commitment to other before self and to depicting sure, noble action in the face of unfavorable circumstance. Shino is one of many characters in *The Seven Samurai* who choose duty to other before self, and I think that commentators on the film have for the most part missed this aspect of it. Some of the samurai, for instance, initially resist the idea of joining with Kambei to protect the village. They have two basic reasons: there is not enough monetary reward in defending farmers, and there is no honor in it. But they finally agree to fight the bandits, primarily because of their attraction to Kambei, their desire to ally with him *as samurai* in a warring cause. The individual, vagrant samurai cohere into a single-minded fighting unit. The young Katsushiro himself becomes Kambei's disciple, at first against the older man's wishes. Katsushiro suppresses self, that is, for devotion to a master. The few farmers outside the village proper want to save themselves, not the village as a whole, but, after some coercion by the samurai, they too forget self and fight on behalf of other. The same goes for the bandits. Every one of them sacrifices self to other: each is killed in the battle with the samurai and the farmers. Not one of them runs, for fear of death at the hands of his chief. (The chief says, pointing to a dead bandit, "Remember! Every coward here will get the same treatment."[4]) No one flees, despite one bandit's remark, "The whole thing is back to front. Now we're burnt out and hungrier than they are."[5]

Circumstance unites man: farmers with farmers, samurai with samurai, bandits with bandits. It "unites" man further: circumstance nearly turns the farmer into samurai-like fighter; it makes the bandit samurai-like in his courage to fight to the end and in his pride at doing so; it makes the samurai farmer-like in his desire to guard the rice crop from the bandits. (It is this crop that the samurai himself now shares, whereas once he had been bandit-like in seizing it.)

Tragedy divides and isolates man. The knowledge that its protagonists derive from suffering is not of the common variety; this is knowledge that can be had only from profound suffering and from the direct witnessing of it. So the message of tragedy is that man will suffer again. The calm at its end is the calm before another storm. Man is steady and united in facing circumstance: it draws him outside himself and gives him an experience common to many; he is unsettled and alone in the face of tragedy, of man's fate. Beneath tragedy's message is buried a more important one, however, which I hinted at earlier: that it is precisely this excessive emphasis on the individual in the West, and in the West's tragic literature, that condemns man to further suffering. Paradoxically, it is the total fascination with and absorption in self, in art as in life, that leads to continued self-destruction. Fate in literature or film becomes almost beside the point, as do individual deeds leading to isolation and suffering in life. The point is that when man lacks a reference outside himself, when he is devoted to nothing but self-fulfillment and self-glorification, he will suffer, however grandly. He will break down. The tragic hero in the West is, then, condemned to defeat before he ever steps onto the page, the screen, or the stage. The very way of life, the world view, that has produced him, condemns him. His fate is not so much "fate" as that word is applied to individuals in works of art. It is *life* as applied to Western man generally.

NOTES TO
"The Circumstance of the East, the Fate of the West: Notes, Mostly on *The Seven Samurai*"

1. Joan Mellen, *Voices from the Japanese Cinema* (New York: Liveright, 1975), p. 242.
2. There is one ceremonial burial (of Heihachi, a samurai) earlier in the film, but, significantly, the human struggle interrupts it: the bandits appear en masse on the horizon.

3. Although the characters in such a Western film as *Elvira Madigan* (1967) appear at first deliberately to choose suicide (actually, he shoots her, then himself) as a means of escape from society's strictures, they are really the victims of the director Bo Widerberg's own absorption with himself and his devices. Widerberg wanted his two lovers to end their predicament by killing themselves, probably because he felt that this was the most romantic way to end his romantic story (recall that we hear the shots but do not see the unromantic dead bodies). The only other explanation, which goes hand in hand with the first, is that the director knew the lovers would commit suicide, because the Elvira Madigan story is true in its outline (and I think it is) and this is why he chose it. But he doesn't for one moment convince us that there is no way out for the army officer and his mistress: it is almost as if they kill themselves for want of something better to do, or out of fear that life outside the bounds of bourgeois society would not be good enough for them. If indeed for the latter reason (although this is not developed in the film), then so much for their concern not to injure the fabric of society or their inability to comprehend society's harsh workings. Just *what* to fill in the outline of the Elvira Madigan story with, just what really happened, no one can know. I am concerned here with how Widerberg, as a Western artist, treated the few facts that came down to him: self-indulgently.

4. Akira Kurosawa, *The Seven Samurai*, trans. Donald Richie (New York: Simon and Schuster, 1970), p. 193.

5. Akira Kurosawa, *The Seven Samurai*, p. 194.

THE ART OF *SHOESHINE*

It is tempting to read de Sica's *Shoeshine* (*Sciuscià*, 1946) as an indictment of post-World War II Italian society. Pierre Leprohon writes that "the theme of *Sciuscià* is the infinitely tragic clash between childhood innocence and adult injustice."[1] Roy Armes states that

> The blame in the film rests squarely on the shoulders of the adults whose actions are indeed often mean and spiteful. Giuseppe's brother callously involves [the boys] in crime, while the police use underhand methods to make Pasquale confess [the brother's name] by pretending to beat Giuseppe (we see what is really happening in the next room: a policeman is beating a sack while a boy shrieks convincingly). The lawyers are cheaply opportunistic, suggesting that Giuseppe put all the blame on his friend, and the prison officials act foolishly and split up the pair (so that Giuseppe is left a prey to bad influences) and then punish Pasquale for fighting a bully.[2]

Peter Bondanella echoes Leprohon and Armes when he says that in *Shoeshine*, "De Sica dramatizes the tragedy of childish innocence corrupted by the adult world. . . . [Pasquale and Giuseppe's] friendship is gradually destroyed by the social injustice usually associated with the adult world and authority figures."[3] Both Bondanella and Leprohon describe a "tragic" conflict between childhood innocence and adult injustice, but by pitting victims against villains in this way, they are really suggesting that the film is a melodrama.

Shoeshine, however, is much more than the story of two boys whose friendship is destroyed at the hands of a villainous and insensate social system. Society may ultimately be responsible for the death of Giuseppe and the destruction of his and Pasquale's friendship, but de Sica does not portray it as villainous, as consciously or indifferently evil and exploitative. As Monique Fong has written,

> *Shoe-Shine* is neither an accusation nor a propaganda work. . . . Great skill is shown in putting the single moral-bearing sentence of the story—"If these children have become what they are, it is because we have failed to keep them what they are supposed to be"—into the mouth of the corrupt lawyer, a man to whom lying is a profession and whom we saw, just a moment earlier, falsely accusing Pasquale in order to save his own client.[4]

Italian society is as much a victim as Giuseppe and Pasquale in *Shoeshine*, and this is perhaps what James Agee had in mind when he wrote that *Shoeshine* "is . . . the rarest thing in contemporary art—a true tragedy. This tragedy is cross-lighted by pathos, by the youthfulness and innocence of the heroes, . . . but it is stern, unmistakable tragedy as well."[5] The real tragic conflict is not between the two boys and society: it is to be found in a society divided against itself; the tragedy of post-World War II Italian society is reflected in the pathetic story of Giuseppe and Pasquale. We are not meant to focus on the misfortune of the boys apart from the world in which they live; the point of the film is that their misfortune derives directly from this world. De Sica is interested as much in having us examine and question (not blame) the society that destroyed the boys' friendship as in having us pity Giuseppe and Pasquale. He is thus a typical neorealist filmmaker according to Roy Armes:

> Deep concern with humanity is common to . . . all [neorealist filmmakers] but there is no attempt to probe beneath the surface into the mind of the individual, so that concepts like *Angst* or absurdity have no place in neo-realist art, and alienation is defined purely in social terms. In place of the traditional cinematic concern with the complexities of the individual psyche comes a desire to probe the basically human, to undertake an investigation into man within his social and economic context. (p. 186)

No critics to my knowledge have investigated the tragic role that society plays in *Shoeshine*; I would like to do so in the following pages.

Italy was, of course, in a state of political and economic turmoil after World War II. Many of its inhabitants, especially those in large cities like Rome, where *Shoeshine* takes place, were finding it difficult to survive, since there was a shortage of food and clothing. A black market arose that traded in goods stolen or bought from the American occupation forces. Giuseppe and Pasquale's problems begin when they agree to sell stolen American army blankets to a fortuneteller as part of a plan by Giuseppe's brother and his gang to rob the fortuneteller's apartment. The boys know nothing of the planned robbery. They use the three thousand lire that they are paid for the blankets to buy a horse; soon afterward they are arrested.

Roy Armes says that "Giuseppe's brother callously involves [the boys] in crime" (p. 148). This statement fails to take into account the environment that produces the crime. Giuseppe's brother may be a thief, but he is one in a society where there is little or no work: he must survive, so he steals. He involves his brother in his crime and pays him well. Giuseppe's brother is callous only when seen from the point of view of someone who has never been in his situation; *he* thinks that he is doing his younger brother a favor. Petty crime is a way of life for them both, and the older brother's justification for robbing a fortuneteller is probably that he is robbing the equivalent of a thief: a woman who legally steals people's money by telling their fortunes. Giuseppe's brother is not a villain. Giuseppe turns on Pasquale when his friend names the brother as one of the thieves to prison officials; his loyalty to his brother—to the person who tried to do him a favor, not to a villain who callously involved him in a crime—leads eventually to his death. Ironically, in attempting to help Giuseppe to survive, the brother has helped to get him killed and has gone to jail himself. Although Giuseppe's brother is not a major character in *Shoeshine*, he is part of the society whose tragedy de Sica is depicting.

While it is true, as Roy Armes writes, that "the police use underhand methods to make Pasquale confess by pretending to beat Giuseppe" (p. 148), it is equally true that they use such methods because they want to capture the gang that robbed the fortuneteller's apartment. Like Giuseppe's brother, the police are not villains. They want to stop the black-marketeering that is threat-

ening an already unstable economy, and they use whatever means they can to do so. The police do not, in
Armes's words, "act foolishly and split up [Giuseppe
and Pasquale]" (p. 148); the pair is split up by chance in
the assigning of groups of boys to cells. The prison in
which the police house the boys is not by design "cruel,
crowded, wretched, and dirty," as Monique Fong believes (p. 15). It is crowded because many of the boys of
Rome have turned to petty crime in order to survive;
wretched and dirty because it is so crowded and because
adequate funds do not exist to provide for the boys; and
cruel because the prison staff is small and overworked,
and therefore prone to solve problems by force instead
of by disputation. The prison was not even built as one:
it was formerly a convent and has been taken over,
presumably because of a shortage of space in other
prisons.

The deception that the police work on Pasquale is not
without its consequences: he and Giuseppe themselves
learn deception. In revenge for Pasquale's betrayal of
his brother, Giuseppe, along with several other boys,
plants a file in his cell; it is found, and Pasquale is
severely whipped by the guards. Later in court,
Giuseppe is forced by his lawyer to put all the blame for
the fortuneteller incident on the older, supposedly
craftier Pasquale. (Armes calls the lawyer "cheaply op-
portunistic" [p. 148]; he is not: he is unscrupulous in the
defense of his client, like many lawyers.) Pasquale, in
revenge for Giuseppe's rejection of him and escape
from jail with his new friend Arcangeli, tells the police
where to find the two. Giuseppe plans to sell the horse
that he and Pasquale had bought and to live off the
money with Arcangeli. The police find them at the

95

stable, Arcangeli flees, and Giuseppe is killed in a fall from a bridge. He slips trying to avoid the angry Pasquale, who is poised to strike him.

Tragically, the prison officials, in "protecting" society from Giuseppe and Pasquale, have brutalized the boys, have robbed them of the very emotion and the very virtue necessary for the survival of humane society: love and trust. Society, in the name of law and order, has destroyed what it should promote: bonding, male and female. When he goes to jail, Giuseppe is torn not only from Pasquale, but also from the mysterious little girl Nana, who had been following him through the streets of Rome and is inconsolable in his absence. Once the boys are placed in separate cells, Pasquale can give his love and trust only to the tubercular Raffaele, who himself is ostracized by the other prisoners and who is trampled to death during a fire; and Giuseppe can give his love and trust only to the scoundrel Arcangeli, who leaves him on the bridge at the end at the first sight of Pasquale.

Shoeshine does not simply portray brutality against children, for which society will have to pay no particular price and for which it is simply "evil." The film portrays society's brutality against *itself* in the person of its future: its children. What makes *Shoeshine* so poignant is that we see more than the love between Giuseppe and Pasquale destroyed: we see a love destroyed that could only have grown and spread to their other relationships as they grew older; a love that meant to solidify itself through the purchase of the horse and take flight, to announce itself triumphantly throughout Rome and its environs.

The very title of this film is a clue to its intentions.

THE ART OF *SHOESHINE*

Shoeshine is the pathetic story of Giuseppe and Pasquale, but, as I have been maintaining, that is not all. The tragedy of post-World War II Italy is *reflected* in their pathetic story. Even as the American GIs in the film see the image of their own security and prosperity in their shined shoes, so too does Italian society find the image of its own disarray and poverty in the story of these beautifully paired boys. *Shoeshine* is an illumination of reality, a "shining" of reality's "shoes," if you will, of the basic problems facing a defeated nation in the wake of war: for the ruled, how to survive amidst rampant poverty at the same time as one does not break the law; for the rulers, how to enforce the law without sacrificing one's own humanity or that of the lawbreakers.

Early in the film we see the shoeshine boys at work, kneeling at the feet of the GIs, who barely take notice of them except to pay. At the end we look over the shoulder of the prison guard at the screaming Pasquale in the river bed: he is on his knees, next to the dead Giuseppe. De Sica holds this shot for a long time—it is the final one. Pasquale and Giuseppe are still the shoeshine boys, and down at them, as if they were shining his shoes, looks the prison guard, a representative of society. He is confronted with the offspring of war-torn Italy, of his own work: a once beautifully matched pair, now driven apart; the kind of pair without which Italy will not be able to move forward.

· · ·

Monique Fong remarks on the cinematography of *Shoeshine*:

It would seem that [the cinematography] might best have been painstakingly realistic, with sharp outline and

> great depth of field. But on the contrary, the use of a
> small-angle lens gives soft effects that help to retain the
> poetic character of the picture and, by contrast, enhance
> the realistic performances of the actors. (p. 25)

Just as the title itself, *Sciuscià*, corrupts or "blurs" the
Italian word for shoeshine (Fong, p. 15), the "soft
effects" of the cinematography blur reality slightly, especially in the last scene on the bridge, where mist also
obscures the image. Fong thinks that this technique, in
addition to giving the film a general poetic character,
"surrounds the adventure with a halo, supplying a new
element to serve the basic idea of the picture—the
presentation of a realistic story seen through the eyes of
children" (p. 25). I would alter this idea and take it one
step further to say the "soft effects" suggest that the
story is seen not only through the eyes of children, but
also through those of the American occupation troops,
the Italian government, the prison officials, and de Sica
himself—eyes that, like those of children, do not comprehend fully what they see, do not have sufficient
knowledge.[6]

The American GI who looks into his shined boots
sees the image of his own victory and prosperity, but his
image is tainted by the Italy that surrounds him—one
that he has helped to destroy and whose rebuilding it is
now his responsibility to oversee. The prison guard at
the end of the film looks down on Pasquale and
Giuseppe and may feel sorry for them, but how aware is
he of society's, of his own, responsibility for their misfortune? De Sica directed the film, but he does not
propose any solutions to the social problem he presents.
There are no clear villains, no easy answers, so de Sica

softens the "blow" of what we see at the same time as he discourages us from seeking answers to all our questions on the screen. We are in a position to contemplate this social tragedy far better than any character in the film; the audience *infers* the tragedy, while the group protagonist, society, plays it out. We are thus able to consider solutions to the problems that de Sica poses, or to consider the idea of abolishing war altogether. We are the ultimate recipients of de Sica's *Shoeshine*.

NOTES TO
"The Art of *Shoeshine*"

1. Pierre Leprohon, *The Italian Cinema*, trans. Roger Greaves and Oliver Stallybrass (New York: Praeger, 1972), p. 101.

2. Roy Armes, *Patterns of Realism: A Study of Italian Neo-Realist Cinema* (New York: A. S. Barnes, 1971), p. 148. Hereafter cited by page number in the text.

3. Peter Bondanella, *Italian Cinema: From Neorealism to the Present* (New York: Frederick Ungar, 1983), p. 53.

4. Monique Fong, "*Shoe-Shine*: A Student Film Analysis," *Hollywood Quarterly*, 4, No. 1 (Fall 1949), pp. 17–18. Hereafter cited by page number in the text.

5. James Agee, *Agee on Film: Reviews and Comments* (Boston: Beacon Press, 1958), p. 279.

6. When writing about neorealism, critics most often follow André Bazin's lead and emphasize its use of nonprofessional actors, the documentary quality of its photography, its social content, or its political commitment. Bazin went so far as to call neorealism a cinema of "fact" and "reconstituted reportage" that rejected both traditional dramatic and cinematic conventions (André Bazin, *What*

Is Cinema?, II, trans. Hugh Gray [Berkeley: Univ. of Calif. Press, 1971], pp. 60, 77, 78, et passim [the first seven chapters—over half the book—treat neorealism]). As Peter Bondanella points out, however,

> Certainly the cinema neorealists turned to the pressing problems of the time—the war, the Resistance and the Partisan struggle, unemployment, poverty, social injustice, and the like—but there was never a programmatic approach to these questions or any preconceived method of rendering them on celluloid. . . . In short, neorealism was not a "movement" in the strictest sense of the term. The controlling fiction of neorealist films . . . was that they dealt with actual problems, that they employed contemporary stories, and that they focused on believable characters taken most frequently from Italian daily life. But the greatest neorealist directors never forgot that the world they projected upon the silver screen was one produced by cinematic conventions rather than an ontological experience. . . . Thus, any discussion of Italian neorealism must be broad enough to encompass a wide diversity of cinematic styles, themes, and attitudes. . . . Directors we label today as neorealists were . . . all united only by the common aspiration to view Italy without preconceptions and to develop a more honest, ethical, but no less poetic language. (*Italian Cinema,* pp. 34–35.)

De Sica himself stated that his work reflected "reality transposed into the realm of poetry" (*Miracle in Milan* [Baltimore: Penguin, 1969], p. 4). And the last scene on the bridge in *Shoeshine* is an excellent example of this poetry: it was shot inside a studio and relies for its meaning and effect in large part on the manner in which it is filmed (a manner more easily controlled indoors than on location). Bondanella notes that the cinematography of the last scene continues the sense of confinement witnessed in "a number of shots through cell windows [that] place [Pasquale and Giuseppe] in a tight, claustrophobic atmosphere and restrict their movement" (p. 54). The boys are trapped in the foreground in the final scene on the bridge, since de Sica's small-angle lens doesn't photograph the image in deep focus in addition to not capturing it in sharp outline.

RE-VIEWING *THE RAIN PEOPLE*

I want to suggest that *The Rain People* (1969) is Francis Ford Coppola's most fully realized, if least spectacular film. Stanley Kauffmann inadvertently touches on the reason for this in the following criticism of the director's career:

> Where Coppola is short is in thought. He stumbles when he thinks, when he thinks he's thinking. . . . *The Conversation* [1974] faltered in its idea-structure. *The Godfather* [1972], both parts, was strongest in its execution (also its executions), not in its adolescent implication of analogy between the Mafia and corporate capitalism. In *Apocalypse Now* [1979] the attempts to dramatize private moral agony and general moral abyss are disjointed, assumptive, weak.[1]

The Rain People is more successful artistically than the films that follow because it is filled, not with thought but with feeling.[2] It has been called a "personal" film, and this is true more than in the others in two senses: Coppola made it on a relatively small budget, unencumbered by his own publicity and huge financial strains; and he seems to have produced it out of felt or at least imagined experience as opposed to the indirect kind:

his ideas about the experience of the Vietnam War, of the Mafia in America, of electronic surveillance in the post-Watergate era. The result is a "road picture," one woman's journey of self-discovery, that was overshadowed at the time of its release by *Easy Rider*, *Midnight Cowboy*, and *Alice's Restaurant* (all 1969)[3]; that draws some of its inspiration, to go back only thirty years, from *Of Mice and Men* (novelette, play, *and* film [1940]); and that is far superior to the once highly touted *Alice Doesn't Live Here Anymore* (1974), which resembles it in many ways.

The picture begins the day that Natalie Ravenna (Shirley Knight), newly pregnant, leaves her husband, Vinny (seen once in the present, asleep, and a few times in silent flashbacks), and their comfortable Long Island home. She tells him by phone that she intends to return but has to get away for a while. She feels trapped, overwhelmed, by her role as wife and childbearer. Natalie is no feminist; she is simply a confused young woman who sees her life mapped out and decides to take a temporary detour or vacation from it. On the road she picks up a hitchhiker, Jimmy "Killer" Kilgannon (James Caan), a former outstanding college football player, and they immediately recognize something in common between them: both are traveling nowhere in particular. What seems to begin as a trite sexual adventure— Natalie says later that she picked Killer up hoping to "make it" with someone new—turns into much more. The hint of sexual liaison hangs over the two until we, and she, discover, perhaps forty-five minutes into the film, that Killer has been left slightly retarded by a football injury, has been given one thousand dollars to leave his campus job as a groundskeeper (in which job he was wholly inadequate and was an embarrassment to college officials), and is without family. He is looking for a friend, a mother, not sex.

Having just left responsibility to her husband, Natalie is of course reluctant to take on the responsibility of looking after Killer. She was even reluctant to pick him up; she stopped her station wagon yards ahead of him, then drove away as he approached, then stopped again to let him in. She tries to leave him at four other points. She drives him to his former girlfriend's house in Pennsylvania, where Killer thinks that he will get the job that the girl's father promised him at a game two years before. The father is willing until he learns about his prospective employee's mental state (not so obvious, because Killer does not say much) from his cruel, selfish daughter. Natalie and her charge hit the road again, and after a night in separate motel rooms, she says that they must go their separate ways. She drives off, then stops, waits for him to get in, and drives on. There will be no easy shedding of Killer: she likes him, and she knows that he is helpless.

Finally, Natalie thinks that she has found the place for him: the "Reptile Ranch," somewhere in Nebraska. She gets him a job there as a clean-up man, provided he entrusts his money to the owner; she knows that he will never see the money again, but she feels it will be worth the loss if the man takes care of Killer. She speeds off, wanting to get as far away from him as possible but happy to have found something for him resembling a home. Gordon (Robert Duvall), a policeman cum sexual opportunist, stops her for speeding and takes her right back to the Reptile Ranch curio shop, where she must pay the fine. Killer is fired for freeing all the animals, especially the chicks in their cramped and dirty cages; his boss drops charges of malicious mischief against him in return for eight hundred dollars. Natalie abandons him in this place again, this time for cutting the telephone lines while she is talking to her husband, whom she calls periodically throughout the film to agonize over what she has done and what it is doing to him. She goes off on a date with Gordon, in whom she thinks she "sees something," then retires with him to his trailer to spend the night.

Through all this, Natalie's relationship with Killer has deepened, despite her desire to be free of him. He says at one point that he loves her; we know that she loves him but will not admit it. He is, of course, a child, and she acts like his mother. Early in the film, in a motel room, she commands him to do various things and he does them without question. She is puzzled by his quick obedience, though happy to dominate a man after being dominated by men all her life; *we* think we are about to witness some kinky sex. We realize later that, as a man with a child's mind, Killer wants to be told what to do, wants to have his life arranged for him by someone else. He eventually follows Natalie to Gordon's trailer, where he plays outside with the latter's young daughter, Rosalie. She is Killer's opposite: an eight- or nine-year-old who behaves like an adult, parading around in a brassiere, staying up late, and possessing intimate knowledge of the lives of the grown-ups who reside in the trailer park. Her mother is dead; her father regards her as an obstacle to his sex life.

Gordon wants no more than to sleep with Natalie. When she rebels, disappointed by his lack of tenderness and repulsed by his treatment of his daughter, he attempts to rape her. Peeping through the window with his new playmate, Killer sheds his gentleness, bursts in, pulls Gordon outside, and proceeds to use him as a tackling dummy. He is on the verge of beating the policeman to death when Rosalie shoots Killer twice with her father's service revolver. He dies in Natalie's arms as she pathetically attempts to drag him away to some type of safety, saying in desperation that they can go back to New York and live as a family with Vinny. The neighbors, who have come out, look on passively.

Natalie's journey is at an end. She has come, with difficulty, to love Killer and by his death is made to realize just how much. He has given her the experience that will enable her to reunite with her husband and have her child.[4] She has not "found" herself in any easy, euphoric sense; her anticipated return to Vinny hardly gives the film a forced happy ending. Natalie has paid, and *had* to pay, a terrible price in order to learn that she is able to love and care; in order to learn that freedom can be its own form of dead end and confinement its own form of liberation. Therein lies her tragedy and the film's achievement. At least five critics—John Coleman, Robert Phillip Kolker, Robert K. Johnson, Joseph Morgenstern, and William S. Pechter—have called Killer's death melodramatic or unnecessary.[5] I am arguing for the necessity of Killer's slaying on the grounds that it is responsible for Natalie's recognition or spiritual transformation. Aside from this, though, the death makes perfect sense within the context of the final scene: Rosalie has no choice but to shoot Killer, because he will doubtless kill her father if she does not. Natalie's very meeting with the little girl's father is charged with inevitability: she wants so badly to rid herself of Killer that she speeds away from him, only to be pulled over by Gordon.

There are also ironic foreshadowings of Killer's death. He received his nickname because of his football prowess, but the name, combined with his size and the one thousand dollars he carries around in a bag and shows off naively, makes him appear initially as a criminal to those he meets. Like most film criminals, he is headed toward demise; unlike them, he is neither a thief nor a real killer. At one point he and Natalie pass a movie theater showing *Bonnie and Clyde* (1967). Except in the sense that they're both on the road and that Natalie is running from something, these two do not appear to have anything in common with the main characters of Arthur Penn's film. The very idea of comparison between the couples seems ludicrous. Like Bonnie, however, Natalie has sexual yearnings that her road companion cannot satisfy; and most important, Killer, like Clyde, dies from wounds inflicted by police bullets.

Natalie's experience in the film is paralleled by Gordon's, who uses his police motorcycle to propel his life as a "free spirit." His wife died when their house burned down. He says that he did not love her before or after her death. It takes his daughter's murder of Killer to penetrate the thick wall with which he has surrounded himself. By the end of the film, there is a broken spirit inside his broken body, but there is at the same time, paradoxically, a spirit elevated by his daughter's act of love toward the father who showed her so little regard.

Natalie is one of the "rain people" of the title; Gordon is not. These people are figments of Killer's childlike imagination, people with whom he can talk, have adventures, and exchange secrets. The opening shot of the film is of the rain falling in puddles outside Natalie and Vinny's house, which is on an island. We see the water refreshing her, even purifying her, in the shower as she prepares to leave her husband. She drives off in the rain, and it falls intermittently during her trip with Killer. It is as if she were a figure of his imagination from the start, destined to find him and then be contained by him. When they reach Nebraska, the weather becomes hot and dry. The Reptile Ranch owner wants only to take advantage of Killer, and Gordon views him in the same way as he does his daughter: as a nuisance. The flashbacks to Gordon's burning house underline the idea of this man, and this area, as hot and hostile, as the antithesis of the sympathetic woman from Long Island. The policeman is hot in two other senses. He is "hot" to have sex with Natalie, whereas Killer, with his child's mind, has no sexual interest in her, is "cool." And, as an official of the law, he is the "heat" to Killer's detached and unintimidating private citizen; his daughter uses his pistol, his "heater," to shoot the oblivious Killer.

Paradoxically perhaps in a film of felt experience, Coppola's camera work is cool and almost distant, as if in imitation of the shy Killer and the rainy-day world of his mind. Like the camera work, the colors of *The Rain People* are cool and muted, not hot and lush—even in Nebraska, where Coppola uses light to fade color instead of to enhance it. Robert Phillip Kolker mistakes the intent of the cinematography and camera work in *The Rain People*. He writes that

> [the film] never achieves a working relationship with the viewer . . . [Coppola] does not know just how much distancing . . . [is] needed. . . . Missing . . . is a clearly

defined and coherent *mise-en-scène* for [the] characters to dwell in, a space for them and for us to share. . . . Its appearance with such power and presence in *Godfather I* is remarkable. Its presence can be partly accounted for by the care Coppola begins to give each image in the film. . . . [He] achieves a richness based on an ability to control light and dark, balance color patterns . . . (pp. 156–157, 158)

Obviously, the *mise-en-scène* that was appropriate to *Godfather I* is not appropriate to *The Rain People*. Kolker, of all people, should realize this, since he writes:

[In *Godfather I*] it is not so much characters to whom we are joined and from whom we are separated but situations, states of being, and places. The film is structured by our desire to move into a world portrayed as being warm, attractive, and protected. . . . The characters . . . function less as individuals than as representatives of an attractive and dangerous world. . . . Our attraction to them, our fears for them, are controlled and are controllable because of the fact that they represent a situation we wish to be part of. (p. 160)

The camera in *Godfather I* invites us into a *mise-en-scène*, invites us to inhabit a place.

The camera in *The Rain People*, by contrast, identifies us with the point of view of a character detached or excluded from a *mise-en-scène*. Just as Killer is slightly distanced from the world, we are distanced from it by the camera: for example, from the home life at the start of the film that he will never know again and to which Natalie will ultimately return; and from the phone booth where she calls Vinny shortly after leaving New

York. The camera remains outside Natalie and her husband's house in the rain for a long time before haltingly going in to find her awakening. And it never places us inside the phone booth with her; we remain outside, listening and observing, in a very long take. Later Killer will be excluded from a phone booth in which Natalie again talks to Vinny, and he will cut the lines in a fumbling attempt to span the distance between himself and other human beings. Just as his perception of his world is not rich in variation, in *difference*, neither is the world we see on screen: its colors are subdued. This film lives by the long take—Coppola gives the characters time to move around within the scene instead of manipulating them through lots of cutting—and so does Killer. In his now simple life, he does not take in a situation by leaps, moving restlessly from one person or object to another; rather, he concentrates his gaze deliberately on the scene before him, struggling to fathom its complexities.

Kolker speaks above of "the care Coppola begins to give each image in [*Godfather I*]" and of characters functioning in it "less as individuals than as representatives of an attractive and dangerous world." The director does not give less care to the images in *The Rain People*; it's simply that he gives excessive care to those in the later films, or in any event emphasizes scenery and lighting over character, which he harnesses to facile ideas. Characters *do* function less as individuals than as representatives of something, to the detriment of the films after *The Rain People*. By the time we get to *One From the Heart* (1982), they function as neither: the visuals finally become everything, and nothing.

Since *The Rain People* is a road film, the camera is

outdoors much of the time, where Natalie seeks her freedom. When it is indoors, even inside her spacious station wagon, we are made to feel the claustrophobia that drove her from her home. In the first scene, Natalie is literally confined in bed by her sleeping husband's arm, which is draped across her chest. At the Reptile Ranch, she is appalled by the chicks' cramped and filthy cages, and she herself looks trapped in the cluttered, gaudy curio shop. Inside Gordon's constricting and dingy trailer, she resists his attempts to embrace her, to confine her. He wears tight jeans, she wears a loose-fitting dress. Coppola shoots much of an early motel scene in mirrors to emphasize Natalie's feelings of entrapment. She views Killer as an extension of that entrapment, so when he enters the room, he is seen in the same mirrors that enclose her. In her car's rearview mirror and in the one in her compact, Natalie confronts the real source of her problems and their only solution in the end: herself. Significantly, she applies make-up in these mirrors. This can be seen as an act of concealment, nullified by the tears she sheds on the phone talking to Vinny and by her weeping in the final scene as she holds the dead Killer.

Just as the "rain people" are figments of Killer's imagination, this film is completely the figment of Coppola's. It is the second film that he wrote *and* directed; *You're a Big Boy Now* (1967) was the first. Killer's mind is incapable of generating thought: his instincts tell him to like Natalie and dislike the owner of the Reptile Ranch, and they are right in both cases. Similarly, the young Coppola trusts his feelings about the characters, not his ideas about the world that produced them. He trusts, if he is not in fact in awe of, his actors; he permits the

story to be told more through them, as acting instru-
ments, than through editing and camera movement. He
is right to do so: Shirley Knight, James Caan, and
Robert Duvall give excellent performances.

Restraint is the hallmark of all three. Caan could
easily have milked his role for sympathy, but he does
not do so. His Killer is touching, less because we feel
sorry for him than because we admire his blind resil-
iency. Duvall's ability to transform himself in character
roles has become legendary: we see an early example
here. He doesn't enter the film until it's far along. I kept
hoping that I would recognize him when I saw his face.
I didn't: that's a form of acting. Before Gordon pulls
Natalie over for speeding, Coppola shows us some
directing, characterizing the policeman in one shot. The
camera is behind a billboard, in front of which sits
Gordon on his motorcycle. We see him only from the
waist down—that is, we see his essence.

Shirley Knight has been criticized in the past for
exhibiting Sandy Dennis-type hysterics. None of that
here. Her "Oh, no" after Killer is shot reminds us of
what "less is more" really means: to give less not for
economy's or ellipsis' sake alone, but so that the audience can imagine more. She says the line in an almost
offhand way, as if she has just remembered that Gordon
would naturally keep a gun on hand at all times. What
we see her realizing is that this is the same weapon she
had pointed at Gordon in an attempt to make him leave
her alone. He quickly grabbed it, tossed it aside, and
tried to rape her. The ease with which Natalie pulled
the gun from its holster on the wall is the same ease with
which Gordon's precocious daughter picked it up and
fired at Killer. Natalie is not to blame for the girl's act;

she comprehends its fatefulness, and we see her doing so. We imagine its fatefulness through her, through just two simple words that she speaks and that Knight inflects subtly. Had the character said more, explained herself, in this sentence, or had the actress done more with it, the moment would have been lost; either literalness or theatrics would have killed it by excluding us. In the same way, had Knight fallen into hysterics on the line, we would have felt the character's suffering far less than we do. We feel it so much because we are enabled to watch the affection for Killer rising up in the woman to break on her face and display itself only for a few moments before he dies. She quietly shows us what she could have given rather than screaming about what has been taken from her. She expresses her love for Killer rather than her grief for herself. We feel her pain precisely because she does not feel it, or has barely allowed it to surface: her own pain is the last thing on her mind; and because her love achieves its greatest expression at the moment Killer can least benefit from it.

Knight has not appeared in another Coppola film. Duvall and Caan went on to achieve stardom in *The Godfather*, as did its director. The measure of his actual decline is in his use of the two actors in the later film. Duvall is again on the side of the law, so to speak. He's cast as a lawyer who defends the Mafia's financial interests: Coppola is interested less in his character than in his function as someone who can beat the system. Caan is again a simple brute, but this time he is riddled with bullets and covered with blood in his death scene. Nothing is left to the imagination: not his agony, not the guilt of those inadvertently responsible for his murder, and not, finally, the film. Perhaps the image from *The Rain People* that remains with us above all others is exactly the one of Killer's death. The sound of the gun is natural; the volume is not increased, as it is in most films, with the result that we need a moment, just a moment, to realize that a gun has been fired. It is dark outside. We see no blood. Killer falls and writhes but barely makes a sound. Gordon and his daughter look on silently. Natalie has spoken her "Oh, no" and continues to speak to the dead Killer as the screen fades to black. This is masterly directing. The scene seems eerie, because it is not filled with film clichés. In fact it is quite realistic, the work of a man who has looked at as well as lived in the world, and who has since seemed content primarily to expound upon it.

NOTES TO
"Re-viewing *The Rain People*"

1. Stanley Kauffmann, *Before My Eyes: Film Criticism and Comment* (New York: Harper and Row, 1980), p. 108.
2. Coppola's most recent film, *One From the Heart* (1982), has neither thought nor feeling behind it. Shot wholly in his Zoetrope Studios for twenty-six million dollars, it attempts to create through optical effects the illusion that the audience is watching a musical comedy on the Broadway stage. The plot and characterization are minimal. Robert Hatch wrote that Coppola made the film to show off the resources of Zoetrope (*The Nation*, 6 March 1982, p. 282); David Denby called it "bizarre and pointless" (*New York*, 1 Feb. 1982, p. 54).

There are precedents for *One From the Heart* in Coppola's work prior to *The Rain People*. *You're a Big Boy Now* (1967) was a light comedy, and *Finian's Rainbow* (1968) was a rendition of the Broadway hit musical; both made ample use of visual effects. (Coppola's first film was *Dementia 13* [1963], a low-budget contribution to the horror genre financed by Roger Corman.) Unfortunately, the director has come full-circle, therefore this seems an appropriate time to mark the achievement of *The Rain People* and to hope that he will return to it. When one considers how much money *One From the Heart* has lost, this may not be such wishful thinking: Coppola may be forced to make films on comparatively low budgets again, on soberer themes that call for real characters in real settings.*

3. *The Rain People* was a commercial flop, disappearing quickly after its release. Joseph Morgenstern panned it in *Newsweek* (8 Sept. 1969), while Stephen Farber and William S. Pechter wrote sympathetic, though finally negative reviews in *Film Quarterly* (Winter 1969) and *Commentary* (Feb. 1970) respectively. Stanley Kauffmann, incidentally, in a rare lapse of critical judgment, wrote this of the film: "[It] is a tedious and affected piece about a wandering young wife who 'finds' herself through her experiences with a simple brute, the most painful bit of preciosity since Jack Garfein's *Something Wild* (1961)" (p. 202 in his *Figures of Light* [New York: Harper and Row, 1971]). Kauffmann's remarks are all the more surprising in light of his fine insight into Coppola's subsequent films, quoted at the start of my essay.

4. Natalie has two other children, but after she looks in on them, asleep in their bedroom, in the opening moments of the film, they are not seen again or spoken of. So it is as if she is pregnant with her first child: the first one to

whom she will be able to give herself fully, as a conse-
quence of her relationship with Killer.

5.   Coleman in *New Statesman*, 15 Dec. 1978, p. 835; Kolker
in *A Cinema of Loneliness: Penn, Kubrick, Coppola, Scorsese,
Altman* (New York: Oxford Univ. Press, 1980), p. 157;
Johnson in *Francis Ford Coppola* (Boston: Twayne, 1977),
p. 82; and Morgenstern (p. 82) and Pechter (p. 81) in
publications already cited in these notes. Kolker's *A Cinema of Loneliness* hereafter cited by page number in the
text.

   *After *One from the Heart*, Coppola did make two films
on relatively low budgets: *The Outsiders* (1983) and *Rumble
Fish* (1983), both adapted from S. E. Hinton novels set in
Tulsa, Oklahoma. Coppola's theme is the teen-ager as
outsider, as spiritual exile, but these films are marred by
artiness and unearned sentiment. They seem to be less
about teen-aged outsiders than about the director's no-
tion of himself as an outsider, a "misunderstood artist," in
the film industry. Coppola's most recent film is *The Cotton
Club*, which was released in December 1984. This saga of
the white gangsters and black entertainers who filled
Harlem's hottest nightclub of the jazz age, cost forty-
seven million dollars, had script and production problems of the kind that plagued the shooting of *Apocalypse
Now,* and combines the director's penchant for spectacle,
musical or otherwise, with his proclivity for half-baked
thinking on large subjects such as crime, capitalism, and
war. *The Cotton Club* seems to signal that Coppola will
never return to the achievement of *The Rain People*, that
he is now completely and irrevocably the prisoner of his
own inflated reputation as well as a devotee to the urge to
impose his ideas on reality rather than filter reality
through his feelings.

117

1. *Room at the Top*

Joe (Laurence Harvey) reveals to Alice (Simone Signoret) that
he is going to marry Susan

2. *Way Down East*

David Bartlett (Richard Barthelmess) has rescued Anna Moore (Lillian Gish) from the icy river and is taking her back to the farmhouse.

3. *Der letzte Mann*

The doorman (Emil Jannings) looks for comfort to the hotel manager (Hans Unterkircher), who has demoted him to washroom attendant

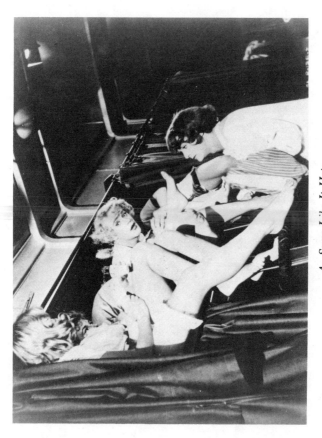

4. *Some Like It Hot*
Jerry/Daphne (Jack Lemmon) and Joe/Josephine (Tony Curtis) get ready for bed aboard the train headed for Florida

5. *Hiroshima, mon amour*

The Girl (Emmanuele Riva) and the German soldier (Bernard Fresson) embrace in Nevers

6. *Day of Wrath*

Anne (Lisbeth Movin) and Martin (Preben Lerdorff Rye) share
a furtive moment in the fields

7. *The Seven Samurai*
The peasants brace themselves for the bandits' attack on their
village

8. *Shoeshine*

Pasquale (Franco Interlenghi), second from the left, and Giuseppe (Rinaldo Smordoni), fourth from the left, undergo questioning by the police

9. *The Rain People*

Natalie's (Shirley Knight) relationship with "Killer" (James Caan) is deepening, despite her desire to be free of him

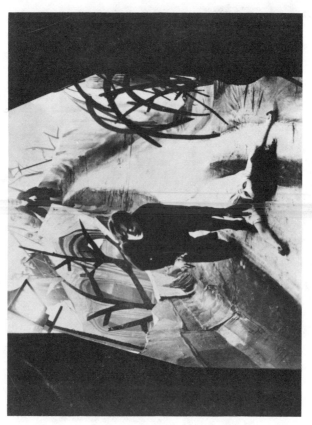

10. *The Cabinet of Dr. Caligari*
Cesare (Conrad Veidt), in flight from the authorities, abandons
the prostrate Jane (Lil Dagover)

11. *Nosferatu*

Nosferatu (Max Schreck) prepares to leave ship in Bremen

12. *L'avventura*
Claudia (Monica Vitti) the outsider

13. *Une femme douce*
The Woman (Dominique Sanda) and The Man (Guy Frangin),
together yet apart

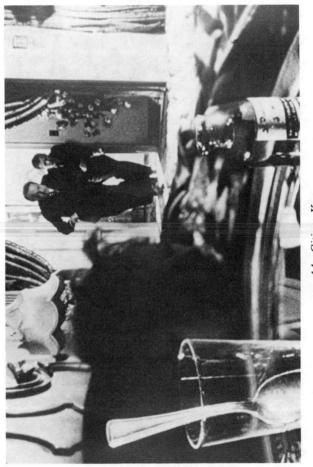

14. *Citizen Kane*

Charles Foster Kane (Orson Welles) rushes in on
Susan Alexander Kane (Dorothy Comingore; in the
foreground), who has attempted suicide.

15. *The Nights of Cabiria*
Cabiria (Giulietta Masina) and The Hypnotist (Aldo Silvani)
onstage

16. *Shoot the Piano Player*

Charlie Kohler/Edouard Saroyan (Charles Aznavour) and Lena
(Marie Dubois) on the run, after Charlie/Edouard has
accidentally killed Plyne

17. *Nashville*
Frog (Richard Baskin) accompanies Albuquerque (Barbara
Harris) as she performs at a speedway, but the lyrics and music
are drowned out by the roar of stock cars circling about them

18. *The Lacemaker*
Beatrice/Pomme (Isabella Huppert) and Francois (Yves
Beneyton) at the American cemetery in Normandy

IV

FILM AND
EXPRESSIONISM

EXPRESSIONISM AND THE REAL *CABINET OF DR. CALIGARI*

I want to consider all of *The Cabinet of Dr. Caligari* (1920), not simply the original story—of a Caligari finally exposed by Francis—which was housed by the director Robert Wiene in a framing story that exposes *Francis* as a madman. Most critics, Siegfried Kracauer significant among them, view the original story, a script by Hans Janowitz and Carl Mayer, as truly Expressionistic, as an exposure of "the madness inherent in authority."[1] Kracauer goes so far as to call the original "an outspoken revolutionary story . . . whose meaning reveals itself unmistakably at the end, with the disclosure of the psychiatrist as Caligari: reason overpowers unreasonable power, insane authority is symbolically abolished" (p. 9). Kracauer feels, as did Janowitz and Mayer, from whom he got his information, that Wiene perverted, if not reversed, the Expressionistic intentions of the original story; that, in answer to mass desires or commercial instinct, "a revolutionary film was turned into a conformist one—following the much-used pattern of declaring some normal but troublesome individual insane and sending him to a lunatic asylum" (p. 11). I want to go against this view, and I want to do so by a careful consideration of what happens in the original story as well as of what happens outside it, in the "frame," and by showing a more than superficial relationship between the original story and the framing one.

Kracauer's opinions about the final film of *Caligari* rest on two erroneous assumptions. Number one, the doctor in the original story, or the story that the insane Francis tells to his older companion seated next to him on a bench, is *not* revealed to be Caligari, as Kracauer believes; he is revealed to be the Director of a mental hospital *posing* as one Dr. Caligari at fairs so that he can carry on experiments with the somnambulist Cesare. The real Caligari is a doctor-mystic from the year 1703 who set out to discover whether a somnambulist, or someone in a trance, can be driven to murder; the Director wants to see if he can duplicate the real Dr. Caligari's experiments. This is not a small point, because it indicates that the "historical"[2] Dr. Caligari is known to the student-artist Francis through his readings as well as to the actual Director of the mental hospital to which Francis has been committed. The one-time student-artist Francis, now insane, makes up a story about the Director of the mental hospital in which the latter takes on the identity of Caligari in secret to carry out his experiments with Cesare. In the story, the somnambulist Cesare murders the Town Clerk, who reluctantly granted "Caligari" a permit to exhibit Cesare at the local fair, and he also kills Alan, Francis' best friend. He almost murders Jane, the young woman whom both Francis and Alan love, before his master is exposed by Francis and the local authorities as the force behind the murders and the Director of the area mental hospital in addition. "Caligari" himself goes crazy at the sight of the dead Cesare (who dies, oddly, of exhaustion—more on this later), is forced into a straitjacket, and is placed in a cell in the very hospital he once ran. This is the end of Francis' story, or hallucination, told to a companion within the insane asylum.

What happens shortly thereafter, back in the "real" world of the insane asylum where Francis resides, leads to the second of Kracauer's erroneous assumptions. At the end of his story, Francis says (on title), "And since that day the madman ['Caligari'] has never left his cell" (p. 96). Then he is astonished to locate Cesare, who dies in his, Francis' story, among the crowd in the hospital courtyard, and he is overjoyed to find Jane, whom he claimed to love in his story and still claims to love, but who totally ignores him. To see the Director again, however, strolling among his patients, is too much for him. In his story, Francis had confined "Caligari" to a cell, and now here he is out and free again! Francis goes berserk and grabs the Director, shouting, "You all believe I am mad. That is not true. It is the Director who is mad. He is Caligari, Caligari, Caligari" (p. 99). He is finally overcome by a group of attendants, placed in a straitjacket, and dragged into the same cell in which the "Caligari" of his story had been incarcerated. As the film ends, the Director turns from Francis' bed and says, "At last I understand the nature of his madness. He thinks I am that mystic Caligari" (p. 100).

Now Kracauer claims that the director Wiene made Francis a "normal but troublesome individual" who, by virtue of the story he concocts, shows why he has been committed to an insane asylum. The Director of the asylum at last understands the case of his patient and feels that he will be able to cure him. "With this cheerful message," states Kracauer, "the audience is dismissed" (p. 11). But Kracauer misunderstands the Director's understanding of Francis' case. Francis is not simply a lunatic who makes up terrible stories about nice people. Yes, he is insane, but he is an insane *murderer*. That is what the Director's line, "He thinks I am that mystic Caligari," tells us. Francis knows who the historical Dr. Caligari is, and so does the Director of the insane asylum. Francis is a murderer, and the nature of his "mad murdering," which the Director now understands, is that he believes the Caligari of his student reading has made him murder, or has hypnotized him to do so. Why else would the Director say that the nature of Francis' madness is his belief that he, the Director, is the mystic Caligari? Would this belief alone make a man a candidate for madness, and even if it did, could such a deviation completely explain the *nature* of his madness? I think not.

Seeking to rerationalize his murdering (his companion on the bench has apparently not yet heard his story), to give it, however misguidedly or unconsciously, the sense or order that it did not have while he was killing, or to exorcise the demon (the mystic Caligari) who, he insanely believes, has driven him to commit murder, Francis, within the confined world of the asylum, has chosen the Director to play the part of, or pose as, Caligari, Cesare to be the murderer (Francis himself) under Caligari's spell, and Jane as the object of his affections. His two victims—people he probably murdered at random in his insanity, but who take on special Expressionistic significance in his story—Alan and the

Town Clerk, are conspicuously missing from his company in the hospital courtyard at the end of the film. Francis does not play himself, for he must be free in his mind to capture and imprison the demon Caligari who is the source of all his problems. What unites the real persons Cesare, Jane, and the Director is the fact that all three are the very opposite of what Francis makes them into in his story. Cesare, all timid and tidy, gazes raptly at a flower throughout the final framing scene. Jane, enamored of Francis in the original story, does not even acknowledge him in the first framing scene (in which Francis is about to tell his story to the older man on the bench) or the last. And the Director is a meticulously dressed, kind and gentle man, hardly the dishevelled, evil, scheming "Caligari." If Francis turns these three into their opposites, then it follows, if my theory about his being a murderer is correct, that he should turn himself into his opposite: a perfectly sane, intent (in his pursuit of Alan's murderer as well as of his studies), upright young man. He does so. He must be such a man in order to be able to track down "Caligari" with impunity. He chooses Cesare to act in his place, because Cesare, as signified by his identification with a white flower, is in real life what Francis thinks that he himself is: peaceful, sensitive, loving. And like Francis, Cesare is *not* a somnambulist (he becomes one in Francis' story, even as Francis believes that he himself must have become one to commit murder). Indeed, it is not even clear his name is Cesare: when Francis calls him this upon locating him in the hospital courtyard in the final "frame," Francis' older companion is somewhat astonished and hurries away. "Cesare" is the name *Francis* has given in his story to the real Dr. Caligari's somnambulist; that is, it is the name he has the Director in the story use for his sleepwalker.

"Caesar" is also the name of the madman kept in "the Doctor's" household in the first Expressionistic drama, Strindberg's *To Damascus* (1898). This "Caesar" functions, naturally, "as the leitmotiv of the hero's megalomania," according to Walter Sokel, while "the Doctor appears as the hated and dreaded leitmotiv of the hero's guilt."[3] I do not think that Janowitz and Mayer could possibly have been unaware of these characters when they wrote their original draft of *Caligari*, given the high regard in which Strindberg's play was held by the dramatists of German Expressionism. I also do not think that they failed to see the similarity between "Caligari," the name of an Italian officer Janowitz pulled from his reading in *Unknown Letters of Stendhal* for use as the name of the imaginary mystic from 1703 (Kracauer, p. 7), and "(Gaius *Caesar*) Caligula," the name of the Roman emperor from 37–41 A. D. Note this description by Siegfried Kracauer of Caligari's character, then recall Caligula's senseless cruelty: "The character of Caligari stands for an unlimited authority that idolizes power as such and, to satisfy its lust for domination, ruthlessly violates all human rights and values" (p. 9). My point is not to make a connection between Caligula's Rome and Germany before the rise of Hitler. I am trying to suggest that Cesare and "Caligari" are aspects of Francis' own insane murderous self (if one pronounces the last "e" in "Cesare" like the last "i" in "Caligari," one will hear a similarity in the names that is not so apparent to the eye); that Robert Wiene saw this in the original script of *Caligari* given to him to direct, but did not see it sufficiently embodied and decided to develop the script's potential. In short, rather than pervert or reverse Janowitz and Mayer's original intentions, Wiene was serving those intentions, was carrying them to their logical conclusion. If Janowitz and Mayer were now denying the intentions inherent *in the script*, that was apparently, as far as Wiene was concerned, their problem.

Francis' very name is an Expressionistic projection or externalization—an "expression"—of what he thinks is his essence: the brotherly love of St. Francis. No one calls him Francis in the framing story; by having others call him Francis in the story he tells, *he* calls himself that. "Caligari" has Cesare murder the Town Clerk for his arrogance and inefficiency. In his will to unlimited authority over another, "Caligari" cannot tolerate anyone else's limited authority over him. In the Expressionist hero Francis' will to unlimited freedom and self-expression, he cannot tolerate the small-mindedness of the bourgeoisie and its omnipresent bureaucracy. So he kills the Town Clerk. "Caligari" has Cesare murder Alan for his naiveté and boyish enthusiasm. Alan is described by R. V. Adkinson in the script of *Caligari* as "a young man of aesthetic pursuits . . . [and] high ideals. He affects the style of the Nineties aesthete—a loosely-tied, flopping bow-tie and hair parted in the centre in the style of Aubrey Beardsley" (p. 44). If he is not Francis' double, then he is only a slightly exaggerated, or condensed, version (the duplication of the "-an-" in the names of Francis, Alan, and Jane is not accidental). When Cesare is stabbing Alan to death in the latter's room, we see *Francis'* shadow, not Cesare's, hovering over Alan. Francis murders in Alan what he hates in himself. He is, again, the consummate Expressionist by Walter Sokel's definition: "A deep conviction of unworthiness runs as a constant theme through the works of the Expressionists. In fact, Expressionism can be viewed as the attempt of a generation to come to grips with and somehow transcend the calamitous self-contempt that has overtaken the modern poet" (p. 83). I add the following, also Sokel's, only because it seems particularly descriptive of Francis' confinement in an insane asylum, and because it points to the peculiar absence of warmth and love from the world of the film, to the coldness and severity that are all it consists of: "The [Expressionist] poet stands on the margin of life, longing to be in the center. But something in himself bars him from ever reaching it, from ever partaking of the world's warmth and love" (p. 83).

"Caligari" has Cesare attempt to murder Jane as much because she is unusually beautiful and charming as because she pokes her nose into his affairs. Cesare gets all the way to the point where he is standing over Jane's body, knife in hand, but he cannot stab her. Something inside himself makes him suddenly stop, "his shoulders move jerkily several times [, and] an almost benevolent expression spreads over his face" (p. 76). He then attempts to take her away for his own. The something inside himself that makes Cesare stop is the animus of Francis. Francis attempts to destroy what he loves but has been unable to attain; when he cannot destroy Jane, he makes one last try at reaching her, at "partaking of the world's warmth and love." Here is Sokel on the Expressionist in love: "His relation to the opposite sex reflects his general feeling of inferiority. If he is not altogether unable to gain a woman's love, he is incapable of holding her affection for any length of time" (p. 83). Francis does not love himself; therefore, he cannot expect the love of another. He kills his double, Alan, who is also in love with Jane. For much of the time in the two framing episodes, "[Francis] gazes wistfully at [Jane] and thinks that if she only condescended to love him she could redeem him . . ." (Sokel, p. 83). Cesare dies of exhaustion from his efforts to carry the prostrate Jane away. His role as Francis' alter ego complete, he can do nothing but collapse and, literally, roll out of the picture. Right after he does, we see Francis looking into the window of "Caligari's" trailer at Cesare's own "double"—the dummy, made to look exactly like him, lying in the "cabinet" for all to see, in order to allay any suspicion that might fall on Cesare while he is off committing another murder. The "real" Cesare collapses, and Francis, eyeing the "double," is immediately disturbed, even though he cannot know of Cesare's death yet and thinks that it is in fact Cesare at whom he is staring. What happens to his alter ego happens, *mutatis mutandis*, to Francis.

Alan and the Town Clerk are dead, Cesare has abducted Jane, and now Cesare is dead. The path of Francis' storytelling consciousness, of his "Ich," can lead only to "Caligari." Jane tells Francis it was Cesare who almost killed her. Francis reexamines the criminal who, the inept police are convinced, is the murderer of Alan and the Town Clerk. He is as puzzled and disbelieving as he was when the suspect was first presented to him as the murderer—naturally enough, since he recognizes no aspect of himself in this bearded, gnarled individual. (Like Francis and Alan, Cesare is pale and gaunt: an aesthete in any other life.) Francis returns to "Caligari's" trailer, goes inside, and discovers that what he thought was Cesare lying in the "cabinet" asleep was really a dummy replacement. "Caligari," who has resisted Francis' attempts to enter the trailer, is now implicated and runs away. As the "co-dramatizer," with Cesare, of Francis' murderous self, "Caligari" can only take the escape route through Expressionistic landscape that Cesare took with Jane. Francis follows him and at one point appears in silhouette in the background as "Caligari" races through the foreground: Francis is the dark consciousness that is responsible for this tale. "Caligari" returns to the insane asylum where he is Director. Only after the Director's books and notes on somnambulism are found does Francis convince the doctors at the asylum that their boss has been assuming the role of Caligari on the side to carry out his investigations with Cesare. The body of the dead Cesare, found in the fields, is returned to the asylum. (Significantly, Francis has not been face to face with Cesare since the night at the fair when the latter predicted Alan's death.) "Caligari," confronted with the dead body of his other half, as it were, loses all control. He is exposed. After he is straitjacketed and locked inside a cell, we see Francis standing outside the huge door to the cell and appearing very bewildered. He is *very bewildered*, not overjoyed, because it is not so much "Caligari" he has succeeded in exposing as himself. That is why he must be straitjacketed in the same way that "Caligari" was and returned to the same cell, once his story ends and we are back in the "real" world of the insane asylum: he *is* Caligari, or Caligari is an extension of him.

So, I go against the grain of most *Caligari* criticism in that I imagine the film less as Janowitz and Mayer's

Expressionistic exposure of "the madness inherent in authority" perverted by Wiene than as Wiene's own exposure, aided unwittingly by Janowitz and Mayer's original story, of *the madness, excess, and ultimate self-destruction inherent in Expressionism itself.* This interpretation becomes more compelling once one considers that *Caligari* was produced at a time when dramatic Expressionism was beginning to exhaust itself as a movement. Wiene uses Francis' insane murdering as a *device* to investigate Expressionism. In no way, do I believe, is he attempting to equate, even remotely, the real Francis with the real-life Expressionists. Wiene gives this away in the final framing scene; he shows that his concern is not with the criminally insane Francis but with the vision he has been able to extract from Francis' mind. The hospital courtyard at the end of the film looks the same as it did during the previous Expressionistic sequences: even though we are back to "reality," perpendicular lines have not replaced oblique ones. The implication is that Francis is more the Expressionist imprisoned by his own vision than the madman imprisoned for murder. In the final "frame" the Director at one moment appears to be the "Caligari" of Francis' story when he puts his spectacles on, at another moment does not look like "Caligari" when he takes them off. There is nothing Expressionistic or not but that "vision" makes it so. Wiene is not suggesting that the real Director of the insane asylum is Caligari-like in the power he wields over human minds. That would be facile. The Director says, just before the film ends, "At last I understand the nature of his madness. He thinks I am that mystic Caligari. *Now I see how he can be brought back to sanity again*" (emphasis mine; p. 100). This *itself* is facile—thinking that Francis can be cured so easily (of his Expressionism? the Expressionists were to plod on for four more years, until 1924). Wiene pokes fun here at the facileness and ineptitude of the bourgeois mentality, perhaps the human mentality itself, in its search for simple answers to complex questions (recall the Director's self-satisfied, foolishly smiling face staring out at the camera during the final iris-out). He manages to give a good, swift kick in the pants to the bourgeois power structure so detested by the Expressionists at the same time as he burlesques or overthrows, in Francis' story, the naiveté and extremism of much dramatic Expressionism itself.

That naiveté and extremism are represented to an unparalleled degree by Janowitz and Mayer's original story taken alone: a fairly melodramatic Francis almost singlehandedly exposes "the madness inherent in authority"; he crushes "Caligari," and he himself escapes all harm (though he does suffer the loss of Alan and Jane). That is pure *silliness*, and perhaps Robert Wiene's real achievement in *Caligari* is to have laid bare less the madness than the silliness, the dead end, inherent in authority, in *formulation*, be it political, social, or artistic. He did something on film that the Expressionists were never able to do on stage: criticize, or laugh at, themselves at the same time as they scored their points.

Tellingly, the Expressionist experiment in film largely ceased with the advent of sound: the situation was too much like the theater again, where the word was primary. The word ultimately destroyed dramatic Expressionism because within the form it tended to lack variety, subtlety, and ambiguity: *richness*. It destroyed cinematic Expressionism because characters talking aloud amid painted sets and artful lighting were some-how less real, even ridiculous. There was nowhere to go from Wiene's criticisms. Wiene meant, I think, to enrich or improve Expressionism. Instead, he has come to represent the final word on it.

NOTES TO
"Expressionism and the Real *Cabinet of Dr. Caligari*"

1. Siegfried Kracauer, "Caligari," in *The Cabinet of Dr. Caligari*, a film by Robert Wiene, Carl Mayer, and Hans Janowitz, trans. R. V. Adkinson (New York: Simon and Schuster, 1972), p. 11. Hereafter cited by page number in the text. Kracauer's essay (pp. 5–26) precedes the script, which includes not only Adkinson's translation of the dialogue, but also his running description of the action.
2. Historical for the purposes of this film. There is no such figure as Dr. Caligari in actual history. He is the screen-writers' invention, if his name is not. The source and connotations of the name "Caligari" are documented on p. 126 of this essay.
3. Walter H. Sokel, *The Writer in Extremis: Expressionism in Twentieth-Century German Literature* (Stanford, Calif.: Stanford Univ. Press, 1959), p. 36. Hereafter cited by page number in the text.

EXPRESSIONISM AND
NOSFERATU

Critics have discussed certain Expressionist features of F. W. Murnau's *Nosferatu* (1922; based on Bram Stoker's novel *Dracula* [1897]),[1] but none has conceived of it as a fully Expressionist work. One reason for this is that most critics' understanding of the Expressionist movement, in drama as well as in film, is superficial. For them a film such as *The Cabinet of Dr. Caligari* (1920) is Expressionistic less for what it means than for how it looks with its "oppressively murky artificial sets" (Perez Guillermo, p. 150). And for Robin Wood, a discussion of Expressionism in *Nosferatu* need only be limited to a catalogue of its stylistic manifestations in the film, in other words, to how the film looks:

> The first shot of the vampire's castle jutting up from the rock, the strange geometrical patterning of arch-forms out of which Nosferatu emerges to meet [Hutter], the use of "unnatural" camera angles as in the shot from the hold of the ship, the trick effects [the speeded-up coach; the shots in negative], the huge shadow as Nosferatu ascends the stairs to [Ellen's] room, the shadow of his fingers clenching into a fist upon her heart. (p. 9)

Expressionism is primarily a drama of the mind, however, whether on stage or on screen. It is concerned with the essence, not the surface, of reality; therefore it, more than other styles, must be defined, not by its own surface characteristics, but by the essence they seek to embody. Roger Manvell and Heinrich Fraenkel have described Expressionism as "essentially a movement designed to get away from actuality and to satisfy the desire to probe seemingly fundamental truths of human nature and society by presenting them through fantasy and dramatized mysticism."[2] Expressionism gets away from actuality through a retreat into the mind and at the same time, paradoxically, through a projection of that mind onto the world. Expressionism externalizes, "expresses," what is inside the mind, it makes "outer" what is "inner." If Impressionism could be said to be the subjective rendering of the visible world, Expressionism is the subjective expression of an inner world, a vision. Many Expressionist plays, dating back to Strindberg's *To Damascus* (1898), a progenitor of the movement, have been called "Ich-dramas," dramas of the "I," the self, on a journey through the mind's inner reaches and the world's outer ones. Many Expressionist works are either explicitly or implicitly political: they react against the social tyranny of the bourgeoisie, on the one hand, and the political tyranny of demagogues, on the other.

Nosferatu's Expressionism has been overlooked, I believe, largely because of its natural, rather than fantastic, settings: the landscape of the Carpathian mountains, the narrow streets and closely packed houses of a small town on the Baltic Sea (where Murnau shot what we are to take as Bremen, Germany, in 1838, a significant time as will later be shown). But the film may be regarded as Hutter's (Jonathan Harker in Stoker's *Dracula*) "Ich-drama," and the two other main characters,

Ellen, his wife (Nina in the novel), and Nosferatu (Dracula in the novel), may be seen as aspects of Hutter's self. Hutter is no conscious, active rebel against society, as are many Expressionist heroes, themselves often extensions of their creators. He is, rather, a passive instrument of Murnau's mythic design; himself no rebel, Murnau doesn't make a rebel of his alter ego Hutter. A witness to or observer of the German sociopolitical scene, Murnau makes Hutter a witness to or observer of the relationship between Ellen and Nosferatu. Hutter himself is "narrated" by a fictitious contemporary of his who serves as a surrogate for Murnau, by a *historian* whose diary provides the story of Hutter's trip to Transylvania and Nosferatu's descent on Bremen. Professor Van Helsing is Dracula's nemesis in Stoker's novel; Van Helsing plays only a small part in Murnau's film (he's renamed Professor Bulwer). He is obviously not Nosferatu's anatagonist: both Annie (Lucy in the novel) and Ellen ask that the Professor be called, once Nosferatu has made his presence felt in Bremen, but the Professor does not go to them and in fact can do nothing to stop Nosferatu. Murnau reduces Van Helsing's role significantly so that Ellen can become simultaneously Nosferatu's destroyer and his victim.

Hutter is clearly linked to Ellen, as an aspect of himself, through marriage. They have recently been married, seem happy—the film begins with Hutter picking flowers for his wife—and together symbolize the bourgeois "correctness" of the Weimar Republic, during which *Nosferatu* was made. He is a clerk in a real estate office in their home town of Bremen. His boss, Knock (Renfield in the novel), asks him to close a property deal—for a house directly opposite his and Ellen's—

with Graf Orlok, known as Nosferatu, of Transylvania. Surprisingly, Hutter is more than happy to go, even though the trip will take him away for months from his bride. He seems exultant when he tells Ellen that she cannot travel with him, that she must not risk the danger of crossing the Carpathian mountains. This is the first indication we get, on a mythic or symbolic level (not a psychological one), of Hutter's attraction-repulsion, love-hate, for his wife, for his own bourgeois existence. In place of this humdrum, stifling existence, he gets to travel on horseback to a remote and different place and to do business with a count. His journey will become less a journey away from Bremen than into himself and as much a linking up with Nosferatu as a leavetaking from Ellen.

Hutter is linked to Nosferatu, as an aspect of himself, through business. He works for Knock, who is obviously demented and acts under the long-range influence of Nosferatu; ostensibly, Hutter volunteers to make the long trip to Graf Orlok's castle in order to improve his own position in the real estate office at the same time as he earns his commission. Nosferatu symbolizes the tyrant, about whose depiction in a group of German films from 1920–1924 Siegfried Kracauer has written:

> In this film type, the Germans of the time—a people still unbalanced, still free to choose its regime—nursed no illusions about the possible consequences of tyranny; on the contrary, they indulged in detailing its crimes and [the] sufferings it inflicted. Was their imagination kindled by the fear of bolshevism? Or did they call upon these frightful visions to exorcise lusts which, they sensed, were their own and now threatened to possess

them? (It is, at any rate, a strange coincidence that, hardly more than a decade later, Nazi Germany was to put into practice that very mixture of physical and mental tortures which the German screen then pictured.)[3]

In 1921–1922, when *Nosferatu* was made, Germany was going through a period of great instability, the result of its defeat in World War I and the overthrow of its traditional monarchy. The new German government was an attempt at democracy, but many officials of the Weimar Republic had rightist political leanings. At the same time, Bolshevism was taking root in Germany. The country was thrown into economic and social plight after the collapse of the currency: bread lines began forming and riots broke out everywhere. Kracauer comments, "The Germans obviously held [at this point] that they had no choice other than the cataclysm of anarchy or a tyrannical regime" (p. 88).

If Bram Stoker's *Dracula* was a novel of Victorian sexual repression, Murnau's *Nosferatu* is a film of Weimar-Republic autocratic repression. At one end, in Bremen, there is Ellen, a pallid, emaciated figure who stands for the weakness, the shakiness, of German democracy in the early 1920s and whose recent marriage to Hutter represents their attempt to fall into line with the surface order of bourgeois life in Bremen, with its closely packed houses, carefully charted streets, tightly knit families, and fastidiously kept living quarters. At the other end, in Transylvania, there is Nosferatu, himself a pallid, emaciated figure who, in his shadowiness, stands for the subterranean impulse in the German people of the time toward autocracy: he represents their skeleton in the closet, as it were, ready to emerge and declare itself at any moment. Nosferatu lives alone in his huge castle; it is as if, in his will to absolute power, he has become the sole inhabitant of his realm: he rules all, he *is* all. Appropriately, Nosferatu emerges only at night, sleeping by day in an earth-filled coffin located in a crypt beneath his castle—he also sleeps in such a coffin in the hold of the ship that carries him to Bremen.

Robin Wood has noted that the arch is a visual leitmotif in the film, that it is used by Murnau "particularly to characterize the vampire as a repressed force who is always emerging from under arches or arch-shapes that seem to be trying unsuccessfully to press down upon him, often forming a background of darkness" (p. 7). (Wood sees Nosferatu, however, as a symbol of repressed sexuality rather than repressed tyranny.) The arch is also used to link Nosferatu with Hutter. There is an arch over the bed in which Hutter sleeps at the inn, just before he enters the vampire's domain. When he enters Nosferatu's castle, Hutter passes under a large arch, just as, when Nosferatu enters Bremen after disembarking from the ship "Demeter," he walks beneath a large arch. When they meet for the first time, Nosferatu emerges from one arch, Hutter from another; they face each other under yet another arch. Nosferatu's crypt is arched, and when Hutter descends into it to find the vampire's coffin, he passes under a huge, oppressive overhang of rock. There are some other scenes in which arches connect Nosferatu with Hutter. At the end of the dinner scene, for example, when Nosferatu is excited by the blood from Hutter's finger (which he cut while trying to slice some bread), the arch in the background strongly resembles the one from which he first emerged. When Hutter awakens the next day at sunrise, he is still beneath an arch of sorts—the arched ceiling of his room. He eats breakfast in front of an arch, goes outdoors through an arched doorway, passes under a dark arch that takes up the entire foreground of the image, then sits down to write a letter to Ellen under the arches of a small pavilion. He is even standing under an arch when he calls to the postman (on horseback) to come pick up his letter. Hutter's daytime movement through this series of arches is later mirrored by Nosferatu's nighttime passage under several arches on his way to suck the sleeping Hutter's blood.

In between the "democracy" of Ellen/Bremen and the "demagogy" of Nosferatu/Transylvania, or beyond them both, lies anarchy, symbolized by the rough terrain, raw or uncontrolled nature, over which Hutter must travel in order to reach Nosferatu's castle.[4] Along the way, he will ride up and down hills, across woods, and through mists and rushing water; he will encounter "spooked" horses (pursued by a jackal), wolves, and eerie birds. The choice for Murnau's Expressionist hero is between a fragile, yet suffocating democracy on the one hand and a steady, yet equally oppressive tyranny on the other hand, with anarchy the route between these two poles. Ellen and Bremen are his projection, his "mindscreen," if you will, just as are Nosferatu and Transylvania. As for the trick photography (the speeded-up coach, the incredibly rapid loading of a carriage with earth-filled coffins), the shots in negative, the odd camera angles, the "supernaturally" opening doors in the castle, and the "supernaturally" propelled ship that takes Nosferatu to Bremen (or rather, "supernaturally" manned sailing ship, the entire crew of which Nosferatu has destroyed), one explanation is not only that these are "endistancing devices" separating the vampire's world from that of the German town, as Gilberto Perez Guillermo believes (p. 153), but also that these devices are the work of Murnau's/the Expressionist hero's consciousness. To underline this point, Murnau has Hutter insist in a letter to Ellen from Transylvania that, even though the frightening things happening to him seem real, they are all part of a dream. The hero's consciousness projects onto the tyrant's world the extraordinary power that it *imagines* this world to have. Low-angle shots, for instance, make Nosferatu loom up in the frame, and shots in negative suggest that this despot has the ability, not only to speed up motion, but also to reverse the usual positions of light and shadow on objects. That Murnau filmed *Nosferatu* "in the world," on location and not in the studio, lends the scenes of trick photography and "supernatural" motion a reality, a convincingness, that they would otherwise not have: these scenes seem to be not merely the products of someone's febrile mind, as they would seem had they been shot within the confines of a studio, but the products of an entire world at the mercy of an omnipotent, nearly godly, tyrant.

Returning to the subject of Hutter's symbolic attraction-repulsion or love-hate toward his wife, toward both his own tidy bourgeois existence and the precarious democratic structure that supports it, I would like to note that, unlike the Expressionist dramatists, who wrote more or less for a coterie audience, Murnau set his story, not in the present, but in what Lane Roth calls "the safety of the past" [p. 311], where the more "democratic" or popular audience could, if it chose, ignore the film's contemporary sociopolitical implications. Thus, whenever I speak in this essay of Bremen, Germany, in 1838, one should transpose its social and political order to the Bremen of 1922. For example, Hutter runs from Ellen to Nosferatu and thus to the promise of financial gain and career advancement. This move makes sense given the seriously troubled German economy in 1922; Germany as a whole was similarly to run over to Hitler's side ten years later when he artificially stimulated the country's economy with his war machine. Hutter has the same love-hate toward Nosferatu, however, that he has toward his wife. Even though he discovers that the count is a vampire and has in fact assaulted him, Hutter does not try to destroy him (as the count was destroyed in the novel by being beheaded and having a stake driven through his heart). When Hutter sees Nosferatu lying asleep in his coffin during the day, he can only draw back in horror—the same reaction he has when, near the end of the film, Ellen tells him of the vampire's designs on her. Despite the fact that Nosferatu would suck the life out of him and his wife, just as a tyrant would suck the life out of his people, Hutter can do nothing to oppose him. Hutter seems repulsed by yet drawn to an aspect of himself that he sees in Nosferatu. He hates the bourgeois in himself, he is suspicious of the capitalistic democracy that would promote the middle class, but he races back to Ellen from Transylvania. He hates the tyrant in himself, he is suspicious of the "benevolent" dictator who promises to make life better for all the people, yet he does not kill Nosferatu; in effect, he allows the count to make the voyage by ship to Bremen.

It is as if Hutter has deliberately sought out the tyrant Nosferatu, so as to make him aware of Ellen's existence. Nosferatu wants her the instant Hutter shows him her miniature, and Ellen seems to want him. Two incidents suggest this. Hutter returns to Bremen the same way he arrived in Transylvania—by land; the vampire travels to Bremen by sea. When we get a shot of Ellen awaiting her husband's return, however, she is looking out to sea. At one point we see her sleepwalking on her balcony; suddenly she collapses, declaring as she does so, "He's coming, I must go to meet him." Murnau implies that she means Nosferatu, because he cuts to her, not from a shot of Hutter on horseback, but from one of the ship with the vampire aboard it. Ellen seems attracted to Nosferatu at the same time as she is repulsed by him. She allows m to ravish her, to suck her blood, and to destroy himself in the process: she intentionally keeps him at her side until dawn, at which moment the rays of the sun cause him to dissolve into nothingness. Nosferatu is similarly attracted to Ellen at the same time as he is repulsed by her. All the while he is making love to her in his way, is sucking her blood, he is draining her of life. She dies, and he vanishes into the air.

Nosferatu has taken with him many of the burghers of Bremen, who have died of the plague spread by rats that have made the journey from Transylvania with him. He is repeatedly associated with these rats—they swarm from his earth-filled coffins in the hold of the ship. Indeed, he himself looks like a rat with his long and pointed, hairy ears, his claws, and his fangs; and he moves like one, especially along the streets of Bremen, skulking and sidling in his fear of being set upon by the citizens. In the Expressionist hero Hutter's mind, the tyrant is both a bloodsucker—a parasite—and a spreader of infectious disease, of a political philosophy that is at once contagious and deadly. Thus Hutter projects Nosferatu as a vampire who looks and moves like a rat and who in effect leads a large pack of rats, his "army," the extension of his will. At least two critics have written of the supposed ambiguous nature of the plague in this film: it is spread by rats, yet the vampire's marks are on the victims' necks, as if Nosferatu had visited each one personally (Perez Guillermo, p. 153; Wood, p. 8). I am arguing that the "ambiguity" is intentional on Murnau's/Hutter's part, that Nosferatu is meant to appear as both rat and vampire, infector and bloodsucker.

Only Hutter, as the generator of this apocalyptic vision, seems to have knowledge of the presence of Nosferatu in town, although the tyrant has been afraid that both Hutter and the townspeople would discover him. Yet Hutter stands passively by as Nosferatu decimates much of the population of bourgeois Bremen. The tyrant destroys them, then one of them—Ellen—sacrifices herself to destroy him. Hutter has watched the bourgeois in himself cancel out, and be cancelled out by, the autocrat in himself. He has pitted social tyranny—the bourgeoisie in its conformity and hegemony—against political tyranny—the tyrant in his isolation and omnipotence. The frightened bourgeoisie, on whose fears any tyrant feeds in a time of economic and social unrest (as Hitler was to feed on the fears of the German middle class), itself helps to pull the tyrant down in the end, to take the life out of him. The Expressionist hero Hutter has witnessed the destruction of the two aspects of himself, each of which he both loves and hates: the democratic bourgeois that he is and the "benevolent" dictator that he would be; his will to equality and his will to power.

Hutter is the Expressionist hero as passive bourgeois, not as active intellectual or artist; as a representative of the people, not as their antagonist. He stands, not apart from society, but as a part of it. There is no escape for him into visionary ecstasy, as there might be for the Expressionist rebel, or into art, as there was for the Expressionist creators themselves. He makes no pronouncements concerning the creation of the "New Man," nor does he offer a prescriptive aesthetics. He is left at the end to mourn the loss of himself, the Nosferatu who is gone (along with his agent and Hutter's boss, Knock, who expires back in jail the moment he senses that Nosferatu has perished) and the Ellen who is dead. A title declares that there were no more deaths from the plague and that happiness was regained, but the camera does not return to the streets of Bremen. We are left with the overwhelming impression of destruction, of loss; a shot of Hutter mourning over Ellen's body is followed by the last shot of the film, which appears to be the product of Hutter's memory: an image of Nosferatu's now vacant castle jutting up into the sky.

The title of Murnau's next film, *Der letzte Mann* (*The Last Man*, 1924, incorrectly translated as *The Last Laugh* in America), could as well be the title of *Nosferatu*. The later work contains Expressionistic elements, but they are fused to a realistic base. We have gone from Hutter's nightmare vision in *Nosferatu* to Emil Jannings' nightmares in *Der letzte Mann*, from the tragic division of one character to the pathetic oneness of another, from the end of the world to a happy ending. Murnau's escape, as Expressionist filmmaker, from the potential artistic dead end of *Nosferatu* was to re-create the everyday world in *Der letzte Mann* and put into it a *character* in a dead end, from which he would be rescued by a dream-come-true: the inheritance, from an American, of a large sum of money. For Murnau, the antidote to Expressionistic nightmare was the opposite extreme: realistic fantasy.

NOTES TO
"Expressionism and *Nosferatu*"

1. Robin Wood, "Murnau's Midnight and *Sunrise*," *Film Comment*, 12 (May/June 1976), p. 9; Lane Roth, "Dracula Meets the 'Zeitgeist': *Nosferatu* (1922) as Film Adaptation," *Literature/Film Quarterly*, 7, No. 4 (1979), pp. 311–312; Gilberto Perez Guillermo, "Shadow and Substance: Murnau's *Nosferatu*," *Sight and Sound*, 36, No. 3 (Summer 1967), pp. 150–151; Tom Milne, "*Nosferatu—Eine Symphonie des Gravens*" [the full title of the film in German: *Nosferatu, a Symphony of Horror*], *British Film Institute Monthly Film Bulletin*, 41 (February 1974), p. 37; and Lotte H. Eisner, *The Haunted Screen: Expressionism in the German Cinema and the Influence of Max Reinhardt*, trans. Roger Greaves (Berkeley: Univ. of Calif. Press, 1969), pp. 102 and 105. Wood, Roth, and Perez Guillermo are hereafter cited by page number in the text.
2. Roger Manvell and Heinrich Fraenkel, *The German Cinema* (New York: Praeger, 1971), p. 13.
3. Siegfried Kracauer, *From Caligari to Hitler: A Psychological History of the German Film* (Princeton, N.J.: Princeton

Univ. Press, 1947), p. 77. Hereafter cited by page number in the text.

4. This anarchy is also symbolized by Hutter's boss and Nosferatu's agent, Knock, who becomes so demented that he reverts to erratic, *animal*-like behavior once he escapes into the countryside from his madman's prison cell. He swings down from rooftops like an ape, crouches behind a tree stump, then hops along like a frog or toad. In addition, like the "vampire *plant*," the Venus' flytrap, whose powers Dr. Bulwer demonstrates to his students, Knock catches and eats insects for his nourishment.

EXPRESSIONISM AND
L'AVVENTURA

The structure of Antonioni's *L'avventura* (1960) reminds me of that of German Expressionist drama, which frequently consists of a series of tableaux or stations depicting the hero's passage through places and events that externally have little, if any, connection. The very title *L'avventura* declares that the film will be about an adventure or a quest. That quest is initially for diversion or excitement, in Anna and Claudia's trip to Sandro's apartment (Station 1) and in the boat trip to the rocky island (Station 2) off the coast of Sicily, where Antonioni shoots his characters traversing the terrain and searching the ancient ruins. The quest soon becomes to find Anna, who has disappeared from the island, but it then quickly turns into Sandro and Claudia's search for a relationship and her unconscious search for self. Thus, although the two are still ostensibly searching for Anna, their stop in an empty town square (Station 4) before going to Noto (where Anna has supposedly gone by bus); their scenes in Noto (Station 5) in the paint shop, the bell tower, and their room; and their scenes in the expensive hotel in Taormina (Station 6), as well as Claudia's experiences at the Princess' villa (Station 3), come outwardly to have little, if any, relation. These sequences are really about

Claudia's growth and her growing to love Sandro, and they are important less for themselves, less for the action they would stimulate in a linear narrative, than for what they reveal about the characters.

The same can be said in retrospect for the scenes at Sandro's apartment and on the island itself: externally, they have small connection. One expects Anna and Claudia to pick Sandro up quickly and go off to an island paradise for fun and relaxation. Instead, Anna and Sandro delay departure by having sex, then they, Claudia, and friends stop at an island where it would be impossible to have a good time in the conventional sense—there is no beach, no hotel, there are no inhabitants, and the nearby islands are also covered with rock. Like the sequences that follow, these two are important, then, less for themselves, for the action that might grow integrally out of them, than for what they reveal about the characters and what the characters reveal about themselves to Claudia.

J. M. Ritchie, among others, has noted that in Expressionism there is constant emphasis on portraying the essence of a situation or character, its deeper image instead of its mere surface appearance.[1] Thus the barrenness of the island and its volcanic rock, under which an ancient civilization lies buried, are symbols, externalizations, of the sterility and callousness of modern civilization, which is epitomized by the wealthy boaters. It is no accident that Raimondo drops the ancient vase (found by a diver) on the rocks when he turns to stare at Claudia and can show only mock sorrow for smashing it. The desolation of the town they stop at on their way to Noto is a reflection of the emptiness of Sandro's life and potentially of Claudia's—she is the outsider in the film, since she is not rich like the rest of the party that originally sets out for the island, and consequently, as one separated from the others by class, she is somewhat akin to the spiritual outsiders of Expressionist drama. The tawdry opulence of the Princess' villa and of the hotel in Taormina is a representation of the material wealth that idlers like Sandro use to cover their spiritual poverty, to fill up their barren lives.

Ritchie notes further that the dynamic, episodic structure of Expressionist drama mirrors the inner turmoil, the spiritual chaos, of the central figure, who often goes through a total moral transformation.[2] The episodic structure of *L'avventura* is designed to mirror the inner turmoil, the spiritual chaos, of Anna; the impulsive search for love and self by Claudia; and the randomness as well as idleness of the lives of the rich. Inside this structure, the couples Sandro and Anna, Patrizia (the Princess) and Raimondo, Giulia and Corrado, Giulia and Raimondo, and Sandro and Gloria Perkins reflect the lovelessness and restlessness or boredom of the Italian rich. Claudia is the outsider, the observer of the sexual encounters (or want of them) between these couples (as she is the outsider or observer at many other moments in the film: see the shot descriptions at the end of this essay). They are not reflections of her central position in the story, as they would be in an Expressionist drama; they are not her inner truth made outer, externalized. These couples are outer truth—the truth about the elite of Italian society—made inner, internalized by Claudia. She is an Expressionist protagonist in reverse. Where the Expressionist hero is active, she is passive, getting her initiation into a way of life that she has known little about. Claudia gets her knowledge less through action and conflict than through observation and introspection, less through her dramatic than through her visual experience. Antonioni literally conveys her "undramatic" quest for love of Sandro and for insight into his social class by means of long takes and lengthy traveling shots of her searching over the extinct volcano, along the passageways of the Princess' vast mansion, through the corridors of the hotel in Taormina. Whereas time is compressed in Expressionist plays, as it is in most drama, in the service of action, time during these shots is real: Antonioni's intention is to make us experience the duration of Claudia's search and thus her frustration at not achieving fulfillment faster.

Where the Expressionist hero is often destroyed in the process of his transformation, Claudia survives to act on her knowledge, however tentatively, at the end of *L'avventura*. The Expressionist hero would destroy bourgeois society and the bourgeois in himself, to create the "new man." Instead of leaving Sandro with the knowledge that he is like all the others she has been observing, or instead of turning quickly to another man, Claudia remains with him. Sandro looked for Anna and did not find her: she may have gone down into the sea and drowned. He looks for Claudia after she runs from the sight of him and Gloria Perkins making love, and he finds her on the hotel terrace. After Anna's disappearance, a squall threatened the island and night was approaching; when Sandro finds Claudia, dawn is breaking and it is still.

Anna was a potential Expressionist protagonist whom Antonioni discarded. She has rightly been described by one critic as having "a neurotic urge to put herself at the center of every stage."[3] She is a wild, even dangerous, figure whose discontent with life and uneasiness in her love for Sandro manifest themselves at every turn. Like many Expressionist protagonists, she has difficulty communicating with her father. She is destroyed, or disappears, before any transformation can take place in her. Antonioni seems not to share the Expressionist faith in the ability of the hero to transform his society and himself through verbal and physical violence, so he gets rid of Anna. By the end of *L'avventura*, Claudia has the knowledge about Sandro and his social class that Anna disappeared with. She gives her pity to the unfaithful Sandro; in not running away from him on the terrace, she acts wilfully against all that she knows about him. She remains, in gentleness and silence, with her hand on his head in the final shot of the film.

L'avventura is, I believe, less an indictment of a social class, as most critics have maintained, than a chronicling of an outsider's initiation into it. Instead of destroying this social class in ecstasy from within, in the manner of the German Expressionist heroes, Claudia attempts to alleviate its distress, through compassion, from without. She is a "new woman" wedded spiritually to an "old man" at the end of the film. We have long since left all the couples in whose lovelessness and disquiet Sandro shared. It is up to Claudia and the tearful Sandro, in "shared pity," to use Antonioni's words,[4] to create a vital and stable order. The rich are a given in this film: they are here, they will always be here, and they are not condemned simply for being rich. What becomes of the lives of the rich is another question, one that concerns Antonioni.

Like Anna, the director was an outsider in his own

upper class: he voluntarily exiled himself at age twenty-seven from the world of his father, a wealthy business-man, and went to live in Rome, where at times he almost starved in order to establish his independence. Before shooting his first feature, *Cronaca di un amore* (1950), he made documentaries that depicted the lower class such as *Gente del Po* (1947), about Po River fishermen, and *Nettezza urbana* (1948), about the street cleaners of Rome. With *Cronaca* he began a series of films about lower-class characters in a world of luxury, returning once to an actual working-class milieu in *Il Grido* (1957). This series culminated in *L'avventura*, with its outsider Claudia from the middle class. Finally, with *La Notte* (1961) and *L'eclisse* (1962), which with *L'avventura* form a loosely connected trilogy, Antonioni was completely at home in the world of the upper class, no longer needing to employ an outsider as his window on it. It is as if, once he reentered prominent social circles through his directorial renown after *L'avventura*, he decided to stay and take an unmediated look around, just as his own character Claudia did after her entry into the same circles through her beauty and grace. In this Antonioni is not unlike Fellini, who, originally from the provincial middle class, made films about it and about the lower class until his reputation gained him entrance into high society. But where Fellini has examined with ebullience and indulgence the moral and spiritual inertia of the upper class, beginning with *La dolce vita* in 1960, Anto-nioni has done so with austerity and concern. One could say that Fellini took the view of a boy at play in a new, if jaded environment, while Antonioni assumed the atti-tude of a man returning deliberately to the home he had deserted.

SHOT DESCRIPTIONS: CLAUDIA AS OUTSIDER OR OBSERVER

1. Claudia observes the conversation between Anna and her father, outside Anna and her father's house. (See the still in *"L'avventura," A Film by Michelangelo Antonioni*, trans. Jon Swan, text reconstruction David Denby [New York: Grove Press, 1969], p. 12.)
2. Claudia waits impatiently outside Sandro's apartment as he and Anna have sexual intercourse inside. (See pp. 15, 16, and 18 of the Grove Press screenplay.)
3. Claudia enters an art gallery and observes first an American couple, then two workers discussing paintings. (See the still, p. 17 of the Grove Press screenplay.)
4. Claudia, in the foreground on the yacht, witnesses this typical exchange between Giulia and Corrado:

    Giulia. All these islands . . . were once volcanoes.

    Corrado. There musn't be a single fact you don't know about third-grade geography. (See pp. 22–23 of the Grove Press screenplay. Also, see the still of Claudia observing Giulia and Corrado *on the island* in *Screenplays of Michelangelo Antonioni*, trans. Louis Brigante [New York: Orion Press, 1963], p. 120.)
5. Claudia observes Raimondo's flirtation with Patrizia on the yacht. (See the still, p. 32 of the Grove Press screenplay.)
6. Claudia stands in the foreground as Corrado, Sandro, Raimondo, Patrizia, and Giulia stand behind her: Claudia has decided to remain on the island with Sandro and Corrado while the others go for help. (See pp. 44–45 of the Grove Press screenplay.)
7. Sandro walks toward the old man, the single person

living on the island (in a hut). In the background, Claudia watches. (See p. 50 of the Grove Press screenplay.)

8. Claudia walks silently past Raimondo, Patrizia, Corrado, Giulia, and a diver. Raimondo turns to look at her and drops the vase. (See p. 55 of the Grove Press screenplay.)

9. Claudia observes Sandro's conversation with Anna's father on the island. (See p. 58 of the Grove Press screenplay.)

10. Raimondo, Patrizia, Corrado, and Giulia make their way down the rocks to leave the island. Claudia stands looking out to sea, away from the others. (See p. 61 of the Grove Press screenplay.)

11. Claudia, later joined by Sandro, observes the flirtation between the young man and the young woman on the train. (See the still, p. 71 of the Grove Press screenplay.)

12. In the background at the Princess' villa, Claudia is standing facing away from Ettore (the Princess' husband), Corrado, Patrizia (the Princess), and Giulia, who speak of Sandro. (See p. 80 of the Grove Press screenplay.)

13. At the Princess' villa, Claudia is in the foreground, her back to the rest, very unhappy at the suggestion that Sandro has found Anna. Ettore, Corrado, and Giulia are behind her. (See the still, p. 80 of the Grove Press screenplay.)

14. At the Princess' villa, Claudia watches Giulia take Goffredo's arm and walk off with him. (See the still, p. 82 of the Grove Press screenplay.)

15. From the terrace outside her room at the Princess' villa, Claudia observes Giulia and Goffredo walk by below. Giulia can be overheard saying, "May I see your work? I admit, I'm curious." (See p. 83 of the Grove Press screenplay.)

16. Claudia observes Giulia and Goffredo on the stairs. (See p. 84 of the Grove Press screenplay.)

17. In Goffredo's art studio, Claudia comes into the foreground and watches him grabbing Giulia and forcing her backward onto a table. (Claudia has been observing their flirtation since she entered the studio; see the still, p. 88 of the Grove Press screenplay.)

18. Claudia watches Patrizia, Ettore, Giulia, Goffredo, and Corrado get into a car and go to a cocktail party. In the foreground, Claudia walks slowly back into the house. (See p. 91 of the Grove Press screenplay.)

19. In Troina, Claudia, with Sandro, observes the rift between the druggist and his wife. (See p. 94 of the Grove Press screenplay.)

20. In Noto, Claudia regards groups of men who lounge about on the street and on the stairway above, staring at her greedily. She walks across the square, attracting more attention, aware of the eyes upon her and of the comments. Further above, on a balcony, men eagerly move to the railing to watch. (See the still, p. 103 of the Grove Press screenplay.)

21. Claudia, alone in the lobby of the expensive hotel in Taormina, looks around at the many well-dressed people wandering about. (See p. 120 of the Grove Press screenplay.)

22. Claudia, a distant relative of the figure in Edvard Munch's Expressionistic painting *The Scream*, runs frantically through the long corridors of the hotel searching for Sandro, then runs away from him and Gloria Perkins and continues running once she leaves the hotel. (See pp. 130, 132, 135, and 136 of the Grove Press screenplay. Also, see the stills, pp. 202 and 205 of the Orion Press screenplay.)

23. (Connected with No. 22) Claudia finds Sandro making love to Gloria Perkins on a couch in the hotel lounge.

(See the stills, pp. 133–135 of the Grove Press screen-play.)

24. On the terrace of the hotel, Sandro sits on a bench with his back to Claudia, who looks at him. She very slowly moves to him, coming up behind the bench. (See the still, pp. 138–139 of the Grove Press screenplay.)

NOTES TO
"Expressionism and *L'avventura*"

1. J. M. Ritchie, *German Expressionist Drama* (Boston: Twayne, 1976), p. 15.
2. Ritchie, *German Expressionist Drama*, p. 18.
3. Penelope Houston, "*L'avventura*," in Jon Swan, trans., "*L'avventura*," *A Film by Michelangelo Antonioni* (New York: Grove Press, 1969), p. 256. Houston's review originally appeared in *Sight and Sound*, Winter 1960–1961.
4. Antonioni quoted in Roger Sandall, "*L'avventura*," *Film Quarterly*, 14, No. 4 (Summer 1961), p. 54.

V

Experiments in Characterization and Empathy

BRESSON'S *UNE FEMME DOUCE*:

A New Reading

What happens in *Une femme douce* (*A Gentle Creature*, 1969), Robert Bresson's ninth film, after the novella by Dostoyevski, and his first one in color? A young woman, unnamed, of certain background and insufficient means, for no apparent reason marries a pawnbroker, also unnamed. She tells this man that she does not love him, and she makes it very clear she disdains his, and all, money; if she is marrying to escape her origins, it remains unclear exactly what those origins were and why she is choosing to escape them in this particular way. She and her husband go through periods of much unhappiness—we even see her with another man at one point, but we cannot be sure that she has been unfaithful—and some calm. She nearly shoots him to death in his sleep. She becomes very ill, and, once she recovers, matters appear to be righting themselves between her and her husband. Then she jumps to her death from the balcony of their apartment.

Dostoyevski's novella, "A Gentle Spirit," is substantially similar to this, allowing for the differences in time and place, with one major exception: the young wife in

Dostoyevski is initially very loving toward her husband, with the result that the main turns of the above plot are easily explained. The husband in the novella—he is the narrator both of the novella and of Bresson's film— distrusts out of his own perversity his wife's love for him, so he decides to test it. He is cold to her and holds over her head the fact that he has rescued her from her poor beginnings. She comes to hate him and almost to commit adultery. Finally, she is ready to shoot him. With her gun at his temple, he awakens but does not move. She cannot fire. A religious woman, she feels great remorse and atones for her "sin" by leaping to her death while clutching an icon. The wife is lying on her bier at the beginning of the novella and the husband is at her side, reviewing his marriage in an attempt to under- stand why she committed suicide. What he winds up understanding is that his own contrariness is the cause of all his unhappiness and that all men live in "un- breachable solitude," in the words of Charles Thomas Samuels, who makes the mistake in his review/essay "Bresson's Gentleness" of allowing Dostoyevsky's no- vella to color his perception of the action in *Une femme douce*.[1]

Samuels' and many others'[2] explanations of what happens in the film pale beside the facts, and the facts are almost all Bresson gives us and all that we should consider if we are to be able to interpret the film justly. I am reminded here of what Bert O. States said of critics' explanations of events in Pinter's *Homecoming* (1965): "It is more a case of the play's not contradicting such ideas than of its actually containing them."[3] One fact that Samuels inexplicably ignores and that I take to be the foundation of any interpretation of *Une femme douce* true to Bresson, as opposed to the critic's own bent, is the young woman's declaration from the start that *she does not love* the man she intends to marry. Put another way, it is not at all clear *why* she marries him, and certainly all the evidence points to the conclusion that they are very different from each other, indeed, nearly exact opposites. (And I reject the "opposites attract" theory here; nothing the young woman does indicates that she is even attracted to the pawnbroker, let alone in love with him.) The pawnbroker for his part, although he may wish to marry the woman, does not make known why he suddenly wants to wed after so many years of bachelorhood. (Bresson makes him thirty-five to forty years old and gives him a live-in maid/assistant whom, significantly, he does not dismiss after his marriage.) He gets little response from his fiancée, and they could hardly be said to carry on a courtship. In a word, these two are simply not meant for each other, and I am maintaining that Bresson makes sure we know this right away. What the director does in *Une femme douce* is the reverse of what Dostoyevski does in "A Gentle Spirit." The latter has his husband test the love of his wife and conclude that all men live in "unbreachable solitude." Bresson has his husband and wife living in unbreachable solitude from the start and tests the love of *his audience* for them through the mediating presence of Anna, the maid, the character he adds and purposefully names. (Although Bresson could just as easily have had the husband think or tell out loud the story of his marriage to himself, he has him tell it to Anna in the same room in which his wife's corpse lies on their bed; like the wife's body lying in the street after her jump to her death, which we see at the *start* of the film, this is

163

another telling image of the-end-of-the-marriage-in-its-beginning.) Dostoyevski uses the spiritual to express the nihilistic; Bresson, the nihilistic to express the spiritual.

. . .

Most of what we learn about the young woman is intended to establish how different from the pawnbroker she is, not to add up to a unified character of depth and originality with whom we can readily identify. She comes to the pawnbroker's shop, and immediately the beautiful Dominique Sanda, in her first screen role, is unsympathetic: her clothing is drab, her hair is dishevelled, she makes very little eye-contact with anyone, and her walk has about it at the same time a timidity and an urgency that make it unnerving. The pawnbroker, by contrast, walks steadily and looks directly at all whom he encounters (Bresson is careful to have him do so, while his customers, for example, avoid his gaze), but with eyes that one cannot look into and with a face that is neither handsome nor plain. He is meticulous in appearance and sparing in gesture. This is a man who "understands" the world and how to get along in it: money is everything to him, and what can't be seen, touched, and stored is not worth talking about. He accumulates item after item in his pawn shop, but we never see him sell anything: he likes his money, but he likes his "objects," too. His wife gives his funds away for worthless objects. He has shelves of books, but we never see him take one down. She pawns her last possessions to get a few more books to read. After they are married he takes her to see *Hamlet*, more because they already have tickets (given to him free of charge?) than because he really wants to see the play. She goes right to the text after the performance. Charles Thomas Samuels writes that "neither husband nor wife can rise above the world of things," and that this is why they fall out (p. 168). The point, however, is that the husband does not wish to rise above "the world of things" and the wife longs to but cannot, and that this chasm between them is clearly established from the start by their behavior and by Bresson's camera. They don't fall out in direct conflict with each other and with themselves over the spiritual way of life versus the material; they are *fallen out* when they first meet.

Early in the film the young woman says something like, "We're all—men and animals—composed of the same matter, the same raw materials," and later we have this truism confirmed visually when she and her husband visit a museum of natural history. At another point she asks whether birds learn to sing from their parents or whether the ability to sing is present in them at birth. Is Bresson trying to mock this woman, to point out that for all her reading and studying, she is intellectually shallow, or worse, a pseudointellectual? I don't think so. I believe that he is trying to set up the major difference in the personalities of husband and wife that I describe above. His interest is less in the revelation of character than in the documentation of behavior. The wife yearns beyond a universe in which all is matter and where even human beings often seem to behave in a preconditioned manner—preconditioned to marry, to gather wealth and possessions, to beautify the self, to respond to art in a certain way. The husband is obsessed with possessing matter and doing the "right" thing. Throughout the film the suggestion is that he responds to situations in a preconditioned or "proper" manner, whereas she responds in the most unforeseen, and sometimes bizarre, ways. The most striking example of this, perhaps, is the amount of money each gives for pawned objects. As I have pointed out, the wife often pays good money for worthless objects; the husband naturally pays as little as he can for things of value. Hers is the unexpected, the selfless or gratuitous, response; his, the predictable and self-centered one. But there are two moments when he behaves as she does, or appears to. Before they are married, he grossly overpays her for a gold crucifix she has come to his shop to pawn, and after their marriage, when she is recovering from her illness, he begins to buy valueless objects and to pay too much for articles that are worth only a little. His is again the predictable and selfish response, however: in the first instance, he wants to get closer to his future wife, to impress her with his generosity; in the second, he is trying to make it appear that he has changed in order to strengthen the delicate balance he and his wife seem to have created in their relationship. His wife behaves true to her self, or I should say her ideal, in both these instances: though she is desperate for money, she refuses her future husband's overpayment for the crucifix; though matters seem better, or in any event calmer, in their marriage, she commits suicide.

Almost all the wife's behavior in the film is choreographed to this ideal of the unexpected or the gratuitous. When she and her husband enter their bedroom on the wedding night, she quickly turns on the television but does not watch it. He does, and what he sees is the image of his own behavior pattern: cars racing around in a circle. (Later horses will be seen racing around in a circle on the same television, then World War II fighter planes in dogfights: there is a contest, there will be a winner, and to him will go the spoils.) The wife nearly runs about the room in preparation for bed, and the towel in which she is wrapped dislodges itself when she goes to turn off the television. Her running about as if preparing to go to work and the towel's coming undone, as opposed to being taken off demurely or enticingly, are inconsonant with the idea of entering the marriage bed for the first time. At one point she carelessly tosses her nightgown onto the bed, in much the same way that she will leave sexy under-clothes strewn about it during the day and will toss her books everywhere: she has no respect for the material, for objects or possessions. Another time, she takes a bath but doesn't drain the dirty water and leaves the faucet running. We see her husband turn the water off. The wife spurns money but likes to eat fancy pastries. She likes jazz but plays Bach and Purcell, too. She picks a bouquet of sunflowers along the side of the road, then quickly tosses them away when she sees that other couples have also gathered such bouquets. She goes to a museum with her husband and contemplates an odd-looking piece of sculpture. He rejects it as too distant from classic art, from the painting in the frame (earlier he had quoted Goethe proudly); she embraces the sculpture simply as a work of art, similar in spirit, if not in form, to all works of art.

The young woman marries, though she does not love, then sees other men, though she is married. We don't learn anything about these men, and we don't learn if she has carried on a sexual relationship with any of them. There may be only one—Bresson is not clear on this or on the issue of adultery, for his true subject is not the rise and fall of a marriage. At a movie—a "costume drama" trading on the wiles of love—the young woman responds to a man making eyes at her, while everyone else, including her husband, is engrossed in events on the screen. We, too, become engrossed in these events, just as we do in the action at two other important moments in *Une femme douce*: at the beginning, during the night drive through the city, and during the performance of *Hamlet.* Bresson identifies his camera with us at these moments, that is. *We* become the audience watching the "costume drama" and the performance of *Hamlet*; *we* become the driver of the car traveling a major Paris boulevard by night. Bresson is teasing us with the kinds of stories we are accustomed to seeing filmed or staged, where we immediately identify with the characters and their worlds; and in the car sequence, he is teasing us with the kind of camera placement (the subjective or point-of-view shot) that is the essence of this character identification. The director is also contrasting our and the husband's responses to the movie and the play with the wife's. She is not so absorbed in the movie that she can't flirt a little with the man next to her. In doing this, she is unconsciously imitating the characters on screen. Yet we cannot identify with her in the same way as we identify with them, which is precisely Bresson's point. During the performance of *Hamlet*, the wife cannot become emotionally involved with the characters onstage because the actors themselves are ignoring the following advice from Hamlet to the players: "In the very torrent, tempest, and whirlwind of your passion, you must acquire and beget a temperance" (III.ii.5–7). So, unlike her husband

and the rest of the theater audience, she does not applaud at the end. She goes home, picks up an edition of the play, and confirms her belief that these very lines from Hamlet's speech had been eliminated in performance so that the actors could, in a word, overact, place the emphasis on themselves as actors instead of on the characters they were playing. Later in the film, she will go to shoot her husband in his sleep and will again be unconsciously imitating a character, in this instance one from the stage. Like Hamlet, she hesitates and is lost (unlike Claudius, her husband sleeps, since, as he himself says, he is unable to pray). We cannot identify with her, even though Dominique Sanda's acting follows in the extreme Hamlet's advice to the players, as does all the acting in every Bresson film. We could identify with Hamlet and the other characters onstage; the wife, as Bresson's stand-in, is overly harsh in her criticism of the actors.

The wife is different from her husband and from us, or she is different from what we expect her to be. Even in dying. We do not get her point of view of the street before she leaps from the balcony. We do not await her fall from below, from the position she will soon be in. She jumps in daylight: we see a potted plant fall off the small table from which she leaped, we watch the table topple over, and we are given a shot of her shawl floating to the ground after her. (She had placed a shawl around her shoulders before she jumped!) She lands in the street and cars screech to a halt. We may assume that it was her husband navigating his car through the Paris night at the beginning of the film, since the wife does not drive. He drives *horizontally* over the streets, and, because of the position of the camera, we seem to be in the driver's seat with him. His wife falls *vertically* into the street, and she is off camera during her fall. The plant, the table, and the shawl imitate her descent. She is apart, she is different, she is dead. We await her husband's discovery of her death. Whereas he responded to her apparent interest in or involvement with other men like any jealous husband—he quickly changes seats with her at the movie theater, for example, and pulls her out of a strange man's car—he responds to her suicide like any guilty person. In the one instance he acts fast, in the other he ponders and paces. His wife's behavior is never so categorizable, is in fact always somewhere in between: we can never quite predict where, and we do not know why. Even in suicide: we assume, of course, that her fall is quick and decisive. But Bresson has her shawl trail slowly and discursively after her, just to remind us for the first and last time of the unpredictability of her nature (her suicide ends as well as begins the film).

Bresson's camera is itself always literally somewhere in between. There are many shots of doors, of empty stairways, of the objects filling the pawnbroker's shop and his apartment. The camera is "in between" in its representation of people: we get hands and arms cut off from bodies, bodies cut off from heads, just torsos, just feet. Bresson makes matter of the human body. The man and the woman live in "unbreachable solitude," and Bresson's camera films the material world, the literal distance between them, to emphasize this fact. As I have remarked, the man wishes to possess the material world, even his wife's body, and the woman wishes to transcend this world, even her own form. She does, in suicide. The last shot in the film is of the lid to her coffin being screwed on: the material world—the actual coffin lid—separates her, in death, from her husband, just as it did in life.

. . .

One may legitimately ask, if this man and woman are simply not meant for each other, why do they marry? I don't know. And I don't think that they know, either. Bresson doesn't care: their relationship per se—its ups and downs, rise and fall, if those terms can even be applied here—is not the focus of his film, as I have observed. Perhaps they get together out of their own perversity, but, again, the film doesn't *contain* this idea: it just doesn't contradict it. Even if the young woman marries the pawnbroker because it is the unexpected thing to do, since she does not love him, this is no satisfactory explanation, since *he* is neither aware of this nor concurs in it. Bresson uses their marriage in the same way that another director might counterpoint the happy marriage of a secondary couple upstairs with the unhappy one of the main couple downstairs. That is, in Bresson's hands marriage becomes a device: marriage is universally thought to be the most intimate state in which two people can live, and Bresson counterpoints this perception of ours with the almost complete lack of intimacy that exists between the husband and wife in his film. In other words, the director does not allow us to identify with the marriage of the pawnbroker and the young woman, to see ourselves in them, because he doesn't indicate that they marry for the reasons *we* usually associate with marrying: love, convenience, desperation, children. They wed, they are unhappy, they reach a fragile understanding, and she kills herself. The

171

husband, in his "narration"—it is not narration in the proper sense, but more on this later—attempts to discover why his wife committed suicide, but he cannot find an answer. He doesn't know why she killed herself, and neither do we. We are not permitted to identify with the wife's suicide, to see ourselves in her, because Bresson doesn't indicate any reason for her action, let alone a reason that we might deem acceptable.

My point is not that every human action in *Une femme douce* is without explanation, without cause or motive—for instance, the wife's near murder of her husband after he discovers her with another man *can* be accounted for—but that these individual explanations become beside the point when one considers that the pawnbroker and the young woman are unsuited to each other and should never have married in the first place. What becomes important is not so much their relationship with each other as our relationship with each of them and Anna's with the pawnbroker. One of the reasons Bresson's camera spends so much time at the beginning of the film on the dead wife, lying face down in the road, is so that we will finally ask, "So what do you want from me? What am I supposed to do?" The reason the camera shifts periodically from *its* illustration of past events to the husband pacing back and forth in the bedroom, telling *his* story, is in order to emphasize that he as character, apart from his story, is the proper focus of our concerns. As is his wife, literally apart from her story in death, lying in the road again at the end of the film, when we should no longer need to ask what is expected of us.

I have already stated that Bresson does not permit us to identify with his married couple, to sympathize with them. He does not allow us to see ourselves, except superficially, in the husband and the wife: he does not permit us to relate back to our own lives what happens to them. Feeling sorry for them for their frailties and obsessions is, ultimately, feeling sorry for ourselves, or it is making them do the work of our living, and this is too easy. Bresson wants more from us. The remarkable aspect of his film is that we do much of the feeling and querying for the actors, not as they do it, not in identification with them, but *in their place*: we literally feel and query for them, as we imagine they would. This has the effect of making us think absolutely about their situation, instead of about theirs plus our own. But we cannot know if our feelings correspond to theirs, or if we have the right answers. That doesn't matter. Bresson has us thinking other instead of self, and this is essentially all he wants from us. But it is a lot. He wants us to feel for and care about characters whom we do not "recognize," who reveal as little that is "like us" as they can, namely, the heights and depths of the strong emotions: love, hate, anger, regret, happiness, sadness. Bresson forces his actors (he calls them "models"[4]) to deny themselves in their portrayal of the characters. He denies himself in his shooting of these characters: the camera is held steady for the most part, in the middle distance; there is no panning, no tracking, there are no high- and low-angle shots. The director asks us in turn to deny ourselves in our perception of characters and events. He demands that we pay attention to the husband and the wife for themselves, no matter how unappealing or inexpressive they may appear, no matter how their story resembles little more than a skimpy newspaper report. This is a perverse demand, that is to say, a religious one. If we can comply, *Une femme douce* becomes for us a religious or spiritual experience.

The fact that Bresson almost always makes his films from preexisting texts should be a signal that he is not primarily interested in the creation of original, arresting, and appealing character in the traditional sense (recall that we never even learn the name of the husband or wife). The fact that he invariably begins his films by telling us what will happen at the end should be a signal that he is not primarily interested in the telling of stories, in the creation of traditional suspense. Related to this, the effect of having the husband narrate parts of the story, the enactment of which parts we then see, is not so much to show us discrepancies in the husband's version as compared with "what really happened," as Charles Thomas Samuels believes (p. 163), but, through this narration and its subsequent repetition in the action, to obliterate the newness or freshness of story, the interest in it per se. Bresson asks us not to understand or follow what happened to the husband and wife, to decipher the how and why of it all, but simply to believe that it occurred and take pity on these people. As I have suggested, an act of faith, of utter selflessness, or a leap of the imagination, is required to do this. Unlike Harold Pinter, who rises above his characters in similar outrageous or exaggerated situations, who triumphs over the conventions of dramatic form through his characters, Bresson kneels before the mystery of his, the mystery of all human behavior. He makes us focus, not on the story in the human beings, but on the human beings in the story and their sometimes complete lack of connection to or understanding of what happens to them. Bresson almost disconnects character from story in this way. His is an extreme reaction to almost one hundred years of "dramatic" films, where character is action and action character; "action" films, where the characters are designed to fit the plot; and films "of character," where the plot is improvised to present interesting characters, those with a "story," that is. To the oversimplifications of character of the cinema before him, Bresson responds by not simplifying anything, by explaining almost nothing. To the self-obsession of the Hollywood star system, the "dream factory," he responds by calling for self-denial.

Harold Pinter points the finger at himself; Robert Bresson, at some other. The young woman pawns her crucifix early in the film and doesn't even want the Christ figure back after the man separates it from the gold. Before she leaps to her death, she fingers the Christ figure briefly, then puts it aside. God punishes those who do not believe? No. God loves without question, absolutely. We must love and pity someone before we know or understand him. We must love absolutely. We must understand that it is art's job not to make people and the world more intelligible to us than they are, but rather to present their mystery or ineffableness, their integrity or irreducibility, if you will, their connection to something irretrievably their own or some other's. Bresson invokes mystery, something we cannot comprehend or that the characters themselves cannot comprehend. He invokes simple otherness, what is beyond our ken as human beings. The husband does not know what has happened at the end of the film, and neither do we. Neither does Bresson. (Another reason he gives us the husband's narrative of events *and* his, the director's, illustration of the marriage is in order to point up that *neither* account provides the "answers.") Bresson suggests that all we really have and can be sure of is one another and that before turning to other pursuits we should pursue the art of being human, of recognizing the humanity in others.[5]

The director has the maid, Anna, utter only a few lines in the film. In her last line she asks if she can have a week off after the wife's funeral. The husband denies her request in as cordial and attentive a tone as we have heard him use, because *he will need her* in the weeks and months to come. The maid says nothing. She does not have to. She believes him. That is all that is necessary. Like all of us, and unlike the husband and the wife, Anna has a name. Like all of us, Anna is a silent and impassive observer of the husband as he tells the story of his and his wife's relationship. She seems to know as little as we do about the motives for and causes of their behavior. (Right before the wife's suicide, the maid asks her if everything is made up between her and her husband—a question we might find ourselves asking at the same time.) As we should be to him, Anna is the husband's dutiful servant. At the end she is trans- formed into a servant of him of her own will, out of her love and concern for him despite what she may perhaps not like about him. She leaves the room before the film concludes, but she will not leave the husband, she will not neglect him. Bresson, by implication, asks the same of us. In so doing, he comes as close to religious art as he can without being denominational. Anna shows abso- lutely no sign of *sympathizing* with the husband through- out his narrative, yet she shows that she truly *feels* for him by accepting without question his need to have her present in the time right after the funeral. She recog- nizes his humanity. If there is anyone in *Une femme douce* with whom we should "identify," it is Anna.

If it can be said we identify with the husband and wife

at all, it is in the sense, as I have implied, that they seem as puzzled by what is happening to them as we are. This is not only "character almost disconnected from story," it is character nearly disconnected *from self*. Thus are we disconnected from *our selves*, our certain egos, and made to look, not for the moral or the balance in the story, the symmetry of color and idea, but simply and inescapably for the tie that binds us to the characters represented on screen, the port in our common storm. We can only love, respect, and serve what we cannot explain away, even as we do the same for ourselves. Even as the husband seems to love the woman he cannot understand and who took herself away from him, and seems to respect and serve her in her death. And just as Anna served the husband and the wife in life, and serves the wife in death and the husband in his solitude and sorrow. Paradoxically, we must acknowledge the existence of the inexplicable in, as well as beyond, art.

Charles Thomas Samuels has said that "Bresson is even more distinguished for his method than for individual films" (p. 161). That is because their subjects pale beside the treatment of those subjects. It is almost as if the director were filming the same film time after time. As of 1983, with *L'Argent* (*Money*), he had made fourteen. How ironic, or perhaps appropriate, that he filmed number nine in color because he felt color was more true to life.[6]

NOTES TO
"Bresson's *Une Femme Douce*: A New Reading"

1. Charles Thomas Samuels, *Mastering the Film and Other Essays* (Knoxville: The Univ. of Tennessee Press, 1977), p. 162. Hereafter cited by page number in the text.

2. See, for example, Eric Rhode, "Dostoevsky and Bresson," *Sight and Sound*, 39, No. 2 (Spring 1970), pp. 82–83; Jean-Pierre Oudart, "Bresson et la vérité," *Cahiers du Cinéma*, No. 216 (Oct. 1969), pp. 53–56; Jacques Chevallier, "*Une femme douce*," *Image et Son*, No. 232 (Nov. 1969), pp. 120–124; Jonas Mekas, "On Bresson and *Une femme douce*," *Village Voice*, 2 Oct. 1969, p. 46; Michel Estève, "Choix des films: *Une femme douce* de Robert Bresson ou le silence du couple," *Etudes*, Oct. 1969, pp. 406–408; and Jean Sémolué, "*Une femme douce*," *Téléciné*, No. 157 (Dec. 1969), pp. 7–18.

3. Bert O. States, "Pinter's *Homecoming*: The Shock of Non-recognition," *Hudson Review*, 21 (1968), p. 475.

4. Robert Bresson, *Notes on Cinematography*, trans. Jonathan Griffin (New York: Urizen Books, 1977), p. 1.

5. I am, of course, not the first to assert that Bresson invokes "mystery" or "otherness" in *Une femme douce*. Amédée Ayfre has written that the characters in Bresson's films, "even in their most extreme confidences, never fundamentally reveal anything but their mystery— like God himself. . . . They are people whose ultimate secret is [not only beyond the viewer, but] beyond [Bresson] too" ("The Universe of Robert Bresson," trans. Elizabeth Kingsley-Rowe, in Ian Cameron, ed., *The Films of Robert Bresson* [New York: Praeger, 1969], pp. 14–15). Paul Schrader has written a book entitled *Transcendental Style in Film* (Berkeley: Univ. of Calif. Press, 1972), which consists of chapters on Bresson, Yasujiro Ozu, and Carl Dreyer. I differ with Ayfre and Schrader in my suggestion that Bresson is not invoking mystery for mystery's sake alone, but for the sake of exalting the human, of calling his audience's attention at once to the divine and the intrinsically worthy in the human.

6. Bresson, *Notes on Cinematography*, p. 55.

THE REAL FASCINATION OF
CITIZEN KANE

One aspect of *Citizen Kane* (1941) has always puzzled me: why, aside from the opportunity it afforded them to display virtuoso technique, did Orson Welles and Herman J. Mankiewicz make a film about the dead Kane instead of about Kane while he lived? To my knowledge, no one has ever attempted to answer this question; yet, probably more has been written about *Citizen Kane* than any other American film. If, as most critics believe, the "message" of *Citizen Kane* is the mystery of the titular character,[1] then couldn't that mystery have been presented in traditional narrative form, a condensed "life of Charles Foster Kane"? Couldn't that mystery have been represented *more subtly* in this way? It is pretty clear once Thatcher's "story" about the young Kane is over and Bernstein's begins, with an immediate contradiction of Thatcher ("It wasn't money [Mr. Kane] wanted. Thatcher never did figure him out"), that what we are going to get in the film is several more or less conflicting viewpoints on the man, none with any real depth, as much because given hastily or sketchily to a newspaper reporter who did not know Kane, as because given by a biased individual. The "storytellers" simplify Kane, to make their own points about him. No matter how many times I see *Citizen Kane*, I always get impatient the moment the reporter, Jerry Thompson, begins his interview of Bernstein, Kane's former business manager and now chairman of the board. I know somewhere inside myself that this method will not deliver—at least not traditional results: an ambiguous but fully developed, complex, *sympathetic* character.

Kane is not sympathetic in the traditional sense because we get to know him only through others' eyes. Bernstein, Leland, and Alexander are sympathetic, because we get to know them through the eyes of the filmmakers, in the "narrative present." But the film is clearly not about these three, or about Raymond the butler, the last of the "storytellers" (Thatcher is dead; Thompson reads Thatcher's "story" of Kane from his memoirs). It is about Charles Foster Kane, and to believe the critics as well as Orson Welles himself, whose obfuscatory words these are, "the point of the picture is not so much the solution of the problem [the mystery of Kane] as its presentation."[2]

But my point is, the presentation is apparently loaded: anyone could tell you that if you ask five different people about a man, you'll get five different stories or interpretations. Those stories will tell less about the man than about the bias of the particular storyteller. They will add up to nothing in particular because a man's motives can never be satisfactorily fathomed by those closest to him. They can, however, be fathomed somewhat by the "objective author," or by this author posing as someone who knew the man. That is, presumably, what much art is all about: the providing of "answers" or motives for particular characters so that larger questions of life and character can be explored.

So I pose my question again: presuming that they were aware of what I have just said, why did Orson Welles and Herman J. Mankiewicz choose to make a film about the dead Kane, through the eyes of others, instead of about the living Kane, through their own eyes? Is *Citizen Kane* one large piece of chicanery, a contribution less to film art, according to Charles Thomas Samuels, than to the art of making films?[3] Or is the film, on the other hand, as David Bordwell claims, a great achievement because it fuses "an objective realism of texture with a subjective realism of structure"?[4] Bordwell believes that the method of *Citizen Kane is* its meaning. He writes that

> *Kane* explores the nature of consciousness chiefly by presenting various points of view on a shifting, multi-planed world. We enter Kane's consciousness as he dies, before we have even met him; he is less a character than a stylized image. Immediately, we view him as a public figure—fascinating but remote. Next we scrutinize him as a man, seen through the eyes of his wife and his associates, as a reporter traces his life story. Finally, these various perspectives are capped by a detached, omniscient one. In all, Kane emerges as a man—pathetic, grand, contradictory, ultimately enigmatic. The film expresses an ambiguous reality through formal devices that stress both the objectivity of fact and the subjectivity of point of view. It is because the best contemporary cinema has turned to the exploration of such a reality that *Kane* is, in a sense, the first modern American film. (p. 105)

Now Bordwell is on to something when he says that Charles Foster Kane is "less a character than a stylized image," and that as a character, Kane is pathetic. But he fails to tell us how exactly we "enter Kane's conscious-

ness as he dies" and who owns the "detached, omni-
scient" perspective at the end of the film that caps the
other perspectives on Kane.

Bordwell's oversights or omissions are characteristic
of his argument in general: unlike the majority of critics
on *Citizen Kane*, he believes that the "message" of the
film, beyond being the mystery of Kane the character, is
the mystery of reality or of life itself. Once one ascer-
tains that the object of a work of art is to present the
mystery of reality, it is very easy to become mysterious
oneself in writing about that work of art: after all, what
else is there to say once one says that the work depicts
the mystery of reality? I don't believe that *Citizen Kane*
presents the mystery of reality any more than *His Girl
Friday* (1940) presents an argument for the equality of
women. I think that the film is first and last about
Charles Foster Kane, as its title indicates, but I do think
it is up to something in its eschewing portrayal of the
living Kane that no one has yet detected, although
David Bordwell begins to touch on it.

Two events occur in the film that, I believe, are clues
to the filmmakers' real intentions and the work's true
status. No one has ever incisively questioned the actions
of Kane's mother toward her son, which actions form a
part of Thatcher's story.[5] Mrs. Kane runs a boarding
house in Colorado with her apparently alcoholic and
abusive husband. It is discovered that some property of
hers contains large deposits of silver, and she instantly
becomes rich. Although she appears to have a very
loving relationship with her son, she now decides to
entrust Charles to the banker Thatcher, who will man-
age the boy's large inheritance and see to his education.
The film does not provide her with sufficient motivation

to commit this act: ostensibly she is worried about her husband's influence on the child. But father and son seem to get on well enough, and Mrs. Kane seems more than in control of her husband's actions (apart from the fact that the "Colorado Lode" is in her name). Let us keep in mind in addition that on the evidence of the film, once she gives her son over to Thatcher, *she never sees him again* (Thatcher takes him back East to live).

Why is Mrs. Kane so eager to do this? She herself is quite rich, so why doesn't she retain custody of her child while having Thatcher look after her business affairs and advise her on her son's education and opportunities? Why can't she simply leave her husband (again, *she* owns the mine), with whom she appears to have anything but a loving relationship, instead of give up her son? I am not saying that Mrs. Kane's action cannot be made believable, although this would require great delicacy, but that Welles and Mankiewicz do not make it so. And I am not interested in whether this happened in real life to William Randolph Hearst, on whom the character of Charles Foster Kane is in part based (I do not know if it did). Truth is often stranger than fiction, it is said; that does not relieve fiction of the burden of believability, however. That does not relieve Mr. Thatcher of the burden of believability, either. He may narrate this part of Kane's life, but Welles and Mankiewicz "narrate" him. In short, neither anything we are told about Mrs. Kane nor all that we know about mothers and their offspring can make Mrs. Kane's act comprehensible. (My argument is strengthened by the fact that Charles is the only child and surely at the same time the last one of the middle-aged Kanes.) It seems an outrage. What, then, is it doing in the film? Of course it is there to motivate Charles's search for love and for control over his environment throughout his life. But, to repeat, why is it not made more believable?

I want to submit that this was not a simple oversight on the part of Welles and Mankiewicz, not another instance of hasty or one-dimensional Hollywood film-making. I believe that this is the first substantial clue we get in *Citizen Kane*, aside from the film's treatment of the dead Kane and not the living one, that what we are witnessing is not intended primarily as a character *study*—the approach most critics take to the film—but as the *experience* of character, the experience of a character's foremost desires and frustrations, not through identification with the figure himself, but through identification with the narrative method of the film that is about him. (This is quite different from David Bordwell's assertion that the film's narrative method per se is its meaning.) Welles and Mankiewicz "clue" us in that their film is not intended as a character study of Charles Foster Kane because he appears, on screen in Thatcher's memory, fabricated from the very start, the unnatural product of his mother's unnatural act.

Looked at in this light, the film's showy camera work, editing, and use of sound make more sense: they are the constant reminder, in their artificiality, of the unreal world the protagonist inhabits, in others' memory. These devices and the world they embellish account for the unsettling effect the film has even on a viewer who has seen it many times. We have been conditioned by most narrative film and literature to want to identify with the main character; in the case of film, we are encouraged to do so by a camera that often comes close up on the main character or otherwise isolates him and that adopts his point of view at crucial moments. We get none of this in *Citizen Kane* (we get everything but this), yet the film purports to be about Charles Foster Kane. We are confused. Even Welles's celebrated deep-focus photography works to unnatural effect, when one would think, with Bazin, that it would work to the opposite end. What deep focus in *Citizen Kane* gives us initially is a sense of life, of dramatic space, continuous with our own. But ironically, at the same time as it seems to be opening Kane up to us more, the "flashbacks," buttressed by salient technique, are frustrating our desire to decipher Kane and thus to identify with him. We are enabled to inhabit this character's space but not him. We are confused. But we are held. That is the advantage of depth of focus over Eisensteinian montage for this particular film, where the use of the multiplaned image is called attention to as never before: the image continually teases us, by seeming to include us within its confines, that we will be able to know Charles Foster Kane completely, even as we know his "space," his entire domain, completely. For this reason, *we* never leave "Charlie," unlike virtually everyone else who knew him.

We never "leave" Kane, yet we cannot be said to identify or empathize with him. On balance, we do not find his personality so appealing; we do not warm to him. As I have already indicated, we are, however, identified with the narrative method of the film that is about him. That method, for which the reporter Thompson supplies the cue, is the search for knowledge of Charles Foster Kane and thus in a sense power over him, and it is by extension therefore the search for love of him, through the finding of what in him is most like ourselves. It is precisely the method of the film *Citizen*

Kane, I am maintaining, that corresponds to (and itself signifies) the major experience of Charles Foster Kane's life: the search for power or control over his environment, for total "knowledge" of it, and the quest to love and be loved by all who surrounded him. One of the reasons, I suspect, that Orson Welles not only played Kane, but also directed the film, was so that identification with the film's narrative method, that is, with the one imposed on it by the director Welles, would substitute even more easily for identification with the character played by the actor Welles. The main character and the director would become almost indistinguishable, and thus the experience of the film's narrative method, charted by Welles, would become all the more the experience of Kane's foremost desires.

Ira Jaffe, in an article entitled "Film as the Narration of Space," gives another reason why we are identified with the narrative method of *Citizen Kane*. Not only does deep focus seem to include us within the confines of the film, to make Kane's space and thus him accessible to us, but Welles's moving camera also does this. The moving camera duplicates for us the central experience or conflict of Kane's life: his search for open space, for the freedom, security, and motherly love of his childhood, and his entrapment in closed space, in the responsibilities that his money brings, in the snares that it plants, and in the materialism and coldness it engenders. Jaffe writes, for example, that

> From the beginning we are caught up in a spatial action as the camera travels up in the night from the forbidding NO TRESPASSING sign on the outer fence of Xanadu, and numerous dissolves through the dark,

often hilly terrain bring us closer to the lit window of the mansion ahead. Almost instantly we experience our-selves as overcoming obstacles in space including the layers of fences, gates, and hills, as bypassing odd senti-nels such as the caged monkeys and the gondolas, and as dissolving space itself. Starting from a position of rela-tive containment outside the fence, we rapidly obtain a certain release by transcending barriers in space, and by penetrating space itself.[6]

Once "we have penetrated the window and gained the access we found ourselves seeking," however, "we also are confined in a new way. For instead of occupying the presumably open, limitless space of the outdoors, we are, though in view of the window and within reach of nature, enclosed in the space of a room in the mansion" (Jaffe, pp. 100–101). In a spatial analogy to Kane's inner experience, we desire knowledge of the character and the freedom to pursue it, only to be hoist by our own petard. The same spatial analogy to Kane's inner experience applies to the reverse camera movement. In the scene at the Colorado boarding house where Mrs. Kane gives responsibility for Charles to Thatcher, the camera begins to pull back from the child, who is outside playing in the snow and seems to revel in the open, unencumbered space. The movement of the cam-era, says Jaffe,

does not reveal, as it would in Kubrick's *Barry Lyndon* [1975], yet more majestic space around the young hero. Instead, the camera retreats through a window into Mrs. Kane's boarding house . . . The camera continues all the way back to a table toward which Mrs. Kane and

Thatcher walk from the window in order to sign the legal agreement which will turn Charles over to the bank and result in his removal from Colorado and his parents. In the move back through the window into the house, the camera diminishes rather than expands the child's space. . . . The camera movement changes the appearance of the space the hero occupies from open to closed. . . . Now he appears tiny within the firm frame of the distant window which remains visible from the table at which sit his mother and Thatcher. (pp. 103–104)

As a result of the camera's retreat, we see, not more of little Charles, but less; we are locked away from him by the window that his father closes on his playful shouts, just as Mrs. Kane is by the agreement that she signs giving custody of her son to Thatcher. No matter how cautious we are in seeking knowledge and freedom, no matter how certain we are that our next move will increase both of them, we become victims of our own curiosity. We are trapped by the narrative method of the film, even as Charles Foster Kane is by his own experience.

The second clue to the filmmakers' intentions and the one that identifies the audience absolutely with the narrative method of their film is the word Kane speaks before he dies: the name of his childhood sled, Rosebud. Now no one is within earshot of Kane on his deathbed when he says this word. The nurse comes in after she hears the glass ball smash onto the floor from the dead Kane's hand. Raymond is nowhere to be seen. How is it, then, that Jerry Thompson and all his news associates know that "Rosebud" was Charles Foster Kane's dying word? No one has ever asked this question; yet, it is clear that no one could possibly have heard Kane's last word—except us, the audience. No one except us finds out that "Rosebud" is the name of Kane's childhood sled, either. That Thompson and his associates, as well as Raymond, know what Kane said before he died is the film's contrivance; it is what makes the film possible, what makes the dead Kane accessible to us. "Rosebud" is the identification of the audience with the search for knowledge of Charles Foster Kane and love of him. We are identified with this search from the start, because we receive information about Kane that no one else does. *We* search for the meaning of "Rosebud," thinking that it will give us total access to Kane, even as he said the word in a last attempt to gain total access to his past, so as to be able to reorder it. We get the meaning and, like Kane's "knowledge," his power, it proves incomplete and unsatisfying. Kane wanted to be President, to be known and loved by all and to govern them. He wound up a recluse. We want to know Kane and to love him, and thus in a sense to be known and loved by him, and what knowledge we get serves only to isolate us from him, in his death, just as he was isolated from himself in life: Kane neither knew nor loved himself, and that is why he needed so much recognition and love from others, yet could not respond to them in kind however much he may have wanted to. We are isolated from Kane, and like him, we are even isolated from all who loved or knew or even just heard about him: we know the meaning of "Rosebud," whereas they do not. That meaning returns us to Kane's childhood and abandonment by his mother. It returns us, in other words, to what I have called the first clue to the strategy of the film about him.

Other interpreters of *Citizen Kane* feel that "Rosebud" returns us to Kane's childhood and abandonment by his mother, but they view the sled as a conventional symbol, whereas I see it, or rather I see the revelation that the sled bears the name Kane called out on his deathbed, much more as a final confirmation of the film's unique artistic strategy. Alan Stanbrook, for example, believes that "'Rosebud' becomes the symbol of [Kane's] youthful innocence, lost when he was adopted into a family of bankers. Money and the pursuit of wealth have robbed him of his humanity and left him isolated and lonely, vainly seeking happiness in an endless acquisition of gimcracks."[7] Peter Cowie takes Stanbrook's interpretation of "Rosebud" one step further when he states that "['Rosebud'] stands as a token of Kane's unhappy relations with people in general. He has no friends, only acquaintances, because he insists on setting himself on a pedestal above those who seek to know him."[8] Stanbrook and Cowie, then, represent the minority view of the film: they believe that the "message" of *Citizen Kane* is not the mystery of Kane the character but his *depiction*, and they find the appearance of the burning sled at the end to provide the information for a definitive interpretation of Charles Foster Kane.

Robert L. Carringer rightly attacks such critics as Stanbrook and Cowie, saying, "If this interpretation were valid, *Citizen Kane* might indeed be vulnerable to charges of intellectual shallowness and of attempting to pass off a creaky melodramatic gimmick in place of real analysis of its subject" (p. 185). But then Carringer goes on, curiously, to interpret in the same way as Stanbrook and Cowie, not the sled, but the little glass globe that

Kane drops from his hand as he dies. The glass globe, he writes, is

> self-enclosed; self-sustaining; an intact world in minia-
> ture, a microcosm. . . . Sealed off to intrusion from
> outside. Free also of human presence—and therefore of
> suggestions of responsibilities to others. But by the same
> token, free of human warmth—a cold, frozen world of
> eternal winter. Suggestive of Charles Foster Kane . . .
> The little glass globe, not Rosebud, incorporates the
> film's essential insight into Kane. It is a crystallization of
> everything we learn about him—that he was a man
> continually driven to idealize his experiences as a means
> of insulating himself from human life. (pp. 191–192)

Carringer wishes to have his cake and eat it, too, however, for no sooner has he found the presence of the
glass globe in the film to provide information for a
definitive interpretation of Charles Foster Kane, than
he is claiming, at the other end of the spectrum from
Stanbrook and Cowie, that the "message" of *Citizen Kane*
is the mystery of the titular character and that "Rosebud" confirms this mystery, for it "does not add significantly to our understanding of Charles Foster Kane . . .
Rosebud finally yields up a figure at once clear and
indistinct who is always less or more than the sum total
of what is said about him. While appearing to give its
assent that sentimental or facile notions like Rosebud
can sum up a man's life, the film actually works to rescue
Kane from them" (p. 192).

Most critics take this view of Carringer's, that the
identification of "Rosebud" only serves to confirm the
mystery of Charles Foster Kane. Significant among

these critics are David Bordwell and Joseph McBride. Bordwell sums up the received wisdom on the film and "Rosebud":

> Although it stands for the affection Kane lost when he was wrenched into Thatcher's world, the sled is clearly not to be taken as the "solution" of the film. It is only one piece of the jigsaw puzzle, "something he couldn't get or something he lost." The Rosebud sled solves the problem that Thompson was set—"A dying man's last words should explain his life"—but by the end Thompson realizes that the problem was a false one: "I don't think that any word can explain a man's life." The appearance of the sled presents another perspective on Kane, but it doesn't "explain" him. His inner self remains inviolate (NO TRESPASSING) and enigmatic. The last shots of the sign and of Xanadu restore a grandeur to Kane's life, a dignity born of the essential impenetrability of human character. (p. 111)

McBride sees the revelation of "Rosebud" as a very necessary part of *Citizen Kane*, not simply as one more piece of a large jigsaw puzzle. "The revelation of Rosebud," writes McBride, "far from explaining the mystery of Kane's futile existence, adds another dimension to it. If Welles had not shown us Rosebud, we would have continued to think that there could be a solution, and that Thompson is merely unable to find it. We would be left to conjure up our own solutions" (p. 42). Also, McBride sees the revelation of "Rosebud" as a character device, not to shed light on Kane, but to "fill in" Thompson: "Thompson is dignified by our realization that we had to see Rosebud to reach his understanding" (p. 42).

Welles himself said of "Rosebud" in a 1963 interview

that "it's a gimmick, really, and rather dollar-book Freud."[9] Certainly "Rosebud" is a kind of gimmick, a "contrivance," as I interpret it, and "Rosebud" *becomes* dollar-book Freud if one interprets it in the manner that Alan Stanbrook and Peter Cowie do. I'll leave the last word on "Rosebud" to Welles's self-styled spokesman, Pauline Kael, who takes the master at his word and elaborates on it in the way only she can: "The mystery in *Kane* is largely fake, and the Gothic-thriller atmosphere and the Rosebud gimmickry (though fun) are such obvious penny-dreadful popular theatrics that they're not so very different from the fake mysteries that Hearst's *American Weekly* used to whip up—the haunted castles and the curses fulfilled."[10]

I have attempted to explain how I think *Citizen Kane* works, but a question still remains, the one I posed at the start: why specifically did Welles and Mankiewicz make a film about the dead Kane instead of about Kane while he lived? Although traditional narrative film form—a film about the living Kane—could not give us the *experience* of the character's foremost desires and frustrations in the same way that *Citizen Kane* does, it could do well enough by a complex *study* of him. The method is different, but the outcome would be about the same: greater understanding of the character and of ourselves. But *would* the outcome be the same in the case of Charles Foster Kane? I don't think so, because I believe that Welles and Mankiewicz conceived of Kane as a fundamentally pathetic character—that is, one not truly aware of what was happening to him—and that they felt the best way to treat him was after his death, through the reports of others. In other words, I am saying that they deliberately chose to make a film about a pathetic character but to do so in a way that would make the film itself rise above pathos. To have told the story of Kane while he lived would have been to achieve pathos and nothing more. Kane is not tragic because he is not self-aware, or is unable to be; he suffers but learns nothing from his suffering. (It would have been easy to feel sorry for Kane in a film of his *life*, because he was helpless. It is much harder to feel nothing more than sorry for a tragic figure, who is not helpless and in whom one therefore imagines that one truly sees oneself.) But to tell the story of the dead Kane, through others, and have us approximate his experience aesthetically, is to resurrect him through us and to show us the Kane in ourselves far better than any identification with the living Kane on screen could have done. We want to possess Kane but cannot. In the same way that Kane sought to dominate the "storytellers" in his life, we seek to "dominate" them in their stories: we almost forget that they are doing the telling as we search restlessly for knowledge and understanding of Charles Foster Kane. By the end of the film our knowledge has got us nowhere, and we are untouched. Like Kane on his deathbed. The filmmakers have ensured that. But unlike Kane we know this, or can admit it to ourselves on reflection.

Kane's "flaw," as I have suggested, was that he did not, or could not, reflect on or criticize himself. The "flaw" of his "storytellers" is that not one of them can see himself in Kane. Each thinks that he has the answer to the riddle of Charles Foster Kane, but not one has the answer to his own problems; not one appears self-critical. (Even Bernstein, who appears the most successful and happy of the "storytellers," has reason to be self-critical: he seems to have devoted his life to Mr.

Kane—his former boss's portrait dwarfs him in his own office—and now that life is made up of distant memories of girls in white dresses, of a life of his own with a woman that was never to be.) On reflection, we do see ourselves in Kane, and we separate ourselves from him. We are left to know and love ourselves before we can know and love another person or conquer the worlds of business, politics, or the arts. That is the triumph of *Citizen Kane* as art: we are enabled by the film's imitation of a subjective experience, as opposed to an objective action, to reflect on ourselves in a way that no character in the film reflects on himself. The characters in the film *assert*; we *reflect*. This kind of art falls, finally, somewhere between pathos and tragedy. It does not make a pathetic figure tragic, but, ironically, through his absence from the film, it helps him to give us what tragedy at its best gives us: knowledge of ourselves. He gets to do more than simply play out his days pathetically, and we get to do more than feel sorry for him.

Citizen Kane's technical daring, I think, pales besides its thematic daring in treating a pathetic figure so.[11] It is time that critics stopped overpraising the film for its brilliant technique, on the one hand, and criticizing it for its supposedly shallow theme and main character in the service of all that technique, on the other. *Citizen Kane* represents a different kind of film art, and one for which it could scarcely be said a sufficient critical language exists at this point. Made on the eve of the dropping of the atomic bomb, *Citizen Kane* is perhaps a new film art for a new era and one whose lead more and more directors may take as they realize that fewer and fewer people in this, the age of narcissism, are reflective, self-critical. Human beings have retreated into themselves in the face of the violence and confusion of modern existence; they have become obsessed with self rather than confront a world seemingly without order or purpose. As a result, characters that are reflective, self-critical, potentially tragic, are not as depictable as they once were. There was a time when a Charles Foster Kane was an anomaly in life as in art. Today he is, in my view, the norm, in both public and private spheres of existence as well as in so much art that approvingly holds a mirror up to the bourgeoisie: incapable of love, untrusting, monstrously ambitious. *Citizen* Kane has actually become in the last forty years or so like many other citizens of this country, of the West. When Welles and Mankiewicz made their film, I have argued, they were raising a pathetic figure from the grave, as it were, and attempting through their narrative method to give his audience more than the experience of pathos. Today's audience may not be capable of anything but admiration, even envy, of Kane and may be able to express nothing more than a paradoxical mixture of regret and pleasure at his ill fortune. A director who wanted to reach them might, in his film, resurrect a tragic figure and attempt through a narrative method similar to *Citizen Kane*'s to make this character's audience conscious of their own pathos.

NOTES TO
"The Real Fascination of *Citizen Kane*"

1.   See especially Joseph McBride, *Orson Welles* (New York: Viking, 1972), p. 42; Andrew Sarris, *The Primal Screen* (New York: Simon and Schuster, 1973), pp. 120–121;

Robert L. Carringer, "Rosebud, Dead or Alive: Narrative and Symbolic Structure in *Citizen Kane*," *PMLA*, 91 (1976), p. 192; and James Naremore, *The Magic World of Orson Welles* (New York: Oxford Univ. Press, 1978), pp. 66–68. McBride and Carringer hereafter cited by page number in the text.

2.   Orson Welles, "*Citizen Kane* is Not about Louella Parsons' Boss," *Friday*, 14 Feb. 1941, p. 9; reprinted in Ronald Gottesman, ed., *Focus on "Citizen Kane"* (Englewood Cliffs, N.J.: Prentice-Hall, 1971), pp. 67–68.

3.   Charles Thomas Samuels, *Mastering the Film and Other Essays* (Knoxville: The Univ. of Tennessee Press, 1977), p. 171. For a doubly negative view, that *Citizen Kane* is both essentially one large piece of chicanery and a *retrogression* in screen technique, see *The Film Criticism of Otis Ferguson*, ed. Robert Wilson (Philadelphia: Temple Univ. Press, 1971), pp. 369–371.

4.   David Bordwell, "*Citizen Kane*," in *Focus on Orson Welles*, ed. Ronald Gottesman (Englewood Cliffs, N. J.: Prentice-Hall, 1976), p. 105. Hereafter cited by page number in the text.

5.   Joseph McBride begins to question the actions of Mrs. Kane in sending young Charles away, but he then ends his speculation by passing everything off unaccountably to fate:

> The family tensions are sketched in quickly and cryptically: the mother is domineering but anguished as she commits her son to Thatcher; the father is pathetic and clumsy in his objections. Why is she sending Charles away? To get him away from his father, who apparently abuses the boy when drunk? Perhaps. But more likely, given the aura of helplessness with which Welles surrounds the entire family, it is simply that the accident which made the Kanes suddenly rich has created its own fateful logic—Charles must 'get ahead.'

What gives the brief leave-taking scene its mystery and poignancy is precisely this feeling of predetermination. (*Orson Welles*, p. 43.)

6. Ira S. Jaffe, "Film as the Narration of Space: *Citizen Kane*," *Literature/Film Quarterly*, 7 (1979), p. 100. Hereafter cited by page number in the text.

7. Alan Stanbrook, "The Heroes of Welles," *Film* (Great Britain), March/April 1961, p. 14.

8. Peter Cowie, "The Study of a Colossus: *Citizen Kane*," in *The Emergence of Film Art*, ed. Lewis Jacobs, 2nd ed. (New York: Norton, 1979), p. 265.

9. Orson Welles quoted by Cowie, "The Study of a Colossus," p. 264, from a 1963 interview with Welles conducted by Dilys Powell of the *Sunday Times* (London).

10. Pauline Kael, "Raising Kane," in *The "Citizen Kane" Book* (Boston: Little, Brown, 1971), p. 5.

11. Peter Cowie states the case for the film's technical daring:

> *Citizen Kane* is of primary importance in the history of the cinema because of the audacity and virtuosity of Welles' technique, and because of the influence that the style was to exert on films in all parts of the world for the next two decades. . . . [Welles's] brilliance stems from his ability to synthesize and harmonize all possible stylistic methods into a coherent instrument for telling his story. ("The Study of a Colossus," p. 267.)

Jorge Luis Borges, writing in 1945, seems to endorse Cowie's view, albeit negatively: "I dare predict . . . that *Citizen Kane* will endure in the same way certain films of Griffith or of Pudovkin 'endure': no one denies their historic value but no one sees them again. It suffers from grossness, pedantry, dullness." (Borges' essay published originally in *Sur* [Buenos Aires], no. 83 [1945]; reprinted in French translation in *Positif* 58 [Feb. 1964], pp. 17–18; and reprinted in Mark Bernheim and

Ronald Gottesman's English translation of the *French* translation, in Gottesman, ed., *Focus on "Citizen Kane"*, pp. 127–128 [this quotation from p. 128].)

Citizen Kane has endured, of course, in a different way: people see it all the time. In my view, that is because it "fascinates" in the manner I describe in this essay. If technical daring were all that *Citizen Kane* had going for it, it would indeed have suffered the fate of, say, *Birth of a Nation* (1915) by now: to be studied in film class for its advances in technique, and to be snickered at in a public screening for its naiveté of theme and primitiveness of characterization.

THE FILM STYLE OF FEDERICO FELLINI:

The Nights of Cabiria as Paradigm

Charles Thomas Samuels once wrote that "[Fellini's] great subject is the reaction to surfaces. Any deeper probing of character is beyond him."[1] Samuels gave *La Strada* (1954) as an example of a film that is ultimately unsatisfying because it attempts both to react to the surface of character and to probe character deeply. Fellini responds to Gelsomina's exterior—that is, he demonstrates her goodness repeatedly, as opposed to analyzing why she is good; at the same time, he attempts to dramatize the spiritual conversion of Zampanò, who, "too bestial to requite Gelsomina, must lose her in order to understand that she was worth loving" (Samuels, p. 100). Gelsomina ends up being the protagonist of *La Strada* through the sheer pathos of her condition, whereas she should have been the agent of Zampanò's internal change. The presence of Zampanò in the film calls for conflict between him and Gelsomina and for his gradual change. Instead, Gelsomina goes mad after Zampanò kills the fool, Zampanò abandons her, and he learns of her death years later by coincidence. Only then do we see his change, his great regret that he rejected Gelsomina's love. We have seen Zampanò's change, but we have not seen how it has occurred; we want to know what he has been feeling about Gelsomina in the years since he left her.

Fellini created another memorable female character in *The Nights of Cabiria* (1957), played by the actress who played Gelsomina, Giulietta Masina. But he wisely decided not to attach her to a single, strong male character and thereby arouse our expectations of conflict between them. He chose instead only to "react to the surface" of his female character. The result is, in my opinion, a better film than *La Strada*, one that marries form to content perfectly.

Samuels has described Fellini's style better than anyone else:

> In the most impressive phase of his career (from *Variety Lights* [1950] through *8½* [1962]), he is, above all, an observer. Insofar as he has a style, it isn't narrowly technical but rather a general method of constructing films through juxtaposition; that is, through setting details of reconstructed reality side by side to point up a common denominator or, more often, to expose the ironic relationship between unlike things. . . . Like his neo-realist forbears, Fellini tries to present the world naturally, without arranging things in order to create plots or entertainments. . . . Scenes are related in his films not by causality or in order to create a crisis but as illustrations of a state of being. . . . Since his subject is [the] incorrigibility [of human hopefulness], repetition is crucial to Fellini's films. (pp. 85–86, 100)

In *The Nights of Cabiria*, Fellini places Cabiria in successive scenes that illustrate the state of her being.

Her boyfriend Giorgio steals her purse and pushes her into a river at the start of the film. She is rescued, and the film chronicles her attempts to bounce back from disappointed love. Cabiria dances at night on the Passeggiata Archeologica, where her fellow prostitutes gather in Rome; but her dance ends in a fight when the aging prostitute Matilda taunts her about rejection by Giorgio. To her astonishment, since she is hardly glamorous, she gets picked up by the film star Alberto Lazzari but is pushed aside when his girlfriend decides to make up with him in the middle of the night. Cabiria next makes a pilgrimage to the Madonna of Divine Love; she wants to pray for a miracle: for a change in her life for the better, for rebirth. Nothing happens. Cabiria is then hypnotized in a theater into believing that she is eighteen again and in the company of a young man who truly loves her. She awakens from her trance to sad reality: no lover in her life and an audience of men jeering at her. Outside the theater, she meets Oscar D'Onofrio, who was a member of the audience and who miraculously falls in love with her at once. Cabiria is at first reluctant to accompany Oscar to a café but eventually dates him regularly, falls in love, and accepts his proposal of marriage. She sells her little house, takes all her money out of the bank, and leaves Rome to marry Oscar. They go to an inn in the Alban Mountains, where he plans to push Cabiria off a cliff into a lake and steal her money. At the edge of the cliff Cabiria finally realizes that she has been duped again and, horrified, offers Oscar her savings and asks him to kill her. He runs off shaken, but not before grabbing the money. We last see her wandering dazed along a road, surrounded by young people singing and dancing to the accompaniment of guitars. A girl says, "Buona sera!" to Cabiria, who smiles.

Cabiria is, then, incorrigibly hopeful: this is the common denominator in her life. She is so incorrigibly hopeful that she seems like a child who has yet to learn from the weight of experience. Indeed, from beginning to end she looks and acts like a child. Richard Gilman remarked in a lecture at Yale that all of Fellini's films, not just the obvious examples like *8 1/2* and *Juliet of the Spirits* (1965), have a dream quality[2]: *The Nights of Cabiria* does in the sense that the childlike Cabiria could be dreaming or having a nightmare that she is wandering through an unaccountably cruel world, a world to which she is a stranger and to which she is unwilling or unable to sacrifice her hopefulness.

Giulietta Masina is a woman with a girl's appearance in the film: she is slim-hipped, has a pixie haircut, and wears bobby socks and penny loafers. When she puts on her shabby fur coat for her nights as a prostitute, she looks like a child "playing adult." In a scene omitted from the final version of *The Nights of Cabiria*, Cabiria says to the Man with the Sack, "Yes, [I'm all alone,] my mother and father both died when I was still a little girl. I came to Rome . . ."[3] She seems to say that she came to Rome as a little girl and grew up alone; it is as if she has remained the little girl she was when her parents died. Fellini is careful never to show her in bed with any of her customers, even though we know that she has saved money from her work as a prostitute. We see her accept a ride from a truck driver, but it is not clear that she will sleep with him: she is making her pilgrimage to the Madonna of Divine Love and may want nothing more than transportation. We see her actually reject the ad-

vances of a potential customer at one point: the man
drives up to the Passeggiata Archeologica, says a few
words to Cabiria, gets no response, and drives on. Even
as Cabiria seems to be "playing adult" when she dresses
up to go out, she seems also to be "playing prostitute."
That is the effect of not showing her in bed with men
and of surrounding her with full-bodied women in high
heels and tight-fitting dresses.

Like a child, Cabiria imitates the behavior of adults.
When a pimp drops her off at the Via Veneto, she tries
to imitate the walk and air of the high-class streetwalk-
ers of the area. When the film star takes her to a flashy
nightclub, she imitates the behavior of the ladies who
surround her. And when she finds herself in the procession to the shrine, she looks around and begins imitating the behavior of the other supplicants. Like a child,
Cabiria is unable to consume liquor: at a picnic after the
pilgrimage, a character says that she gets drunk after
one drink. Cabiria even throws tantrums like a child.
Twice she goes into a rage at people who mean well: at
the men and boys who save her from drowning, and at
her next-door neighbor, Wanda, who tries to comfort
her and learn what is wrong when she returns home
muddy and wet. Of course we understand the source of
Cabiria's anger—not only has she been robbed and
pushed into a river, she has also been deserted by the
man she loves—yet it seems irrational and inconsider-
ate. The childlike Cabiria gives her love as freely as she
displays her anger: to Giorgio, to Oscar, to one of her
chickens, to the film star's puppy. Cabiria becomes
excited as easily and completely as a child: while Alberto
Lazzari is drivng her to the nightclub, she stands up on
the front seat and shouts proudly to the prostitutes who

line the streets, "Look at me! Look who I'm with!" When they arrive at the club, Alberto must coax her out of the car and through the front door as one might coax a shy or frightened child.

Two images especially fix Cabiria in my mind as a child-woman, both photographed at Lazzari's garish mansion. The first image is of Cabiria climbing the stairs to Alberto's room—he has gone ahead of her, just as he did at the nightclub. Cabiria looks like a child climbing stairs that are too large for her: Fellini shoots the scene from the bottom of the staircase, so that the already small Cabiria appears smaller the higher she goes and the stairs appear larger. The second image is of Cabiria peeking through the keyhole of Alberto's spacious bathroom, where she's hiding from his girlfriend. It is as if Cabiria, holding Alberto's puppy, is a child peeking through the keyhole at two adults, a father- and a mother-figure, who are getting ready to go to bed. Indeed, Alberto seems like a father to Cabiria: he dwarfs her, as does his home. Like a good father, he urges her to eat supper, and when his girlfriend arrives he sends her out of the room with her meal and the dog.

Alberto is one of four parental figures Fellini gives Cabiria in the film. Wanda, the prostitute who lives next door to her, is a mother-figure. She seeks to comfort the distressed Cabiria and offers common sense where Cabiria can plead only her hope and her dreams. When Cabiria says of Giorgio, "Why would he shove me in the river for a mere forty thousand lire? I loved him," Wanda replies, "*Love*. . . . You only knew him a month—you know nothing of him." When Cabiria wants to know, after the pilgrimage, why her life has not yet changed for the better, Wanda stares at her in disbelief, saying, "What do you mean, *change?*" Wanda is the first to suspect that Oscar is deceiving Cabiria, and, like a mother, she cries when Cabiria departs from Rome to marry him, complaining that she has not even met the fiancé. The Madonna of Divine Love is Wanda's spiritual counterpart, just as Giovanni, the lay brother, is Alberto's. Like Alberto, Giovanni disappoints Cabiria: he is not at the church when she calls on him, and even had he been there he would not have been able to hear her confession, since he is not an ordained father. (When Cabiria hears this, she reacts with characteristic hopefulness: she says that she will wait for him anyway.)

Fellini gives Cabiria surrogate siblings to complement her surrogate parents. Many children populate this film. Three boys dive into the Tiber and save Cabiria from drowning. Children play outside her door on something resembling the "monkey bars" of American playgrounds; boys have started the fire into which she throws Giorgio's pictures and clothing. Boys and girls run after Cabiria to say good-bye when she is leaving to marry Oscar; the husband and wife who move into Cabiria's house the moment she vacates it have four or five children. Laughing, frolicking children fill the street as Cabiria and Oscar leave the inn in the Alban Mountains to take their fateful walk. Finally, boys and girls revive Cabiria's spirit at the end of the film with music, song, joy, and kindness.

Fellini said that *The Nights of Cabiria* "is full of tragedy."[4] It is, in a sense. One childlike quality of Cabiria's—her resilience, her inexhaustible energy—enables her to endure many setbacks; yet, another childlike quality—her impulse to love and to trust—is responsible for those very setbacks. There is apparently no way out for her *except* to endure, to suffer in her humanity. Cabiria achieves no tragic recognition; she does not change but remains hopeful to the end. If anything has changed in the film, it is the attitude of Fellini's camera and, by extension, our attitude as viewers. Like a shy child, the camera has come upon Cabiria and Giorgio from afar in the opening long shots, has decided to stay with Cabiria, has then followed her through her experience unobtrusively yet doggedly, and in the final shot has come up close to embrace her in love and compassion. The camera has been quintessentially childlike in the sense that it has seemed content to observe and record Cabiria's experience rather than analyze and explain it. Fellini's camera may be naive, but it is not sentimental. No one is blamed for Cabiria's condition; we never learn why she is the way she is, or why she cannot change. The greatest tribute to this film may be that we don't resent not knowing. We accept Cabiria as she is presented to us, and we care about her. We have been removed from the temporal world of causality, of psychology, and transported to the eternal world of wonder and play. That is, we have been transformed from adults into children.

Paradoxically, in reacting only to Cabiria's surface, Fellini has placed her character more firmly at the center of his film than he would have had he probed her character deeply through plot complication, through an agon. He has, in a sense, rescued her from plot. Just as *The Nights of Cabiria* has no structured beginning and middle, no conflict leading to climax, it doesn't really have an end, a dénouement, as Leo Braudy has pointed out[5]: we just leave Cabiria after her betrayal by Oscar, as she walks down the road into the group of strolling boys and girls. I began by quoting Charles Thomas Samuels' remark that the deep probing of character is beyond Fellini. I would argue the opposite: that Fellini is beyond such character analysis; that he is wise rather than naive. Although *8½* with its self-referential and dream qualities seems to be the first of his films to locate him among the modernists in all the arts, Fellini in fact was already a modernist in such an apparently realistic film as *The Nights of Cabiria*, where he celebrated not only the incorrigible hopefulness of human character, but also its ultimate inscrutability.

NOTES TO
"The Film Style of Federico Fellini:
The Nights of Cabiria as Paradigm"

1. Charles Thomas Samuels, *Mastering the Film and Other Essays* (Knoxville: The Univ. of Tennessee Press, 1977), pp. 99–100. Hereafter cited by page number in the text.
2. Richard Gilman, Prefatory Remarks to a Screening of *The Nights of Cabiria*, Yale Univ., New Haven, Ct., 4 Nov. 1982.
3. Gilbert Salachas, ed., *Fellini: An Investigation into His Films and Philosophy*, trans. Rosalie Siegel from 1st French ed. (New York: Crown, 1969), p. 146.
4. Federico Fellini, *Fellini on Fellini*, trans. Isabel Quigley (London, 1976; rpt. New York: Delacorte Press/Seymour Lawrence, n.d.), p. 66.
5. Leo Braudy, *The World in a Frame: What We See in Films* (Garden City, N.Y.: Anchor Press/Doubleday, 1976), p. 248.

STYLE AND MEANING IN
SHOOT THE PIANO PLAYER

Critics agree that *Shoot the Piano Player* (1960) has a disorienting and unsettling quality that results from its mixture of tones and forms. The film is part crime thriller, part love story, part psychological case study; scenes that are a matter of life and death are filled with comic moments, other scenes seem to be the products of Truffaut's whimsy rather than of a tight narrative intention. What follows is a sampling of critics' unanimity of approach to the film and at the same time a description of several important sequences:

> The opening . . . presents us with the totally unexplained situation of a man fleeing from unseen pursuers (represented only by the sound and headlights of their car). . . . We are unsettled visually by the circumstances of the filming: . . . only available light is used, with the result that Chico (the main being chased) moves abruptly and disconcertingly from the full glare of a street lamp into complete darkness, then back into half-light again, and into shots of this kind are intercut jarring flashes of the headlights of the pursuing car. . . . We see [Chico] stumble and hurtle, in almost comic fashion, into a lamppost; laughter at the awkwardness of his fall is stifled by our realisation that he seems to be hurt. . . . We see someone bend over him

ominously and slap his face. The newcomer helps him up, we expect him to be an enemy and are prepared for violence, but . . . the two walk off together like old friends. They begin a conversation . . . and Chico's helper takes the opportunity to tell a perfect stranger details of his private life which he could tell no one else . . . , his voice competing with the sound of their footsteps and the roar of traffic. They stop at a corner and say goodbye, the other leaves, Chico looks round and abruptly begins to run again—we are suddenly reminded that the danger to him was neither imaginary nor forgotten.

Almost every feature of this sequence is designed to disorient the audience: Raoul Coutard's deliberately rough camera style, the lighting (or lack of it), the total absence of background music that might help the audience to develop an appropriate emotional response, and especially the confusion as to whether and when we should experience fear, relief or laughter, and to what extent we are intended to identify with the characters. This uncertainty continues throughout the film.[1]

Our next view of [Chico] is when he enters a cabaret, greets his brother "Charlie" Saroyan, the piano player, and talks vaguely of his troubles. When Charlie refuses help, the desperate runner simply begins to enjoy himself dancing with the local whores. Once again we are surprised. Surely no man in danger would dance with such abandon at such a time. We are further misled by a scene which raises *Shoot the Piano Player* to high comedy. A waiter gets up onto the bandstand to sing . . . deadpan, verse after verse of what must be the wittiest song yet heard in films . . . While we are still laughing, the pursuing gangsters catch up with our "desperate" man. And it is no joke. They carry loaded revolvers. Once more a desperate chase begins and we wonder: where

are we? in comedy? In the shock of ironic juxtaposi-
tions?[2]

The reappearance of the gangsters (Ernest and Momo)
next morning, heralded by a burst of melodramatic
suspense music, points up again their role as comic
characters, as Fido, Charlie's younger brother, bombs
their car windscreen from on high with a carton of
milk—another example of the consciously incongruous
interpolation of gratuitous humour into an otherwise
plausible love story, and typical of the film's abrupt
switches of tone. . . . This capacity to surprise (and
mislead) the audience is what distinguishes this from
every other Truffaut film.[3]

Charlie . . . and Léna [are] bustled into the gangsters'
car while passers-by look calmly on; once in the car,
however, captors and captured get on well together,
joke and reminisce about their childhood. . . . One of
the gangsters pleads for his mother to drop dead if he is
lying and, framed in an antique oval design, an old lady
clutches her heart and falls flat on her back. (Petrie, pp.
26, 30.)

Consider the scene in *Shoot the Piano Player* when Charlie
is about to ring Lars Schmeel's bell for his audition.
Rather than accompany him inside at this climactic
moment, Truffaut follows an attractive young woman
with a violin case—someone we do not yet know and will
not see again. The camera remains with her as she goes
outside . . . *Shoot the Piano Player* continually surprises
us in this fashion, deliberately disrupting tone.[4]

The final gun battle with the gangsters . . . epitomizes
the disturbing clash of tones which has characterized the
film. First, comedy—the ease with which Fido escapes
from the crooks as they slip on the ice; then burlesque of

the gangster film's traditional finale—gun butts shatter windows, one of the gangsters twirls his gun again, but it still looks like a toy gun. We have been manipulated into identifying with Charlie and Léna. We have been willing a happy ending, ignoring the carefully planted omens of tragedy—. . . the suspense music, the gun. . . . The continuing aura of comedy surrounding the gangsters has cushioned us in our expectation that the situation cannot be unhappily resolved. Then suddenly Léna is hit by a bullet, and in an agonizingly prolonged shot her body slides down the slope, insistently proclaiming the reality, and the finality, of this moment. (Allen, pp. 84–85.)

Shoot the Piano Player's mixture of tones and forms is not merely an expression of the director's freedom and versatility, not merely his affectionate explosion of genre, as still another critic, Leo Braudy, believes.[5] Nor does Truffaut, in Graham Petrie's words, "by breaking down our accepted notions of cause and effect, by destroying our normal expectations and assumptions about pattern and order and neat categorisation of experience, [give] us a means of apprehending the real world around us more intelligently and perceptively, for it is the real world he has shown us" (p. 27).[6] Truffaut shows us, not the "real" world, but Charlie's: the unsettling style of the film is meant to imitate the central experience of Edouard Saroyan/Charlie Kohler's life. We get a cinematic or aesthetic equivalent of what Charlie has been trying to avoid socially (and does until Chico rushes into the café where his brother works, looking for protection from the two crooks whom he has apparently cheated): surprise, uncertainty; we are made to feel in our viewing of the film what Charlie does in life. He retreats to the café in an attempt to seal himself off from the vagaries of his existence: his meteoric rise to success as a concert pianist from obscure origins; the steady decline of his marriage and the eventual suicide of his wife under the pressure of that success. Charlie's idea of certainty or security (however minimal) is to sit impassively at his honky-tonk piano night after night playing the same monotonous tune.

Roy Armes has written that *Shoot the Piano Player*'s

> chief flaw lies in the central character, for the two halves of Charlie-Edouard's life never coalesce . . . He is consecutively typical Truffaut hero (hesitantly accosting Léna), *série noire* hero (sleeping with a statuesque prostitute who worships him, and killing the pub-owner Plyne) and melodramatic concert pianist (thumping out Chopin in the Salle Pleyel, and watching his wife leap to her death). . . . We never feel that the various aspects add up to a single coherent character.[7]

Precisely. *Charlie* does not feel that the various aspects of his life add up to a single coherent character; in reaction to this feeling, he has tried to make his life as simple as he can: he has withdrawn to the café, where he performs a routine job and sees as few people as possible. The film's mixture of tones and forms is not only an attempt to create in the audience, *mutatis mutandis*, the disorientation and uncertainty that Charlie experiences; it is also an attempt to reflect the splits in its chief character's life, the jumble of tones and forms that *he* is.

The style of *Shoot the Piano Player* seems to herald that Charlie's existence will remain uncertain, full of surprises and excursions. Charlie appears to be locked into his way of life because, not only does he live it, the style of the film of which he is the subject mirrors his way of life, seemingly reinforcing it. Style is in this sense an augur of inevitability, whereas the almost documentary style of, for example, *The 400 Blows* (1959), is neutral, auguring neither stasis nor change in Antoine Doinel's life. In Truffaut's words, this film follows "a single character simply and honestly."[8] Antoine's situation could improve or remain bad beyond the film; it became better to judge by what happened to Truffaut, on whom the character of Antoine is based. At the end of *Shoot the Piano Player*, Charlie returns to his job in the café to find that Léna has been replaced by a new waitress, with whom he immediately makes strong eye-contact; we recall that after Léna was shot, Ernest and Momo chased after Chico and Richard. Could Charlie's two brothers be headed for shelter at the café, just as Chico was at the start? Will Charlie get together with the new waitress, just as he did with Léna? The fact that the film opens and closes with the same image, of the inside of a piano with the hammers pounding out Charlie's mechanical tune, suggests that the story will repeat itself in the same unsettling, disjointed manner. The only certainty, in Charlie's life as in any Truffaut film of it, will be uncertainty.

The question that remains is, aside from the unity of form and content, of form and content and spectator, that this style afforded, why did Truffaut choose it for Charlie's story? Why didn't he follow Charlie's character "simply and honestly"? Because, unlike Antoine Doinel, Charlie epitomizes less a unique, complex psychological portrait than he does the spirit of an age—the atomic age of post-World II Europe. Truffaut shows us, not the "real" world as it truly is and always has been, as Graham Petrie believes, but an aesthetic equivalent of the world as Charlie perceives it and as it has increasingly come to be viewed after 1945: a place of moral, spiritual, and psychic uncertainty, if not chaos; a world without absolutes and without grace, where the unthinkable can occur and often does. (Thus the title of the film, which is the opposite of what we expect: "Please don't shoot the piano player—he's doing the best he can.") Charlie is the representative and product of his age: this is why Truffaut does not chart or "explain" in any detail the discovery and growth of his musical talent or the disintegration of his marriage. What happens to Charlie is as attributable to the time in which he lives as it is to his "psychology." Charlie's character is not the focus; we are not meant to identify with or have sympathy for him apart from or in opposition to the world in which he lives, as we are in the case of Antoine Doinel. Through the style of his film, Truffaut *gives us Charlie's experience*, his world, as directly as he can; he approximates it aesthetically. We identify not so much with the character as with the manner in which the film proceeds; we identify with a world.

This is possible partly because in the postwar period, what could be called the age of narcissism (lately known as the "me generation"), in our retreat into ourselves from the violence and confusion of modern existence, we have come to view the world less as an objectively verifiable place populated by other human beings worthy of our attention than as our own projection, of which we are simultaneously the sole creator and creation. So we shouldn't mind not being presented with an in-depth study of Charlie's personality: it is not his character that we ought to become interested in, but his world, whose absurdities and incongruities we recognize as aesthetic variations on those in our own. It is not other people that Charlie is interested in, but the little world he has created for himself around his honky-tonk piano. (It was not other people that he was interested in when he was a famous, high-living concert pianist; he was completely self-absorbed, but married at the same time—a fatal combination.) Charlie leaves the world of his piano for Léna, for his brothers, at his and their peril. He returns to the piano at the end of the film only, it seems, to be lured away from it again. We are identical to Charlie, and he is to us, primarily in this sense: that in this age we are all fundamentally cut off from one another, feel safest that way, and venture forth from ourselves with forebodings of doom, therefore with the greatest caution.

None of this is to say that *Shoot the Piano Player* is "anti-humanistic," although I suppose that one could look at the film in this way if one took its title literally: shoot the piano player and put him out of his misery, end his isolation by the easiest, most flippant route. Men are as the time is, said Edmund in *King Lear*, and this goes for Truffaut's film as well as for Charlie Kohler. *Shoot the Piano Player* is the product of its age, which was the culmination of the reduction in stature of the human figure, a process that began early in the twentieth century in art as in life. The film is courageous—avant-garde, let us call it—and consequently in keeping with the best in the human spirit: it tells what it sees as the truth about the human condition at a certain period in history, and it does so at the same time as it lovingly mocks the artistic forms that contrive through their rigidity to tell outdated truths or even fabrications.

Truffaut never experimented again as he did in *Shoot the Piano Player*, which made film history in its unmaking of traditional screen characterization (the split Charlie; the deadly yet comic Ernest and Momo; the mysterious woman with the violin case) as well as of the traditional structures inhabited by screen characters; the director stopped being a product of his time and became instead the product of his own publicity. In my view his career was in one long descent after this film, until all he could do was package Gallic charm and "quote" film history, hoping that no one detected the absence of substance in his work. Rather than being the explorer of a world in the throes at once of narcissism and anxiety, he became merely one more narcissistic inhabitant of it. Narcotized by his own success, he cut himself off from everyone else's anxiety.

NOTES TO
"Style and Meaning in
Shoot the Piano Player"

1. Graham Petrie, *The Cinema of François Truffaut* (New York: A. S. Barnes, 1970), pp. 23–24. Hereafter cited by page number in the text.
2. Judith Shatnoff, "François Truffaut—The Anarchist Imagination," *Film Quarterly*, 16, No. 3 (Spring 1963), p. 5.

3. Don Allen, *François Truffaut* (New York: Viking, 1974), pp. 80, 85. Hereafter cited by page number in the text.

4. Annette Insdorf, *François Truffaut* (New York: William Morrow, 1979), p. 24.

5. Leo Braudy, Intro., *Focus on "Shoot the Piano Player"* (Englewood Cliffs, N. J.: Prentice-Hall, 1972), p. 4.

6. Pauline Kael holds the same view as Petrie: "We never quite know where we are, how we are supposed to react—and this tension, as the moods change and we are pulled in different ways, gives us the excitement of drama, of art, of *our* life. Nothing is clear-cut, the ironies crisscross and bounce." (*I Lost It at the Movies* [Boston: Atlantic-Little, Brown, 1965], p. 213.)

7. Roy Armes, *French Cinema since 1946*, II: *The Personal Style* (New York: A. S. Barnes, 1966), p. 52.

8. François Truffaut, *The Films in My Life*, trans. Leonard Mayhew (New York: Simon and Schuster, 1978), p. 276.

VI

FILM AS THE
CHARACTERIZATION
OF SPACE

THE SPACE IN THE DISTANCE:

A Study of Robert Altman's *Nashville*

In an article entitled "Let Us Not Praise *Nashville*'s Failures," the novelist John Malone made the following statements:

> The real measure of Altman's visual imagination . . . is taken in the . . . traffic jam sequence. The initial pile up of cars is very well done. But from that point on, the scene is a visual . . . shambles. It has no pace, no rhythm, no real cinematic interest.[1]

His remarks are priceless in their thorough misunderstanding of the traffic jam's function and design. Even Malone's attempt to be magnanimous—I hesitate to say condescending—backfires. The pile-up is not "realistically" well done. Altman deliberately and conspicuously stages it. He does not photograph the scene in extreme long shot or from high overhead, showing the lead crash and the immediate reaction to it of every vehicle in its vicinity, then cut systematically from car to car as most of the film's major characters are encountered anew or introduced for the first time. *That* would be "realistic." Instead, he films first the rear-end collision of one automobile into another pulling a trailer laden with an oversized boat; then he shoots the unrealistically delayed intrusion into the frame of numerous vehicles swerving and skidding to avoid a pile-up, and looking as if they were auditioning miserably for some tire commercial. The point of this artificial, ironic staging is to distance the spectator from the action by disappointing his Hollywood-conditioned expectations, and so to jolt him into the awareness that there will be more to be derived from this sequence than the few cheap, safe thrills provided by a "true-to-life" multiple-car crackup, replete with mangled and bloody bodies, twisted wreckage, and perhaps an explosion and fire here and there. Altman's camera and direction steer the spectator's attention away from merely *what* happens on screen to *how* it happens; they turn the traffic jam from something common, typical, readily assimilable, into an object singular, arresting, and unforeseen,[2] and consequently begging serious examination.

It is thus not accidental that "the spatial relationships of the various cars in which the characters sit are not clear" (Malone, p. 13), nor that the camera does not for a moment dote on what little wreckage there is once the pile-up has been completed. Neither is it miraculous that no one is injured, remarkable that no one seems unusually put off by the delay, or incredible that no one appears to give anything more than passing attention to the cause of the delay up ahead. Altman simply did not intend to film his backed-up cars "with extraordinary virtuosity combining visual wit and social satire to ferocious effect" (Malone, p. 13), as did Godard in *Weekend* (1967). The traffic jam as cultural-semiological phenomenon and the conventional responses of the bourgeoisie to it are not the subject of his camera; the traffic jam as a contextual phenomenon of the organic world of his fictionalized Nashville is. One need not look outside the film for the traffic jam's signification, except secondarily. Its meaning within *Nashville*, its definition by the film, should be one's primary concern.

Altman does not so much advance the highway traffic jam *sui generis*, then, as a pure, all-embracing emblem for America, as he does ground it subtly in the reality of his *Nashville* to evoke on screen what he perceives to be the dominant quality of American life today. It is one man's tragicomically exaggerated vision of contemporary American society, and by implication contemporary Western civilization as a whole, that is the real subject of this film, the timeless universal to be conveyed through the particular vehicle of spatially defined *Nashville*. Altman's method in building and equipping such a vehicle is to be compared with that of the novelist of character or the writer of comedy. Unlike the dramatic novelist or the tragedian, Altman is never at one with any of his characters, never at pains to pursue each's fate as he or she comes into being. Their dialogue is anything but profound, they themselves nothing if not ordinary. We do not identify with them as they move linearly from a beginning to an end in time and come to some insight about their lives. The particular actions of the people of *Nashville* are not intended, in this way, to evoke the complete range, the absoluteness, of human experience and hence to work as Altman's personal, boundless metaphor for or aesthetic vision of the character of human life in general. As the polar opposites of "round" introspectionists, these "flat," self-presenting characters, having sprung full-blown from the mind of their creator, have their fates (or want of them) imposed on them from the start. They exist spatially rather than temporally, much as the figures in a painting. That is, they do not change, are "complete" from the beginning, tangible enough to endure as they are in the service of Altman's social vision. Their three-dimensionality is sufficiently suggested rather than fully realized, their existence defined more by the presence of people and things, in space, than by their own thoughts, actions, and interactions in time. These characters do not so much act *upon* one another to produce change in time as act *at* one another to isolate themselves in space. They thus point more to the significance of that space as the artistic extension of Altman's selective social vision than to one another as separate and unique incarnations of his personal, temporal assessment of the human experience.

Appropriately, no one in this film appears alone for very long, if at all. Sueleen Gay is filmed alone in her bedroom, it is true, but certainly not in a reflective pose. She primps and shimmies before a mirror—presents her body to it—in a stunning *spatial* revelation of character. It is clearly her relationship to the space she occupies that defines Sueleen in this scene, not the unveiling of her thought processes in time through monologue or through conversation with other characters. Kenny, Barbara Jean's eventual assassin, is also portrayed alone, first in his room and then just outside it on the telephone, in one of the film's few purely introspective moments, only to have his conversation with his mother pointlessly interrupted by the groupie L. A. Joan. Her mere unthinking presence, in a garish outfit of hot pants, halter top, and platform shoes, as the quintessential projection of the morally and intellectually bankrupt societal space Altman seeks to document, is enough, significantly, to put an abrupt end to the dialogue that might have saved Barbara Jean's life and returned Kenny safely to his home. In a film by design noticeably lacking in introspectionists, it thus becomes wholly if cruelly fitting that Kenny, who had struggled alone in his room to achieve some self-awareness or self-acceptance but failed, should in the final scene maniacally destroy Barbara Jean (and complete his spiritual destruction in the process), whose fumbling, distracted onstage contemplations of her past aimed at a naive self-justification were themselves cut short by the impatience of the crowd and the intervention of her husband.

Typical or general situation, texture—Sueleen fatuously prepping in her bedroom for a concert début she never makes, Kenny lost in thought in a rented room—defines action in *Nashville*, and action in turn is designed to bring out the various attributes of characters, which were there at the beginning, or to introduce new characters. Such figures are comparable to those described by Edwin Muir as being "like a familiar landscape, which now and then surprises us when a particular effect of light or shadow alters it, or we see it from a new prospect."[3] Plot in *Nashville*, a film of character, is improvised to present the characters, even as in Richard Lester's *The Three Musketeers* (1974), for example, a film of action, the characters are designed to fit the plot. On the other hand, in Josef von Sternberg's *The Blue Angel* (1930), a dramatic film, no such hiatus exists between plot and characters. The dramatic film, like the dramatic novel, "shows that character is action, and action character," and consequently "that both appearance and reality are the same" (Muir, p. 47), that characters are and do as they appear and say (or at least are aware of and made to take responsibility for the moments when this is not true). In contrast, the film of character, like the novel of character, "is concerned immediately only with the outside show of reality, and implies beneath, not something corresponding to that, but something relatively incongruous with it. [The film of character] brings out the contrast between appearance and reality, between people as they present themselves to society and as they are" (Muir, p. 47). If the dramatic film at its greatest can be equated with poetic tragedy for its depiction of man as he ought to be and rarely is—of thinking man aspiring nobly and suffering with dignity—then the film of character at its greatest can be equated with high comedy for its depiction of man as he most often is—of enduring man achieving limited objectives while failing to come to terms with himself in a society of which he is at once creation and creator.

Nashville at its greatest is just such a film of character, cinematic in style, novelistic in form and idea, tragic in substance, comic in superstructure. Its aim is to expose the discrepancy between appearance—illusion—and reality in contemporary American society, to uncover our nation's glaring contradictions: "a flagrant, nearly frenzied, workaday energy and a kind of moral deadness; a proud regard for history and heritage and an abiding need to construct a synthetic mythology; a sweeping national certitude and the hypocrisy that comes with it."[4] To this end, paradoxically, the film circumscribes time from the start so as to make it inexhaustible and hence unimportant or unreal. We do not come gradu-

ally to feel, as we do in the dramatic film, "a development reproducing the organic movement of life," that
"time moves and will therefore move to its end and be
consumed" and with it action be resolved (Muir, pp. 80–
81, 85). Since we are immediately informed that the film
will span five days, we *assume* that, in its selection and
portrayal of events from this time period, it does so, no
matter how long or short it finally turns out to be (in the
case of *Nashville*, anywhere from the two hours and
forty minutes of the print distributed by Paramount to
the eight hours of footage that Altman shot with the
intention, however unrealistic, of including the greater
part of it in his film). Of course, as Muir writes, "the
more time is [thus] slowed down or ignored—the more
all urgency is taken from it—the more favorable does it
become for the emergence of characters" (p. 81).
Twenty-four of them emerge in *Nashville*, the complete
and unchanging inhabitants from the first of a specific
world that, in its annihilation of time for the screening
of life in space, from the perspective of space, exists
beyond time, thereby achieving the universality or absoluteness of art.

To criticize the "flatness" of these characters from the
world of *Nashville*, to claim, as Greil Marcus does, that
"the open possibilities all interesting fictional characters
hold are [here] falsely foreclosed in order to make a
statement,"[5] is not to evaluate the film Robert Altman
has made, but to argue for the film one feels he should
have made. It is, to exaggerate only slightly, akin to
criticizing comedy for not being tragedy. For Marcus to
maintain further that Altman is not "for a moment
implicated in the story he tells, the lessons he draws, or
the actions of his characters," and from this to conclude

that such "a deadening distance ultimately kills his work" (p. 61), is to deny his film unjustifiably the objective view of its characters that it shares with both comedy and the novel of character. As I implied earlier, *Nashville* is much more than the sum of its characters. Indeed, it transcends them even as it presents them by framing them largely from the relatively objective distance of the medium and the long shot in the company of one another, at the same time as it detaches us from them somewhat by withholding what, in the context of the dramatic film, would be deemed vital information about their characters.

We do not once feel cheated by this "flat" characterization or that character is being unaccountably obscured, because we know all along as much (or as little) about the characters as they know, or care to know, about one another. Again, these figures exist not so much engrossed in time, for one another, as suspended in space, in the company of one another, in the service of Robert Altman's social vision. And it is their very suspension in relief in a space, in a *situation*—the bedroom and the party, the traffic jam and the auto graveyard, the superhighway and the airport, the recording studio and the concert, the nightclub and the political rally—that serves to point up the gap between the real moral deadness of that space, the failure of imagination to transmute it, and the flagrant and frenzied but finally specious vitality of those who inhabit it. The people of *Nashville* are trapped in a vicious circle, frozen in time, as it were. The like and limited offspring of the space that they themselves have created, the victimizers in turn victimized, they are doomed to extend indefinitely the life of their space because they are unable to expend anything but the inflated energies it generates alone.

Scenes—"modes of existence in society," in the words of Muir (p. 60)—change often throughout *Nashville*, if characters themselves do not. However, in changing, in shifting, even the scenes remain essentially the same to the extent that they always reflect in their major characters the single overriding trait that attends the rest of the film's twenty-four. Thus the animus of the participants in the multiple-car crackup is presented as the passive reflection of an inoperative, "dead" space, the traffic jam, to which Nashvillians have become so accustomed, so "dead," as a given of urban living that they now regard one not as an environmental eyesore and a gross inconvenience, as an abuse of space and a pointless consumption of valuable time, but as yet another means of mindless distraction and even a cause for celebration of sorts. Albuquerque is herself presented as the empty reflection of a similar space, as is country-and-western music as a whole ultimately, when the words and music to the song she performs at a speedway are drowned out by the roar of stock cars circling madly about her. And Tom, the up-and-coming rock star, has the insincerity of his designs on Linnea revealed by a tape recorder in his bedroom, which repeats the vacuous lyrics of his hit, "I'm Easy," in the background as he "performs" in bed with her, even as it did previously for his seductions of Mary, Opal, and L. A. Joan. Haven Hamilton, the reigning king of the country-and-western scene that Tom endeavors to conquer, sings his proud testament to America, "200 Years," in a Nashville that seeks to legitimize itself as "the Athens of the South" by pointing to its elaborate replica of the Parthenon, the consummate objectification, ironically, of its own hollow patriotism. The BBC reporter Opal, interviewing Hamilton's son at his father's large outdoor party, leaves him abruptly to chase down Elliott Gould once the son becomes introspective and begins to speak seriously about his life in and out of Nashville. Gould, who plays himself, represents the fabricated energies of a Hollywood that for years catered to the desire of Americans to escape momentarily from everyday life and become something grander or more heroic than what they were. The film industry thus helped inadvertently to sustain the very moral torpor and passivity of imagination that begot Nashville and continues to plague it as well as other cities all over the country. Opal, the Englishwoman, is similarly plagued when she rejects the warm, human contact she might have had with Hamilton's son for the opportunity merely to gaze upon the visage of Elliot Gould, movie star.

In attendance at the same party, and somewhat more discreetly enamored of Gould, are John Triplette and Linnea's husband, political front men for the presidential campaign of Hal Phillip Walker. Their way of soliciting votes and contributions for their candidate from a large group of prominent Nashvillians is to organize a night on the town for them. The festivities come complete with a striptease act, and Altman's camera is careful to isolate the two men standing off to the side of the show floor overseeing their political manipulation of space. They themselves go virtually unheeded by the hundred or so fat cats who, as Andrew Sarris has observed, like their hosts look at one another as much as

they do the stripper.[6] As self-important political contrib-
utors (investors?), "they are more concerned with the
cameraderie of watching a striptease [that is, with themselves as reflections of one another] than with the striptease itself" (Sarris, p. 64), even as Triplette and his
sidekick are more concerned with their mirror images,
in which each sees himself advancing his career. The
stripper, Sueleen Gay, looks down out of shyness at her
body and at the floor more than she does at the audience, in a neat spatial variation on normally temporal
dramatic irony. She does not know it, but her downward
gaze at herself is her confrontation with—a visual un-
masking of—her essence: the waitress Sueleen with
absolutely no singing ability exchanging her body in
space for what she envisions will be her big break in
time. (Earlier in *Nashville*, Sueleen had stood before her
mirror adjusting the falsies that she ludicrously tosses to
the audience of her striptease.) Altman photographs
her striptease and its audience at an ominous, unre-
lieved distance, as if to trap with his camera everyone
present in blame for the perverseness of an event whose
unmitigatedly absurd cultural-political foundations
they cannot realize.

. . .

Richard Gilman once said of playwright Jack Gelber,
"He represents the latest manifestation of Yeats' cautionary figure: the man who instead of making poetry
out of his quarrel with himself, makes rhetoric out of his
quarrel with others."[7] Instead of "killing" and thereby
immortalizing, paradoxically, that part and projection
of himself which he at once loves and embraces, hates

and fears, he "kills" only what he loathes in others. The first act is imbued with the completeness, the infiniteness of art, and comes ultimately to stand for something beside itself: it transcends its particularity to make a universal statement about the human condition or about the condition of society in which man finds himself obliged to live. The second act is bound by the finiteness, the topicality, of its own polemic.

Gilman by implication was holding up the achievement of Yeats as an example to such a "cautionary," marginal figure as Gelber. And although I am in no way suggesting that Altman's work be placed on a level with Yeats's, I *am* suggesting that he be lauded for the breadth and pith of *Nashville*'s thematic ambitions as well as for the ingeniousness of their technical execution. To be sure, the film has its weaknesses, among them some uneven performances; several overextended improvisatory scenes that contrast harshly and pointlessly with the frequent crosscutting; a few obvious, empty transitions; and, the most serious weakness, a proclivity to employ strictly visual imagery to convey complex ideas. Still, *Nashville* must be judged a sizable achievement as is. If, as Greil Marcus asserts, the film is "not about the passivity and failure of imagination that now oppresses us in daily life, but merely examples of such things" (p. 62),[8] then it is so out of choice, I submit, and to controlled, compelling, and important end. The product of an unchecked and irresponsible, deadening and empty "substitution of form for substantial, intriguing ideas, artistic courage, emotion, and risk" (Marcus, p. 62), the film simply is not.

Its visual style, furthermore, is far from being the disappointing and dull sum of its "mundane" shooting angles and "prosaic" editing, arrived at by John Malone. If technique in *Citizen Kane* (1941) is a reflection and projection of the inhuman quality of its protagonist in the very showiness of the camera work, the editing, and the use of sound,[9] then technique in *Nashville*, I propose, is a deliberate reflection and projection of the passivity and failure of imagination of its characters by means of the distance the relatively static camera maintains from events, the seeming randomness of the editing, the apparently casual selection of dialogue to make intelligible, and the finely disguised writing, composing, and singing of songs by nonprofessionals (the actors themselves). Altman's cinema of distance is fashioned to discourage our totally passive, hypnotic, unthinking absorption in events and lives on screen, and to goad us into bringing some intelligence and reason to bear on what passes before our eyes. We are made to stand outside this cinema, "estranged" from it, to the extent that its constituent parts call attention to themselves as aesthetic devices and demand integration into a unique artistic universe.

For all the distance it maintains from the object of its social vision-artistic creation, *Nashville* is never cold and condescending. Accordingly, there are no cardboard figures in this film, no vicious caricatures by turns ominously unsettling and comically reassuring. Altman's quarrel, unlike Jack Gelber's, is not so much with his subject matter as with himself. His *Nashville* may be finally and most accessibly a coolly, almost deceptively desperate example of the moral deadness that can infect a society. In the dialectic it sets up between distanced camera and animated action, however, the film is perhaps equally an ironic intimation of the static decadence of the self-conscious "I" of this camera as juxta-posed against the animal vitality (illusory as it may be) of the aimless "they" on screen. For Altman clearly loves the country-and-western scene for the quasi-primitive vitality of its animal aimlessness; he himself would emulate its unreflective, simple *living* from day to day, but *ipso facto*, as artist and thinker, he is unable to. Yet he hates and would transform this same scene for the absence of real inspiration and invention from its motions. In the unresolved tension of its love-have, his dilemma is at the core of his art. It is the basis for the benign and enduring antagonism between *Nashville*'s form and content, for the necessarily unresolved tension of the film's will to gratify even as it edifies.

· · ·

Jay Cocks and John Simon, among others, have criticized Robert Altman for his deployment of the BBC correspondent Opal at the very heart of *Nashville*. Simon claims that "it is foolhardy and self-destructive for a film that so trades in metaphors to hold up to our unmitigated ridicule the one character in it who likewise spouts them."[10] Cocks writes that "it is this kind of coyness—the eagerness both to use the rather parched symbolism and mock it too [through the character of Opal]—that is the movie's most serious flaw" (pp. 67–68). Neither man seems to realize, however, that Opal is more device than character. Simon is on the right track but misses the mark when he adds, "No one that unprofessional, foolishly garrulous, and ineptly pushy would work for the sedately respectable BBC" (p. 38). Altman and his screenwriter, Joan Tewkesbury, are no doubt just as much aware of this as Simon, which is precisely the reason, I suspect, that they characterized Opal as the nearly imbecilic sycophant she is.

It became more and more apparent to me as the film went on that Opal in fact could not work for so sedately respectable an organization as the BBC, that she could be no more than a zealous impostor cum groupie attracted to the country-and-western scene for the same reasons as L. A. Joan and Sueleen Gay. This conclusion is strongly supported by three facts. First, Opal neither conspicuously displays nor once produces credentials proving that she is a BBC employee, as members of the media of any country are wont to do. Second, it is rather odd that the cameraman assigned to her never once appears to film the documentary she is supposedly making. The suggestion is that Robert Altman is doing the filming and that the truth of Nashville is just as much contained in his fiction film as it would be in any "objective" documentary. Third, no one in the film takes Opal's rhetoric or her purported mission seriously— indeed, some characters are put off by her, especially when she resorts to pushiness to get an interview or gain entrance to some event.[11]

As an impostor cum groupie, Opal represents, in her total obsession with microphone and tape recorder, an additional, foreign embodiment of the moral deadness and failure of imagination afflicting the America of *Nashville*. Altman withheld the evidence that would prove Opal an impostor neither out of caprice nor out of his conviction that such evidence, for reasons of economy and priority, was simply better left on the cutting-room floor. Rather, he withheld the proof, I submit, in the belief that to expose her as an impostor would have been to draw unwanted attention to the *content* of her character—to her motivations, intentions, and objectives—as opposed to the *form* of her function. And to do so would have been to obliterate the dialectic between object and subject, between the world of *Nashville* and his own directorial self.

Opal is Altman's Shakespearean fool in reverse, his inversion of the wise and temperate servant of Restoration comedy, who functions, as device, to distance the audience from the action at key moments. Cocks is correct when he accuses Altman of using parched symbolism. But it is the figure of Opal that enables the audience to take seriously what it would otherwise dismiss as wildly clichéd; it is not Altman who, through this character, coyly mocks the very images he seems to be advancing in earnest. Paradoxically, the audience can take, for example, "a yard filled with auto wrecks, symbolic of the violent rape and waste of the whole country" (Cocks, p. 67), more seriously, precisely because it does not have to take Opal seriously for so presenting it. Were she to comment on such a scene with the sobriety and determination of, say, Howard K. Smith, instead of with her own effervescence and ostentation, we would indeed be justified in rejecting the scene's banality of image and idea out of hand, in refusing to examine it more closely for the essential truth beneath its clichéd surface.

It thus surely cannot be by accident that Opal is the only character in the film who speaks with a British accent. Altman elected to have her speak with one, I maintain, so as to separate her language in sound as well as style from the unadorned idiom of the rest of the film's characters; that is, so as to isolate her further, to make her conspicuous, in her function as his agent of Brechtian "defamiliarization." Thirty years prior to the making of *Nashville*, Brecht similarly chose to have the Storyteller in *The Caucasian Chalk Circle* (for one example among his plays) recite verse to music instead of speaking in prose, like the other characters, when he stepped forward to "alienate" the audience by summarizing the action of the scene to come or by commenting on the one just past. Opal, too, comes forth to underscore her role as perpetrator of the film's "alienation effect," speaking into her microphone and facing an imaginary audience (addressing us?) after she is carefully isolated by Altman's camera. Sometimes she is suddenly left standing alone by characters who, fittingly, appear either as puzzled by her behavior or as indifferent to it as the film audience is "estranged" by it. Altman has Opal describe, "You Are There"-style, the ongoing action of several scenes—what we can see happening right before us—in order to quiet by indirection the voice within us that performs the same function and deflect our attention to how the scene has been filmed as well as to why the characters act as they do. He even has her comment on the action at one point by invoking assuredly, but nevertheless inanely, another filmmaker. At the outdoor party on the grounds of Haven Hamilton's log-cabin retreat, Opal suddenly turns to the camera and remarks, "Pure, unadulterated Bergman. Of course, the people are all wrong for Bergman, aren't they?" The very ring of her hollow words is enough to cause us to reject them outright for the larger process of which they are a part: incidents and ambience on screen, framed by a distant and relatively stationary camera that is a stranger to the subjective shooting angle and the close-up. Opal and the camera combine here and elsewhere to encourage our detached observation of the course of a scene over our emotional anticipation of its outcome, our scrutiny of characters and events over our absorption in them.

Nashville is not to be dismissed simply as good entertainment, as Pauline Kael's "orgy for movie-lovers"[12] or Stanley Kauffmann's cinematic equivalent of "a good read,"[13] and it is quite possible Altman had in mind it would be when he insisted to the screenwriter Joan Tewkesbury that one of the characters die at the end, as well as when he inserted Opal in his film. The assassination of the singer Barbara Jean is not intended to be the inevitable and disastrous outcome of ritualistic tragedy, as Molly Haskell thinks.[14] Nor is the assassination supposed to be the comprehensible, believable act of a strongly motivated, if somewhat mad killer, as John Simon would like it (p. 38). Rather, the singer's murder is meant to frustrate the expectations and wishes of audience members. Unable to empathize fully with a disturbed woman about whom they know very little really, they are unable moreover either to like or loathe the young killer whose motives they cannot divine and whom they have found up to this point to be a sympathetic, if enigmatic figure. The assassination is thus freed to act as a device of Brechtian "defamiliarization." It becomes Altman's final admonition to his audience not to reflect lightly on *Nashville* as the amusing and tidy sum of the story strands of its twenty-four characters, but instead to seek the film's vision and authority in the peculiar quality of its action that subsumes characters as it reveals who they are.

Altman's camera does not pursue the mortally

wounded Barbara Jean as she is carried from the stage, nor indulge in close-ups of the unsuspecting young singer as she performs for the last time (even as it did not follow the abashed Sueleen Gay as she ran naked from the nightclub floor, nor employ close-ups of her as she stripped), because she *as character* is not the primary object of his concern. He is interested above all in the character of the *situation* from which she departs and that engendered her senseless murder. The stage and the crowd therefore remain in cold long shot as the oddly engaging Albuquerque takes over with the song "It Don't Worry Me." Again, Albuquerque's character is not so much Altman's concern here; it is her function that is important to him. That her fine singing was not the truly moving personal triumph it might have been (in another film) for John Malone is unimportant. It simply was not intended to be, and to this end the director deliberately denied Albuquerque the requisite empathetic details of character[15] and avoided close-ups of her face in song. That she captivates the crowd and leads its members in a sing-along is vital.

The reaction of the concert audience to Barbara Jean's murder has been called unrealistic in its heartlessness.[16] But the audience's reaction could be explained, if not excused finally, from a realistic point of view. The crowd—that part of it nearest the bandstand—does swarm all over Kenny, the assassin, and it resists giving him up to the police. Furthermore, it is so large that very likely a good percentage of it, distracted as audiences can become at outdoor concerts, simply did not look to the stage in time to experience directly the shooting of the singer; they witnessed only the murder's brief aftermath. Since Albuquerque comes on stage so quickly after the removal of Barbara Jean's body, it is not unreasonable to assume that crowd members in general were responding to the call of the moment in joining the new performer in song; that they were ready, if perhaps too willing, to grasp at anything that might restore a festive air to the concert. Apart from this "realistic" explanation, however, the crowd's heartless reaction to Barbara Jean's murder can be justified on purely aesthetic grounds as the logical conclusion of a work that would stand as a metaphor for America, and thus necessarily indict by implication the American film audience for the same insensibility it uncovers in the concert audience.

The concertgoers know little more about Barbara Jean *the woman* than we the film viewers do. Accordingly, they respond with relative indifference to or acceptance of the violence visited upon her, even as we do the same in our inability to identify with her as we would have liked to, as the movie industry in this country has conditioned us to. Altman himself has thwarted our expectations, it is true, and with good reason. But it is a measure of the unresolved tension between the form and content of *Nashville* that what initially discourages our involvement with a character, distances us from her, should return to chide us indirectly for our powerlessness to respond instinctively with complete shock and horror to her brutal murder. We are one in lamentable numbness with the live audience of Barbara Jean's concert as well as with her Nashville *television* audience, Altman seems to be saying. And to awaken us gradually to this and at the same time to embody once and for all the tension between form and content in his film, he frames Albuquerque in cool long shot as she appealingly sings a song that, paradoxically, comes to worry us even as it thrills us, precisely because it does *not* worry the concert audience that thrills to it during the final minutes of *Nashville*.

. . .

In a brilliantly reasoned essay, Gilberto Perez wrote that in Dovzhenko's *Earth* (1930), people and things

> are taken out of their spatial context by close-ups; their intrinsic reality, the sense of their independent life, matters more than where they are exactly within a vast space. . . . The spatially discontinuous [or fragmented] shots are linked together by their inner arrangement, not from some [dramatic] perspective that takes us outside the shot itself. Dovzhenko prefers to bring out correspondences, connections between things, to juxtapose elements that have an intrinsic similarity. . . . Chiefly by means of the editing, by the way he brings things together in the assembling of the shots, he . . . gives the film its forward movement. It is not the movement of pure pattern, as in musical composition, but the movement to establish pattern against the weight of concreteness, to incorporate into a larger design the individual energy that people and things possess.[17]

Perez described Dovzhenko's cinematic style as "of the foreground," after Erich Auerbach's description of the style of narration in the *Odyssey*, where "Homer knows no background. What he narrates is for the time being the only present. We get a fully externalized description of things that leaves nothing dark or incomplete, no room for their taking on a subjective significance; in this absolute present, things are simply themselves, seen without perspective." Perez went on to distinguish between *Earth* as an example of "the cinema of solid objects" and Murnau's *Nosferatu* (1922) as its opposite, an example of "the cinema of empty space." He brought up in the process Ortega y Gasset's argument that close and distant vision are two different ways of seeing: in close vision we look at solid objects; in distant vision we look more at the space between objects, at the air in which objects are submerged.

Like *Nosferatu*, Robert Altman's *Nashville* may be said to be one example of "the cinema of empty space"; like *Earth*, it may be said to eschew portraying its characters and events from the dramatic perspective of time for presenting them from the geometric perspective of space. (Where *Nashville* opts to subjugate the interweaving and resolution of its stories to the vision inherent in its overall design, however, *Earth* eliminates the flow of narrative almost completely.) But, in the uncertain, uneasy distance of *Nosferatu*, in Perez' words, "what is actually in the world affects us less than what we fear might be there." And, in the sure, restful closeness of *Earth*, "what things are in themselves, in their enduring aspect," is more important than the space that surrounds them. In the ambivalent, anticipatory distance of *Nashville*, by contrast, what people are in close relation to their space, how they are simultaneously its products and producers, its pawns and its manipulators, is offered up for our scrutiny. Even as Gilberto Perez argued that the style of *Earth* could be termed "of the foreground," so too would I argue, then, that the style of *Nashville* could be termed "of the background."

"Now the camera [committed neither to the foreground nor to the background]," writes Perez, "automatically reproduces things as they appear from a particular point in space, which automatically tends to give some things—those closer to the camera, or in sharper focus—a greater stress than it gives to others. The camera tends to place an uneven stress on the visual field, to create a kind of foreground and background." This is, roughly put, the method of the dramatic film, whose subject is the action of character and whose perspective is subjective, expressing a particular point of view that makes some things stand out and others recede in importance. In the dramatic film, theoretically, close-ups and soft focus are used to concentrate our attention on one or more individuals, the main characters in a situation of conflict or intimacy; long shots and deep focus are employed to establish and enhance place; and medium shots to take in several characters during a conversation or in a moment of intense interaction.

Altman's method is of the film of character, whose real subject is the character of action, of situation or milieu, and whose perspective is objective. To everything on the screen he gives an equal stress. But it is not the evenness of stress of "all in the foreground," as in *Earth*. Dovzhenko, according to Perez, "shows things often one by one, with the equal clarity given by close-ups. . . . Every shot is thus on some equality with every other shot." With Altman, too, one might say that every shot is on some equality with every other shot. His is the evenness of stress of "all in the background," however, where people and things are often viewed from a distance, in a *mise en scène*, occupying and in turn being enveloped by their space. It is not as if "different things were brought, one after another, into the same space, a kind of constant, a common ground," as in Dovzhenko, but as if different spaces were made, one after another, to be inhabited (and revisited) by the same people, themselves a kind of constant. Just as in *Earth* what different things have in common is enforced by their being placed successively within the same frame, so too in *Nashville* what different spaces have in common is enforced by their being made successively to host the same people.

Unlike Dovzhenko's humanistic vision, Altman's is essentially a social one, then, which needs to take the long view, the objective one available from the perch of distance. Thus, seldom is a character seen alone in long shot in *Nashville*.[18] This would be to give the individual too much weight at the expense of the company of the film's characters, as it would be to give space too much weight at the expense of character per se. Rather, groups of characters are observed in long shot, the empty reflections of spaces of their own creation. Unlike the people of Dovzhenko's *Earth*, the people of *Nashville* cannot be firmly apprehended for what they are in themselves, in their essence, and *hence are rarely viewed in close-up.* They can be apprehended only in relation to the continuous space they inhabit, and to which they have all but sacrificed the intrinsic nobility and vitality of the human spirit. What is left is mere appearance, photographed at a distance, accordingly, so as to give us the elusive impression, the passing glimpse, the oblique view, of figures of light, animated more from without than within.

NOTES TO
"The Space in the Distance: A Study of Robert Altman's *Nashville*"

1. John Malone, "Let Us Not Praise *Nashville*'s Failures," *New York Times*, Sunday Ed., 10 Aug. 1975, Sec. 2, p. 13. Hereafter cited by page number in the text.

2. John Willett, ed. and trans., *Brecht on Theatre* (New York: Hill and Wang, 1964), p. 143.

3. Edwin Muir, *The Structure of the Novel* (New York: Harcourt, Brace and World, n. d.), p. 24. Hereafter cited by page number in the text.

4. Jay Cocks, "From the Heartland," *Time*, 16 June 1975, p. 67. Hereafter cited by page number in the text.

5. Greil Marcus, "*Ragtime* and *Nashville*: Failure-of-America Fad," *Village Voice*, 4 Aug. 1975, p. 61. Hereafter cited by page number in the text.

6. Andrew Sarris, "Where I Stand on the New Film-Crit," *Village Voice*, 11 Aug. 1975, p. 64. Hereafter cited by page number in the text.

7. Richard Gilman, *Common and Uncommon Masks* (New York: Random House, 1971), p. 176.

8. One such example is the Tricycle Man, whom Stanley Kauffmann unjustly called "a regrettable link with the consciously fey style of earlier Altman" (*The New Republic*, 28 June 1975, p. 33). As Andrew Sarris has pointed out, the Tricycle Man is more a "visual figure of style" than a temporal character (*Village Voice*, 9 June 1975, p. 81). He is not meant to refer back in time to the freedom and nonconformity symbolized by the Peter Fonda and Dennis Hopper characters of *Easy Rider* (1970), but to embody in stasis the failure of imagination afflicting Nashville and, by extension, American

society. The Tricycle Man is one more projection of a morally and intellectually bankrupt space; he is a parody of the Fonda and Hopper characters, since his only claim on our attention is his imitation of their appearance and his complete obsession with his motorcycle. Significantly, Altman has the rest of the characters in *Nashville* regard the Tricycle Man with wonder and curiosity—another indictment of the failure of their imaginations.

9. This idea of Andrew Sarris' is noted in Edward Murray, *Nine American Film Critics* (New York: Frederick Ungar, 1975), p. 64.

10. John Simon, "The Amazing Shrunken *Nashville*," *Esquire*, Sept. 1975, p. 38. Hereafter cited by page number in the text.

11. After this was written, Ernest Callenbach, the editor of *Film Quarterly*, in a letter postmarked 10 Dec. 1975, informed me he had heard that "in the original script she *was* 'exposed' as not from the BBC."

12. Pauline Kael, "The Current Cinema," *The New Yorker*, 3 March 1975, p. 79.

13. Stanley Kauffmann, "On Films," *The New Republic*, 28 June 1975, p. 33.

14. Molly Haskell and Andrew Sarris, "A Critics' Duet on *Nashville*," *Village Voice*, 9 June 1975, p. 82.

15. Albuquerque's argument with her husband, Star, during the traffic jam cannot be heard, for example. The shot of them inside their pickup is designed only to introduce her (and secondarily her husband)—to outline her credibility as a participant in the Nashville scene—and to prefigure her mute performance at the speedway later in the film.

16. Eliot Fremont-Smith, "Making Book," *Village Voice*, 11 Aug. 1975, p. 39.

17. Gilberto Perez, "All in the Foreground: A Study of

Dovzhenko's *Earth*," *Hudson Review*, 28, No. 1 (1975), pp. 68–86. Since I quote often from this article here and on the following pages, I have elected simply to refer the reader to it for consultation in its entirety rather than list the page from which each quotation is taken.

18. An exception is Opal, who appears alone in long shot in the auto graveyard and in the school-bus parking lot. In these shots, Altman intends to give space more weight at the expense of character. As I described her earlier, Opal is a device that enables the audience to take more seriously the parched symbolism of the auto wrecks and of their antithesis, the school buses, because the audience does not have to take *her* seriously for presenting them as revealing comments on American society.

THE FALL OF BÉATRICE, THE SALVATION OF POMME:

Simultaneity and Stillness in Goretta's *Lacemaker*

Claude Goretta's *Lacemaker* (1977) tells a deceptively simple story. Béatrice, nicknamed Pomme, is a young apprentice in a Paris beauty salon. She lives with her mother and appears to have only one friend: the older Marylène, a beautician where she works who, in worldliness, ebullience, and appeal to men, is just the opposite of Béatrice. The latter seems content with her lot, patient with life; Marylène is ever on the move, currying favor with her customers, tending to her relationship with a well-heeled married man, buying the latest fashions, keeping a chic apartment. But Marylène's "movement" is suddenly halted one day: her lover leaves her, and she is distraught. She needs to get away, so she talks Béatrice into accompanying her to Cabourg for vacation. Once there, Marylène takes to chasing men, while Béatrice is left to herself. Along comes François, a literature student from the Sorbonne, to keep Béatrice company. He is highly articulate and not a trifle conceited, but manages to charm a girl so different from himself because he pays attention to her and is "nice." Béatrice is inexperienced and lonely; although she does not appear at first to be as infatuated with François as he is with her, she grows to love him in spite of the differences in their backgrounds and interests, because he has reached out to her and in addition seems to need her love.

Back in Paris, they move into a small apartment together. She continues to work as an apprentice in the beauty salon, while he resumes his studies at the Sorbonne. But François, in his way, is just as naive as Béatrice. He finds that her love is not enough for him, that he wishes she were more eager to get an education and a better job. His intelligence does not threaten her, because in her love for him she simply is not concerned with this aspect of his character. Her ignorance bothers him, because he finds that he cannot talk to her as he does to his friends and hence that *she* cannot talk to his friends as he does. François does not love Béatrice for what she is. She has been a novelty in his life, an infatuation; he has "read" her as if she were a new book, thought about her briefly, and, his curiosity satisfied, he is ready to return her to the shelf. He does not know what love is yet; she, correctly, construes it as a form of devotion. François more or less asks her to leave, and she quietly does. Béatrice is crushed, for she does not understand a world in which people pick up and discard other people as they might a car or a piece of clothing.

Béatrice is pregnant when she and François separate, but she loses the child. It is as if, as a last taunt, she is forced by a cruel world to do something that she could never do on her own: expel a loved one from her life. When we last see her, she is in a mental hospital, completely alienated from a world she did not understand and that did not understand her. She is there less because she has "lost her mind" than because she has lost her heart, her desire to love and be loved.

Simply put, then, the aim of *The Lacemaker* is to chronicle the destruction of a young working-class girl through her involvement with a literature student of good bourgeois stock. But Goretta does something about one third of the way through the film that belies this aim. He intercuts a scene of Béatrice's mother mysteriously approaching her sleeping daughter from the background and placing a hand on her shoulder, with a scene of Béatrice and Marylène rowing a boat along a river. Now the common denominator of both these scenes is Béatrice's mother, who is sitting on the bank of the river watching her daughter and Marylène, and who apparently flashes back to the scene in Béatrice's bedroom. The mother is the common denominator as well of the very next two scenes: she seems to fantasize that she is walking arm-in-arm with her daughter in the present, then seems to flash back to Béatrice walking arm-in-arm with her after first Holy Communion. The scenes can easily be justified as oblique glosses on Béatrice's character of a piece with the images or objects that the French surrealists were so fond of juxtaposing in their poetry: apparently unrelated on the surface, these images or objects are in fact deeply connected.

In her shyness and innocence, Béatrice could be said to "live in the moment" at the same time as she allows the moment to touch her. That is, she is not particularly self-conscious or reflective—she works, she cleans, she eats, she sleeps—but neither is she totally unreceptive to how she is different from those around her, how she affects them, and how they regard her. She is, in short, far more the child-woman than most girls her age; instead of playing unselfconsciously much of the time as children do, she must now work and help her mother. So when Goretta juxtaposes a scene of Béatrice "playing"—boating with Marylène—against one of her asleep, he is suggesting the correspondence between the mind of the sleeping Béatrice and that of the waking Béatrice. He is saying that Béatrice, for all her self-consciousness while awake, might just as well be asleep. When Goretta juxtaposes the scene of Béatrice walking with her mother in the present against the one of the daughter walking with her mother after first Holy Communion, he is saying something very similar: that, in its unselfconsciousness, Béatrice's mind has remained essentially unchanged from the time she was eleven or twelve to the time she is eighteen (nearly nineteen: the director gives her a birthday later in the film to let us know that increased age is not going to affect Béatrice's nature very much).

But the above "justifications" of the intercut scenes depend for their exclusive validity on the place of Béatrice's mother in the film. And she has very little place, really. She is not a central character, let alone the film's narrator, and the flashbacks or free associations reveal nothing about her. I would like to submit that each of the intercut scenes can stand alone, apart from their apparent emanation from the character of the mother and apart from the fact that when juxtaposed against each other in the order I have stated, they reinforce something about Béatrice that we should already know from her mere presence on screen. It is as if

Béatrice is a figure in a painting in these four scenes, which for reasons that will become clear I shall call the film's "interlude." If the camera pulls back to reveal Béatrice's mother observing her daughter and Marylène in their boat, it does so not to place emphasis on the mother as a character, but to suggest that she is like an audience before a painting (Béatrice and Marylène do not acknowledge her, and she does not acknowledge them), and an audience for whom this "painting" triggers mental images, other "paintings." These "paintings" or "painterly scenes" of "Pomme," as she is called throughout the film, do not so much advance the story as isolate her in her own world, a painter's world of deftness and suggestion, of the ineluctability and irreducibility of each moment. The scenes are less interested in revealing Pomme's character than in depicting her relation to space, her place in an event.

It is, of course, not only these four scenes in which Pomme appears like a figure in a painting. But these four come at a crucial moment in the film, right before she is to meet François and begin her decline. That is why I call them an "interlude." They are the calm before the storm, the "form in suspense" that Susanne Langer speaks of in relation to dramatic form. They seem to slow down Pomme's decline, to freeze her fate within the eternity of the frame, to secure her for the moment in the eyes of her friend and the arms of her mother. And that, I would maintain, is precisely what the entire film of *The Lacemaker* is trying to do: freeze Pomme's fate within the eternity of the frame, take her back to the genre painting, secure her in time's eye.

The very title of the film copies the title of a genre painting—Vermeer's *Lacemaker*; Goretta's title has nothing directly to do with events in the film. The director has chosen this title for the anonymity it confers upon Pomme, even as Vermeer chose his for the anonymity it ᴄonferred upon his lacemaker. A genre painting by definition depicts human figures anonymously; it treats them as types rather than as unique personalities. The genre painter, like the painter of still lifes, makes no judgments: he is interested, above all, in the objective contemplation of everyday life. Goretta actually places such a painter in his film in order to symbolize his own relationship to Pomme. As she and François sit in a park, an artist sketches her face. When François, who cannot see the man's hands drawing, tells him to keep his eyes off other men's girlfriends, the artist shows his sketch. It is roughly Pomme, but it could roughly be some other girl in the park, too. The sketch could be entitled as a genre painting might have been: "Girl Sitting on a Park Bench." Goretta has given us the secret to the casting of Isabelle Huppert as Pomme: we do not so much see Huppert's face when we look at her as her essence, her silence and serenity. Her features are indistinct; her solidity is clear. She is the perfect anonymous subject.

By taking Pomme back to the genre painting, by conferring anonymity on her, Goretta is through his art removing or repudiating the stain and pain of her involvement with François. Pomme says so little, reveals so little about her feelings, not only because it is in her character to behave in this way, but also because through her reticence Goretta further preserves her anonymity, her opaqueness or integrity, if you will, in a modern-day world that clamors to know everything about everybody. The last shot of the film has Pomme knitting in the recreation room of the mental hospital, where garish travel posters of Greece cover the walls, and slowly turning out to the camera as the background goes to soft focus. She is at last and forever like the sole subject of a genre painting: there are no others, there is not even a hint of the outdoors. She has just seen her last of the outdoors with her visitor, François, and he has remarked on how good the air and scenery are for her. There is no sound, even as there was none during the interlude.

. . .

Everything in *The Lacemaker* has led up to this point, to this isolation yet at the same time restoration of Pomme within the frame, within the genre painting. Pomme's father left her and her mother when she was a child. Marylène leaves her at Cabourg to move in with an American. François's parents reject her as unsuitable for their son. Her mother gives Pomme permission to live with François a little too quickly, with words something like, "Whatever is best for her." François himself rejects Pomme, then her own mother again sends her away, in a manner of speaking, when she commits her daughter to the mental hospital. There Pomme is visited and abandoned for the last time by François, and there even her own doctor is oblivious to her as he passes by on the hospital grounds. Finally Pomme is alone, much as she has been in the individual frames that fill in the above outline of her fate.

She is alone at work, immersed in her chores as an apprentice, hoping only to become a stylist. As if in recognition of Pomme's aspirations, the camera follows hands *at work* on heads, faces, and other hands during the opening sequence. The other employees sit around idly; Pomme works constantly. She is alone at home in her room, closing its latticed door—it is like a door to the outside—on her mother and the television. She is alone in her hotel room at Cabourg, stripping to go to bed and then carefully laying out her nightgown on top of the covers, as if to make it her companion in place of the missing Marylène.

At Cabourg, after François and Pomme have met and spoken briefly at a café, Goretta intercuts scenes of him feverishly searching for her and of her unconsciously looking for him. François locates her, but it is as if he interrupts her in her isolation. He finds her after he has all but given up his search. The effect of this is to make the "search" scenes stand for themselves, separating François and Pomme from each other, and characterizing him as the goal-oriented, nervous young littérateur and her as the process-oriented, placid young worker. They should not meet, we are told by everything that Goretta's camera does. But they do. They sit at the table in Pomme's hotel room for a small meal. But they do not belong together, so Goretta interrupts their silence with the sounds of a couple making love in the room next door (a couple truly together, in other words), then has the embarrassed Pomme turn on the radio to ensure an interruption to the other couple's lovemaking as well as to her and François's silence. Her mother and François sit at the former's table back in Paris after a meal. Pomme is alone in the kitchen, cleaning up. She is then alone in her room, packing her suitcase carefully for the move to François's apartment. She is not at the table because she does not belong there. She cannot idle, and she will soon be excluded forever from these two persons' lives. She leaves the table at the home of François's parents after she has choked on some food: Goretta thus tells us that she is out of place at this table, too.

Pomme would rather touch than speak. Touching is her way of speaking, of communicating in her isolation. At the Normandy cemetery for American soldiers who fell on D-day, Francois, Marylène, and John (the American) talk of the more than ten thousand dead who lie beneath them. Pomme says nothing, but as the others are leaving, she places a seashell that she had solicitously picked up at the beach on one of the crosses. This is a physical, significant gesture, of the sort that a painting can best isolate. Pomme is momentarily alone and in communion with these war dead. They are as important as she; she acknowledges them: it is this simultaneity that the image, the painting, can best capture. Pomme achieves/attributes peerage here in the same way as she does, for example, when she goes to pet (not run from) the barking dogs at François's parents' home; when she fingers the fruits and vegetables at market—Goretta makes her shopping seem like the most important and exquisite of tasks; when she runs her hand over the books she has never heard of in a bookstore; when, before painting her and François's apartment, she carefully covers all his belongings with clean, white sheets.

The Lacemaker is a series of these "significant gestures" and studied isolations, I say "paintings," because I think that Goretta, in the making of the film, was aware of how the heightened image could ennoble Pomme where words would only have diminished or talked around her. The heightened image could make her part of a world in body that she was never very much a part of in spirit. As I have noted, Pomme is not a creature of words; she is without the ability or desire to communicate complexly through language. Therefore the painting, an art form without words, is best equipped to portray her, is best suited to evoking, through her physical relationship to objects and people, her virtue, simplicity, and contentment. It mediates less between her and us. The painting's equivalent in cinema is, of course, the image, and in order to enhance further this idea of his film as a succession of still images, of paintings, of which Pomme is the primary subject (even as a "pomme" may be the subject of a still life), Goretta often holds a shot several seconds after the characters have left the screen, or he holds the camera on them after they have finished speaking and before he cuts to the next scene. Like Pomme throughout most of the film, they become silent, seeing, still. Unlike Pomme, they are not comfortable in this pose, and their uncomfortableness, conveyed through the image, reveals more about them than their words. To those who would argue that all films, regardless of content, deal in images, in the placement of people and things in space, that all films are in essence a series of "pictures" put into motion, I would say that few films have less dialogue than *The Lacemaker* and few contain more still moments. None do what Goretta does in his last frame: exclude all other characters and turn a shot of a single character into a virtual genre painting. To those who would argue in addition that *The Lacemaker* was first a novel by Pascal Lainé, that Goretta merely translated it faithfully into film, I would say that, on the contrary, Goretta and Lainé, who wrote the screenplay, have probably done for Pomme in images what Lainé could not do in words alone (his novel has not been available to me). Lainé's novel most likely told Pomme's story well. His screenplay and Goretta's *mise-en-scène* have transformed her.

Goretta has chronicled Pomme's destruction in today's world, but at the same time, paradoxically, through his gradual isolation of her, he has been returning her to the world of the genre painting, a world in which she would have been most comfortable and would have survived, her mind intact. He returns her to a time when class distinctions were more strictly observed, when she would have survived if only because someone like François would never have figured prominently in her life. Certainly the uneducated and uncultured of the seventeenth century (when Vermeer lived) were not looked down upon less than their counterparts of today—indeed, they were held in greater contempt— but at least they were for the most part left to themselves, left to marry among one another and to live their own lives, however politically disadvantaged and poor they may have been. That a seamstress, water girl, or lacemaker occasionally became the subject of a genre painting is an indication, not of an improvement in the lot of the worker, but of a curiosity on the part of the middle and upper classes about the daily lives of those beneath them, and of the beginning of the desire on the part of artists to embrace everything and everyone as their subject matter.

Pomme is destroyed, but she is restored. This is *The Lacemaker*'s working tension and what makes a screening of it at once saddening and exhilarating, what makes it high art as opposed to "fictional documentary"—the kind of film John Cassavetes has tried to create with

Husbands (1970) and *A Woman Under the Influence* (1974), one that tells a story (usually of misfortune), sometimes using non-actors, so unobtrusively and unadornedly as to make it appear actually to be happening as it is being photographed. Goretta knows that there is less room these days for the Pommes of the world. To live simply and to work, to "help mother," is not enough, it seems. One must achieve something great, or make a lot of money, or be beautiful, or one will not be noticed. Pomme's crime is her lack of self-consciousness, her inability, or the absence of desire in her, to reflect on her condition and the world's. Goretta's film imitates Pomme: like her, it makes no value judgments, and it is not self-important. That is its true homage to her. Pomme herself becomes momentarily "self-conscious" at the end when she turns from her knitting to face the self-conscious Goretta and his camera tracking in; she seems almost to be aware of the filmmaker and the audience, with its potential biases. But Goretta will not have her any different than she is, and he himself will not be elevated in importance: he has his pose, and he disappears quickly, and the unselfconscious camera and the unselfconscious Pomme are allowed to become one. The credits come up. We are moved not so much to judge Pomme or to feel sorry for her, as to consider and honor her, as well as all like her, in her simple *being*, and that alone. We leave her in her own world, and we leave her mother, Marylène, François, and all the rest to the Paris she never really knew, and that will continue to hold its mysteries for them.

FILM CREDITS

Room at the Top
Great Britain, 1958

PRODUCTION COMPANY: Remus.
PRODUCER: John and James Woolf, a Romulus Production.
ASSOCIATE PRODUCER: Raymond Anzarut.
DIRECTOR: Jack Clayton.
SCREENPLAY: Neil Paterson, based on the novel by John Braine.
PHOTOGRAPHY: Freddie Francis.
ART DIRECTION: Ralph Brinton.
MUSIC COMPOSER: Mario Nascimbene.
MUSIC CONDUCTOR: Lambert Williamson.
MAKE-UP: Tony Sforzini.
SOUND SUPERVISOR: John Cox.
SOUND RECORDIST: Peter Handford.
EDITOR: Ralph Kemplen.
ASSISTANT DIRECTOR: Ronald Spencer.
PRODUCTION MANAGER: James Ware.
CONTINUITY: Doreen Francis.
CAMERA OPERATOR: Ronald Taylor.

CAMERA ASSISTANT: Derek Brown.
DUBBING EDITORS: Stan Hawkes, Alastair McIntyre.

CAST:
Joe Lampton: Laurence Harvey.
Alice Aisgill: Simone Signoret.
Susan Brown: Heather Sears.
Mr. Brown: Donald Wolfit.
Mrs. Brown: Ambrosine Philpotts.
Charles Soames: Donald Houston.
Mr. Hoylake: Raymond Huntley.
Jack Wales: John Westbrook.
George Aisgill: Allan Cuthbertson.
June Samson: Mary Peach.
Elspeth: Hermione Baddeley.
Miss Gilchrist: Avril Elgar.
Aunt: Beatrice Varley.
Darnley: Stephen Jack.
Mayor: John Welsh.
Mayoress: Everley Gregg.
Miss Breith: Thelma Ruby.
Janet: Anne Leon.
Joan: Wendy Craig.
Gertrude: Miriam Karlin.
Teddy: Richard Pasco.
Mavis: April Olrich.
Priest: Basil Dignam.
Man at Bar: Paul Whitsun-Jones.
Girl at Window: Yvonne Buckingham.
High-stepping Girl: Doreen Dawn.

RUNNING TIME: 115 minutes.
FORMAT: 35mm, black and white.

Way Down East
United States of America, 1920

PRODUCTION COMPANY: D. W. Griffith, Inc.
DIRECTOR: D. W. Griffith.
SCREENPLAY: Anthony Paul Kelly, elaborated by D. W. Griffith, from the play by Lottie Blair Parker, Joseph R. Grismer, and William A. Brady.
PHOTOGRAPHY: G. W. Bitzer and Hendrik Sartov.
ART DIRECTORS: Charles O. Seessel and Clifford Pember.
MUSIC: Louis Silvers and William F. Peters (the film was re-released in 1931 with a musical soundtrack).
COSTUMES: Lady Duff Gordon and O'Kane Cromwell.
DECORATIVE TITLES: Victor Georg.
EDITORS: James and Rose Smith.
ASSOCIATE DIRECTOR: Elmer Clifton.
TECHNICAL DIRECTOR: Frank Wortman.
PRODUCTION ASSISTANT: Leight Smith.

CAST:
Anna Moore: Lillian Gish.
Her Mother: Mrs. David Landau.
Mrs. Tremont: Josephine Bernard.
Diana Tremont: Mrs. Morgan Belmont.
Her Sister: Patricia Fruen.
The Eccentric Aunt: Florence Short.
Lennox Sanderson: Lowell Sherman.
Squire Bartlett: Burr McIntosh.
Mrs. Bartlett: Kate Bruce.
David Bartlett: Richard Barthelmess.
Martha Perkins: Vivia Ogden.
Seth Holcomb: Porter Strong.

Reuben Whipple: George Neville.
Hi Holler: Edgar Nelson.
Kate Brewster: Mary Hay.
Professor Sterling: Creighton Hale.
Maria Poole: Emily Fitzroy.
"The fiddler and many of the merrymakers in country
  dance scenes are from White River Junction, Vermont."

RUNNING TIME: originally, 150 minutes; re-issued at
  110 minutes.
FORMAT: 35mm, black and white, silent.

The Last Laugh (*Der letzte Mann* [*The Last Man*])
Germany, 1924

PRODUCTION COMPANY: Universum-Film-Aktienge-
  sellschaft (Decla Film der Ufa).
DIRECTOR: F. W. Murnau.
SCREENPLAY: Carl Mayer, under the supervision of
  Erich Pommer.
PHOTOGRAPHY: Karl Freund.
PRODUCTION DESIGN: Robert Herlth and Walter
  Röhrig.
MUSIC: Giuseppe Becce.

CAST:
The Hotel Porter: Emil Jannings.
His Daughter: Maly Delschaft.
Her Fiancé: Max Hiller.
The Porter's Aunt: Emilie Kurtz.
The Hotel Manager: Hans Unterkircher.

A Young Hotel Resident: Olaf Storm.
A Hotel Resident: Hermann Valentin.
A Thin Neighbor: Emmy Wyda.
The Night Watchman: Georg John.

RUNNING TIME: 73 minutes.
FORMAT: 35mm, black and white, silent.

Some Like It Hot
United States of America, 1959

PRODUCTION COMPANY: An Ashton Picture. For the Mirisch Company.
PRODUCER: Billy Wilder.
ASSOCIATE PRODUCERS: I. A. L. Diamond, Doane Harrison.
DIRECTOR: Billy Wilder.
SCREENPLAY: I. A. L. Diamond, Billy Wilder; idea suggested by an unpublished story by R. Thoeren and M. Logan.
PHOTOGRAPHY: Charles B. Lang, Jr.
ART DIRECTOR: Ted Haworth.
SET DECORATOR: Edward G. Boyle.
MUSIC: Adolph Deutsch.
SONG SUPERVISOR: Matty Malneck.
SONGS: "Running Wild," music by A. H. Gibbs, lyrics by Leo Wood; "I Want to Be Loved by You," music by Herbert Stothart, lyrics by Bert Kalmar; "I'm Through with Love," music by Matty Malneck, lyrics by Gus Kahn.
SOUND: Fred Lau.

COSTUMES: Orry-Kelly.
EDITOR: Arthur Schmidt.
ASSISTANT DIRECTOR: Sam Nelson.

CAST:
Sugar Kane: Marilyn Monroe.
Joel/Josephine: Tony Curtis.
Jerry/Daphne: Jack Lemmon.
"Spats" Columbo: George Raft.
Mulligan: Pat O'Brien.
Osgood Fielding III: Joe E. Brown.
Little Bonaparte: Nehemiah Persoff.
Sweet Sue: Joan Shawlee.
Sig Poliakoff: Billy Gray.
Toothpick Charley: George E. Stone.
Beinstock: Dave Barry.
Spats's Henchmen: Mike Mazurki and Harry Wilson.
Dolores: Beverly Wills.
Nellie: Barbara Drew.
Paradise: Edward G. Robinson, Jr.
Bouncer: Tom Kennedy.
Walter: John Indrisano.

RUNNING TIME: 121 minutes.
FORMAT: 35mm, black and white.

Hiroshima, mon amour
France/Japan, 1959

PRODUCTION COMPANY: Argos Films/Como Films (Paris)/Daieï (Tokyo)/Pathé Overseas.

EXECUTIVE PRODUCER: Samy Halfon.

DIRECTOR: Alain Resnais.

SCREENPLAY: Marguerite Duras.

PHOTOGRAPHY: Sacha Vierny (France), Michio Takahashi (Japan).

CAMERA OPERATORS: Pierre Goupil, Watanabe, Ioda.

ART DIRECTORS: Esaka, Mayo, Petri.

MUSIC: Giovanni Fusco, Georges Delerue (also two records of Japanese music for the procession and the jukebox).

SOUND: Pierre Calvet (France), Yamamoto (Japan).

MIXING: René Renault.

COSTUMES: Gérard Collery.

EDITORS: Henri Colpi, Jasmine Chasney, Anne Sarraute.

ASSISTANT DIRECTORS: T. Andréfouet, J.-P. Léon, R. Guyonnet, I. Shirai, Itoi, Hara.

LITERARY ADVISOR: Gérard Jarlot.

PRODUCTION MANAGERS: Sacha Kamenka, Shirakawa Takeo.

CAST:

She: Emmanuèle Riva.

He: Eiji Okada.

The German: Bernard Fresson.

The Mother: Stella Dassas.

The Father: Pierre Barbaud.

RUNNING TIME: 91 minutes (88 minutes in U.S.A.).

FORMAT: 35mm, black and white.

Day of Wrath (*Vredens Dag*)
Denmark, 1943

PRODUCTION COMPANY: Palladium Film.
DIRECTOR: Carl Dreyer.
SCREENPLAY: Carl Dreyer, Mogens Skot-Hansen, Poul Knudsen. Based on the play *Anne Pedersdotter*, by Hans Wiers-Jenssen.
PHOTOGRAPHY: Karl Andersson.
ART DIRECTOR: Erik Aaes.
MUSIC: Poul Schierbeck.
COSTUMES: Lis Fribert, K. Sandt-Jensen, Olga Thomsen.
EDITORS: Edith Schlüssel, Anne Marie Petersen.
HISTORICAL ADVISOR: Kaj Uldall.

CAST:
Absalon Pedersson: Thorkild Roose.
Anne Pedersdotter: Lisbeth Movin.
Merete, Absalon's Mother: Sigrid Neiiendam.
Martin: Preben Lerdorff Rye.
Herlofs Marte: Anna Svierkier.
The Bishop: Albert Høberg.
Laurentius: Olaf Ussing.
Kapellmeister: Sigurd Berg, Harald Holst.
With: Emilie Nielsen, Kirsten Andreasen, Sophie Knudsen, Preben Neergaard, Emanuel Jørgensen, Hans Christian Sørgensen, Dagmar Wildenbrück.

RUNNING TIME: 92 minutes.
FORMAT: 35mm, black and white.

The Seven Samurai (Shichinin no Samurai)
Japan, 1954

PRODUCTION COMPANY: A Toho production.
PRODUCER: Shojiro Motoki.
DIRECTOR: Akira Kurosawa.
SCREENPLAY: Shinobu Hashimoto, Hideo Oguni, and
    Akira Kurosawa.
PHOTOGRAPHY: Asakazu Nakai.
LIGHTING CAMERAMAN: Shigeru Mori.
ART DIRECTOR: So Matsuyama.
ART CONSULTANTS: Seison Maeda and Kohei Ezaki.
MUSIC: Fumio Hayasaka.
SOUND: Fumio Yanoguchi.
FENCING DIRECTION: Yoshio Sugino.
ARCHERY DIRECTION: Ienori Kaneko and Shigeru
    Endo.
COORDINATOR OF WRESTLING STUNTS: Yoshio
    Sugino.
ASSISTANT DIRECTOR: Hiromichi Horikawa.

CAST:
The Samurai:
Kambei, Leader of the Samurai: Takashi Shimura.
Kikuchiyo: Toshiro Mifune.
Gorobei: Yoshio Inaba.
Kyuzo: Seiji Miyaguchi.
Heihachi: Minoru Chiaki.
Shichiroji: Daisuke Kato.
Katsushiro: Ko Kimura.

The Farmers:
Gisaku, the Village Patriarch: Kuninori Kodo.

Manzo: Kamatari Fujiwara.
Rikichi: Yoshio Tsuchiya.
Yohei: Bokuzen Hidari.
Mosuke: Yoshio Kosugi.
Gosaku: Keiji Sakakida.

The Villagers: Jiro Kumagai, Haruko Toyama, Tsuneo Katagiri, Yasuhisa Tsutsumi.
Shino, Manzo's Daughter: Keiko Tsushima.
Grandfather: Toranosuke Ogawa.
Husband: Yu Akitsu.
Wife: Noriko Sengoku.

Masterless Samurai: Gen Shimizu.
Tall Samurai: Jun Tasaki.
Other Samurai: Isao Yamagata.
Laborer: Jun Tatari.
Stall Keeper: Atsushi Watanabe.
Minstrel: Sojin Kamiyama.
Rikichi's Wife: Yukiko Shimazaki.
Thief: Eijiro Higashino.

The Bandits: Kichijiro Ueda, Shimpei Takagi, Akira Tani, Haruo Nakajima, Takashi Narita, Senkichi Omura, Shuno Takahara, Masanobu Okubo.

RUNNING TIME: original version, 200 minutes; cut version, 160 minutes.
FORMAT: 35mm, black and white.

Shoeshine (*Sciuscià*)
Italy, 1946

PRODUCTION COMPANY: Alfa Cinematografica.
PRODUCER: Paolo W. Tamburella.
DIRECTOR: Vittorio de Sica.
SCREENPLAY: Cesare Zavattini, Sergio Amidei, Adolfo Franci, Cesare Giulio Viola, and Vittorio de Sica; from a story by Zavattini.
PHOTOGRAPHY: Anchise Brizzi.
PRODUCTION DESIGNER: Ivo Battelli.
MUSIC: Alessandro Cicognini.
EDITOR: Nicolo Lazzari.

CAST:
Giuseppe: Rinaldo Smordoni.
Pasquale: Franco Interlenghi.
Raffaele: Aniello Mele.
Arcangeli: Bruno Ortensi.
Vittorio: Pacifico Astrologo.
L'Abruzze: Francesco De Nicola.
Giorgio: Enrico Da Silva.
Righetto: Antonio Lo Nigro.
Siciliano: Angelo D'Amico.
Staffera: Emilio Cicogli.
Avv. Bonavino: Giuseppe Spadaro.
Commissario P.S.: Leo Caravaglia.
Il Panza: Luigi Saltamerenda.
Fortuneteller: Maria Campi.
Giuseppe's Mother: Irene Smordoni.
Mannarella: Anna Pedoni.

RUNNING TIME: 93 minutes.
FORMAT: 35mm, black and white.

The Rain People
United States of America, 1969

PRODUCTION COMPANY: Warner Brothers-Seven Arts.
PRODUCERS: Bart Patton, Ronald Colby.
DIRECTOR: Francis Ford Coppola.
SCREENPLAY: Francis Ford Coppola.
PHOTOGRAPHY: Wilmer Butler.
ART DIRECTOR: Leon Ericksen.
MUSIC: Ronald Stein.
SOUND: Nathan Boxer, Walter Murch.
EDITOR: Blackie Malkin.
PRODUCTION ASSOCIATES: George Lucas, Mona Skager.
ASSISTANT DIRECTORS: Richard C. Bennett, Jack Cunningham.
MUSIC ASSOCIATE: Carmen Coppola.

CAST:
Natalie Ravenna: Shirley Knight.
Jimmie Kilgannon: James Caan.
Gordon: Robert Duvall.
Mr. Alfred: Tom Aldredge.
With: Marya Zimmet.

RUNNING TIME: 102 minutes.
FORMAT: 35mm, Technicolor.

The Cabinet of Dr. Caligari (*Das Kabinett des Doktors Caligari*)
Germany, 1920

PRODUCTION COMPANY: Decla Filmgesellschaft, Berlin.
PRODUCER: Erich Pommer.
DIRECTOR: Robert Wiene.
SCREENPLAY: Carl Mayer and Hans Janowitz.
PHOTOGRAPHY: Willy Hameister.
PRODUCTION DESIGNERS: Hermann Warm, Walter Reimann, and Walter Röhrig.
COSTUMES: Walter Reimann.

CAST:
Dr. Caligari: Werner Krauss.
Cesare: Conrad Veidt.
Francis: Friedrich Feher.
Jane: Lil Dagover.
Alan: Hans Heinz von Twardowski.
Dr. Olson: Rudolf Lettinger.
A criminal: Rudolph Klein-Rogge.

RUNNING TIME: 90 minutes.
FORMAT: 35mm, black and white (originally tinted in green, brown, and steely-blue).

Nosferatu, a Symphony of Horror (*Nosferatu, eine Symphonie des Grauens*)
Germany, 1922

PRODUCTION COMPANY: Prana-Film, Berlin.

DIRECTOR: F. W. Murnau.

SCREENPLAY: Henrik Galeen. Based on the novel *Dracula*, by Bram Stoker.

PHOTOGRAPHY: Fritz Arno Wagner and Gunther Krampf.

ART DIRECTOR: Albin Grau.

MUSIC: Hans Erdmann.

COSTUMES: Albin Grau.

CAST:

Graf Orlok, Nosferatu the Vampire [Count Dracula]: Max Schreck.

Knock, an Estate Agent [Renfield]: Alexander Granach.

Hutter, His Assistant [Jonathan Harker]: Gustav von Wangenheim.

Ellen, Hutter's Wife [Mina]: Greta Schroeder.

Harding, a Shipbuilder [Westenra]: G. H. Schnell.

Annie, His Wife [Lucy Westenra]: Ruth Landshoff.

Professor Bulwer, a Paracelsian [Professor Van Helsing]: John Gottowt.

Professor Sievers, Town Medical Officer: Gustav Botz.

Captain of the Ship "Demeter": Max Nemetz.

First Mate: Wolfgang Heinz.

Second Mate: Albert Venohr.

The Innkeeper: Guido Herzfeld.

Hospital Doctor: Hardy von François.

With: Heinrich Witte.

RUNNING TIME: 74 minutes.

FORMAT: 35mm, black and white.

L'avventura
Italy/France, 1960

PRODUCTION COMPANY: Produzione Cinemato-
grafiche Europee, Cine del Duca (Rome), and Société
Cinématographique Lyre (Paris).
PRODUCER: Cino Del Duca.
DIRECTOR: Michelangelo Antonioni.
SCREENPLAY: Michelangelo Antonioni, Elio Bartolini,
and Tonino Guerra; from a story by Antonioni.
PHOTOGRAPHY: Aldo Scavarda.
ART DIRECTOR: Piero Poletto.
MUSIC: Giovanni Fusco.
SOUND: Claudio Maielli.
COSTUMES: Adriana Berselli.
EDITOR: Eraldo da Roma.
ASSISTANT DIRECTORS: Franco Indovina and
Gianni Arduini.
PRODUCTION SUPERVISORS: Enrico Bologna and
Fernando Cinquini.
OPERATING CAMERAMAN: Luigi Kuveiller.
SPECIAL ASSISTANT TO THE DIRECTOR: Jack
O'Connell.

CAST:
Claudia: Monica Vitti.
Sandro: Gabriele Ferzetti.
Anna: Lea Massari.
Giulia: Dominique Blanchar.
Anna's Father: Renzo Ricci.
Corrado: James Addams.
Raimondo: Lelio Luttazzi.

Patrizia: Esmeralda Ruspoli.
Goffredo: Giovanni Petrucci.
Gloria Perkins: Dorothy De Poliolo.
Old Man on the Island: Joe, fisherman from Panarea.
Ettore: Prof. Cucco.
With: Enrico Bologna, Franco Cimino, Giovanni Danesi, Rita Molé, Renato Pinciroli, Angela Tommasi di Lampedusa, Vincenzo Tranchina.

RUNNING TIME: 145 minutes.
FORMAT: 35mm, black and white.

Une femme douce
France, 1969

PRODUCTION COMPANY: Parc Film/Marianne Productions.
PRODUCER: Mag Bodard.
DIRECTOR: Robert Bresson.
SCREENPLAY: Robert Bresson, from the novella "A Gentle Spirit," by Fyodor Dostoyevsky.
PHOTOGRAPHY: Ghislain Cloquet.
ART DIRECTOR: Pierre Charbonnier.
MUSIC: Jean Wiener; Henry Purcell's overture "Come Ye Sons of Old"; Mozart.
SOUND: Jacques Maumont, Jacques Lebreton, Urbain Loiseau.
SOUND EFFECTS: Daniel Couteau.
MAKE-UP: Alex Marcus.
COSTUMES: Renée Miguel.
EDITOR: Raymond Lamy.

ASSISTANT EDITORS: Geneviève Billon, Christine Gratton.
ASSISTANT DIRECTORS: Jacques Kébadian, Mylène Van der Mersch.
PRODUCTION MANAGERS: Philippe Dussart, Michel Romanoff, Michel Choquet.
CAMERA ASSISTANTS: Paul Bonis, Emmanuel Machuel.
CONTINUITY: Geneviève Cortier.
PROPS: Eric Simon.

CAST:
The Woman: Dominique Sanda.
The Man: Guy Frangin.
Anna: Jane Lobre.
With: Dorothée Blank, Claude Ollier.

RUNNING TIME: 88 minutes (original version).
FORMAT: 35mm, Eastmancolor.

Citizen Kane
United States of America, 1941

PRODUCTION COMPANY: A Mercury production at RKO.
PRODUCER: Orson Welles.
ASSOCIATE PRODUCER: Richard Barr.
DIRECTOR: Orson Welles.
SCREENPLAY: Herman J. Mankiewicz, Orson Welles, and (uncredited) John Houseman.
PHOTOGRAPHY: Gregg Toland.

ART DIRECTORS: Van Nest Polglase, Perry Ferguson.
SET DECORATOR: Darrel Silvera.
MUSIC: Bernard Herrmann.
SOUND: Bailey Fesler, James G. Stewart.
COSTUMES: Edward Stevenson.
SPECIAL EFFECTS: Vernon L. Walker.
EDITORS: Robert Wise, Mark Robson.
CAMERA OPERATOR: Bert Shipman.

CAST:
Charles Foster Kane: Orson Welles.
Jedediah Leland: Joseph Cotten.
Bernstein: Everett Sloane.
Susan Alexander: Dorothy Comingore.
Jim Gettys: Ray Collins.
Jerry Thompson and Newsreel Narrator: William Alland.
Mary Kane: Agnes Moorehead.
Emily Norton: Ruth Warrick.
Walter Parks Thatcher: George Coulouris.
Herbert Carter: Erskine Sandford.
Jim Kane (Kane's father): Harry Shannon.
Rawlston: Philip Van Zandt.
Raymond: Paul Stewart.
Signor Matiste: Fortunio Bonanova.
Curator of Thatcher Library: Georgia Backus.
Kane, age 8: Buddy Swan.
Kane, Jr.: Sunny Bupp.
Head Waiter: Gus Schilling.
Hillman: Richard Barr.
Georgia: Joan Blair.
Mike: Al Eben.
Entertainer: Charles Bennett.
Reporter: Milt Kibbee.

Teddy Roosevelt: Tom Curran.
Dr. Corey: Irving Mitchell.
Nurse: Edith Evanson.
Orchestra Conductor: Arthur Kay.
Chorus Master: Tudor Williams.
City Editor: Herbert Corthell.
Smather: Benny Rubin.
Reporter: Edmund Cobb.
Ethel: Francis Neal.
Photographer: Robert Dudly.
Miss Townsend: Ellen Lowe.
Gino the Waiter: Gino Corrado.
Reporters: Alan Ladd, Louise Currie, Eddie Coke, Walter Sande, Arthur O'Connell, Katherine Trosper, and Richard Wilson.

RUNNING TIME: 119 minutes.
FORMAT: 35mm, black and white.

The Nights of Cabiria (Le Notti di Cabiria)
Italy/France, 1957

PRODUCER: Dino De Laurentiis.
DIRECTOR: Federico Fellini.
SCREENPLAY: Federico Fellini, Ennio Flaiano, Tullio Pinelli.
ADDITIONAL DIALOGUE: Pier Paolo Pasolini.
PHOTOGRAPHY: Aldo Tonti, Otello Martelli.
ART DIRECTOR: Piero Gherardi.
MUSIC: Nino Rota.
SOUND: Roy Mangano.

EDITOR: Leo Cattozzo.
ASSISTANT DIRECTORS: Moraldo Rossi, Dominique
  Delouche.
PRODUCTION MANAGER: Luigi De Laurentiis.

CAST:
Cabiria: Giulietta Masina.
Mario, the Actor: Amedeo Nazzari.
Oscar: François Perier.
Wanda: Franca Marzi.
Jessy: Dorian Gray.
The Hypnotist: Aldo Silvani.
Giorgio: Franco Fabrizi.
Crippled Uncle: Mario Passante.
Matilda, Cabiria's Enemy: Pina Gualandri.
With: Ennio Girolami, Christian Tassou.

RUNNING TIME: 110 minutes.
FORMAT: 35mm, black and white.

Shoot the Piano Player (*Tirez sur le pianiste*)
France, 1960

PRODUCTION COMPANY: Les Films de la Pléiade.
PRODUCER: Pierre Braunberger.
DIRECTOR: François Truffaut.
SCREENPLAY: François Truffaut, Marcel Moussy.
  Based on the novel *Down There*, by David Goodis.
PHOTOGRAPHY: Raoul Coutard.
ART DIRECTOR: Jacques Mély.

MUSIC: Georges Delerue.

SONGS: "Dialogues d'amoureux," by Félix Leclerc; sung by Félix Leclerc, Lucienne Vernay. "Vanille et Framboise," by Bobby Lapointe; sung by Bobby Lapointe.

SOUND: Jacques Gallois.

EDITORS: Cécile Decugis, Claudine Bouché.

ASSISTANT DIRECTORS: Francis Cognany, Robert Bober.

PRODUCTION MANAGER: Roger Fleytoux.

CAMERA OPERATOR: Claude Beausoleil.

PRODUCTION SUPERVISOR: Serge Komor.

SCRIPT GIRL: Suzanne Schiffmann.

CAST:

Edouard Saroyan/Charlie Kohler: Charles Aznavour.

Léna: Marie Dubois.

Thérésa: Nicole Berger.

Chico Saroyan: Albert Rémy.

Momo: Claude Mansard.

Ernest: Daniel Boulanger.

Clarisse: Michèle Mercier.

Fido Saroyan: Richard Kanayan.

Richard Saroyan: Jean-Jacques Aslanian.

Plyne: Serge Davri.

Lars Schmeel: Claude Heymann.

Passerby Who Helps Chico: Alex Joffé.

Mammy: Catherine Lutz.

Singer in Café: Bobby Lapointe.

RUNNING TIME: 80 minutes, American version; other versions, 84 and 86 minutes.

FORMAT: 35mm (in Dyaliscope), black and white.

Nashville
United States of America, 1975

PRODUCTION COMPANY: ABC Entertainment/Paramount Pictures.
EXECUTIVE PRODUCERS: Martin Starger, Jerry Weintraub.
PRODUCER: Robert Altman.
ASSOCIATE PRODUCERS: Robert Eggenweiler, Scott Bushnell.
DIRECTOR: Robert Altman.
SCREENPLAY: Joan Tewkesbury.
PHOTOGRAPHY: Paul Lohmann.
MUSIC DIRECTION: Richard Baskin.
SONGS: "200 Years" (lyrics by Henry Gibson, music by Richard Baskin); "Yes, I Do" (lyrics and music by Richard Baskin and Lily Tomlin); "Down to the River" (lyrics and music by Ronee Blakley); "Let Me Be the One" (lyrics and music by Richard Baskin); "Sing a Song" (lyrics and music by Joe Raposo); "The Heart of a Gentle Woman" (lyrics and music by Dave Peel); "Bluebird" (lyrics and music by Ronee Blakley); "The Day I Looked Jesus in the Eye" (lyrics and music by Richard Baskin and Robert Altman); "Memphis" (lyrics and music by Karen Black); "I Don't Know If I Found It in You" (lyrics and music by Karen Black); "For the Sake of the Children" (lyrics and music by Richard Baskin and Richard Reicheg); "Keep a Goin'" (lyrics by Henry Gibson, music by Richard Baskin and Henry Gibson); "Swing Low Sweet Chariot" (arrangements by Millie Clements); "Rolling Stone" (lyrics and music by Karen Black); "Honey" (lyrics and music by Keith Carradine); "Tapedeck in

His Tractor (The Cowboy Song)" (lyrics and music by Ronee Blakley); "Dues" (lyrics and music by Ronee Blakley); "I Never Get Enough" (lyrics and music by Richard Baskin and Ben Raleigh); "Rose's Cafe" (lyrics and music by Allan Nicholls); "Old Man Mississippi" (lyrics and music by Jonnie Barnett); "One, I Love You" (lyrics and music by Richard Baskin); "I'm Easy" (lyrics and music by Keith Carradine); "It Don't Worry Me" (lyrics and music by Keith Carradine); "Since You've Gone" (lyrics and music by Gary Busey); "Trouble in the U.S.A." (lyrics and music by Arlene Barnett); "My Idaho Home" (lyrics and music by Ronee Blakley).

SOUND: Jim Webb, Chris McLaughlin.

EDITORS: Sidney Levin, Dennis Hill.

ASSISTANT DIRECTORS: Tommy Thompson, Alan Rudolph.

CAST:

Norman: David Arkin.

Lady Pearl: Barbara Baxley.

Delbert Reese: Ned Beatty.

Connie White: Karen Black.

Barbara Jean: Ronee Blakley.

Tommy Brown: Timothy Brown.

Tom Frank: Keith Carradine.

Opal: Geraldine Chaplin.

Wade: Robert Doqui.

L. A. Joan: Shelley Duvall.

Barnett: Allen Garfield.

Haven Hamilton: Henry Gibson.

Pfc. Glenn Kelly: Scott Glenn.

Tricycle Man: Jeff Goldblum.

Albuquerque: Barbara Harris.
Kenny Fraiser: David Hayward.
John Triplette: Michael Murphy.
Bill: Allan Nicholls.
Bud Hamilton: Dave Peel.
Mary: Cristina Raines.
Star: Bert Remsen.
Linnea Reese: Lily Tomlin.
Sueleen Gay: Gwen Welles.
Mr. Green: Keenan Wynn.
Jimmy Reese: James Dan Calvert.
Donna Reese: Donna Denton.
Trout: Merle Kilgore.
Jewel: Carol McGinnia.
Smokey Mountain Laurel: Sheila Bailey and Patti Bryant.
Frog: Richard Baskin.
Themselves: Jonnie Barnett, Vassar Clements, Misty Mountain Boys, Sue Barton, Elliott Gould, Julie Christie.

RUNNING TIME: 161 minutes.
FORMAT: 35mm, Panavision.

The Lacemaker (*La dentellière*)
France/Switzerland/West Germany, 1977

PRODUCTION COMPANY: Action Films/F R 3 (Paris)/ Citel Films (Geneva)/Filmproduktion Janus (Frankfurt).
EXECUTIVE PRODUCER: Yves Peyrot.
PRODUCER: Yves Gasser.

ASSOCIATE PRODUCERS: Klaus Hellwig, Lise Fayolle.

DIRECTOR: Claude Goretta.

SCREENPLAY: Pascal Lainé, Claude Goretta. Based on the novel by Pascal Lainé.

PHOTOGRAPHY: Jean Boffety.

ART DIRECTORS: Serge Etter, Claude Chevant.

MUSIC: Pierre Jansen.

SOUND: Pierre Gamet, Bernard Chaumeil.

SOUND RECORDING: Alex Pront.

SOUND RE-RECORDING: Claude Villand.

SOUND EFFECTS: Jérôme Levy.

EDITORS: Joëlle van Effenterre, Nelly Meunier, Martine Charasson.

ASSISTANT DIRECTORS: Laurent Ferrier, Patrick Grandperret.

CAST:

Béatrice, known as Pomme: Isabelle Huppert.

François Beligne: Yves Beneyton.

Marylène Thorent: Florence Giorgetti.

Pomme's Mother: Anne Marie Düringer.

Marianne, François's Friend: Renata Schroeter.

Gérard, the Painter: Michel de Ré.

M. Beligne: Jean Obé.

Mme. Beligne: Monique Chaumette.

The Student: Sabine Azema.

Voices: Anne Deleuze and Rosine Rochette.

With: Christian Baltauss, Christian Peythieu, Héribert Sasse, Jeanne Allard, Odile Poisson, Gilberte Géniat, Valentine Albin, Agnès Chateau, Berterand de Hautefort, Suzanne Berthois, Yan Brian, Barbara Cendre, Luc Chessex, Nicole Chomo, Maud Darsy,

Jacques Dichamp, Gilbert Gaffiot, Daniel Guillaume, Michèle Hamelin, Lucienne Legrand, Martine Mauclair, Rebecca Potok, Joëlle Robin, Simone Roche, Simone Saniel, Sophie Thiery, France Valéry, Catherine Vidon, Jean-Pierre Vivian.

RUNNING TIME: 107 minutes.
FORMAT: 35 mm, Eastmancolor.

Bert Cardullo
(Photo by Bill Carter)